Adobe
Premiere Pro 2024

Your Ultimate Toolkit to Learn the Newest Features, Techniques, and Secrets for Seamless Video Editing in Adobe Premiere Pro 2024 from Beginner to Pro

McBunny Albert

TABLE OF CONTENTS

INTRODUCTION

Adobe Premiere Pro is like a super cool workshop for making videos! Your unfinished video clips can be turned into great movies or videos that people will love with its help. When it comes to creating videos, Adobe Premiere Pro is the best. It's used by professionals and people who just like videos. It's an easy-to-use, efficient, and adaptable method that makes editing videos a pleasure. It is cool that it can work with many types of videos, audio, and pictures without you having to change them. You can work faster and come up with better ideas. Premiere Pro has many strong tools that can help you with any issue you have while editing or putting together your videos. Premiere Pro will help you with everything, from editing to production to making sure everything runs smoothly. Getting great work done is what it's all about. Let's talk about how users feel! It's so simple to use because Adobe made it. It's meant to be easy to use and adaptable, and it looks the same in all Adobe programs. It's really simple to try new things and find better ways to complete tasks. Adobe Premiere Pro is more than just a tool; it's a whole experience that makes making videos easy and quick. Premiere Pro is great because it's simple to use, even if you've never done it before. It's also very powerful, though, so you can do a lot of cool things to your videos even if you're new to it. Here, you'll learn how to make your videos look professional and unique as we go along. Premiere Pro helps your videos stand out, whether you're making them for work, fun, or something big like a movie. Let's look around Adobe Premiere Pro together. Get ready to edit your videos so well that they look great and wow everyone. Let's work together to make some cool videos!"

Adobe Premiere Pro 2024 Features

If you want to edit videos professionally, Adobe Premiere Pro 2024 is the most recent version. People who work in movies, TV, and streaming businesses use it a lot because it has many tools for cutting, color grading, and VFX.

Here are some of the features:

The most recent update to Premiere Pro makes some great improvements to how text-based editing is done. The **Filler Word Detection** tool is one of the best. It can find annoying ***"um"*** *and* ***"uh"*** sounds in your timeline and remove them instantly. This is a huge step forward in improving sound quality. Speech will sound better and more professional.

- **Managing Motion Graphics Templates (MOGRTs)** has also been changed to make it easier to keep track of and organize. Streamlined sequence settings make starting new projects faster and easier. It's also now easier to see the past *Team Project versions* and use **Auto Save**. Even though these changes may not seem like much, they greatly enhance the editing experience in Premiere Pro and help editors do their jobs faster and better.

Filler Word Detection with bulk delete for Text-Based Editing

You can find **"uh" and "umm"** filler words and delete them all at once with Text-Based Editing to make your recordings sound better. You can delete a filler word from your sequence record by clicking on it, just like you can delete a stop. Filler words can be used in any language, so they can be used in all 18 languages that **Speech to Text** supports.

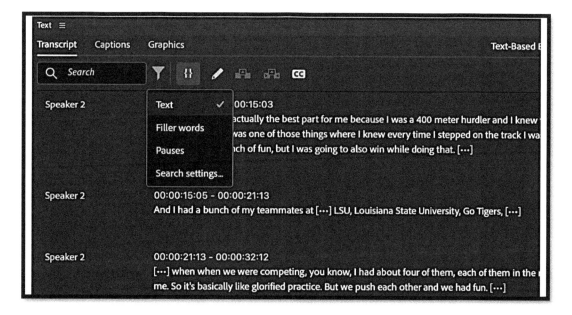

Redesigned MOGRT management

Motion Graphics Templates (MOGRTs) are like After Effects motion graphics, but they come in the form of templates with simple settings that can be changed in Premiere Pro. We're making **MOGRT control** easier to understand based on what users have told us. It's easier to find, view, and organize the **MOGRT files** you need in more places, like folders on your hard drive.

Instead of a dropdown menu, we now show MOGRTs as separate rows with check marks. This makes it easier to look through a collection from different places. You can now look through MOGRTs in two different ways. The Browser Tree View shows you where you are in MOGRT. The MOGRT view below shows all the miniature layouts from the chosen places. You can change how much room each view has by moving the window up and down or clicking on the funnel button at the top to turn the **Browser Tree View** on and off.

New sequence presets

New sequence settings for HD, UHD, HDR, and social media projects make it easy to get your sequence going quickly. You can now quickly and easily find the most-used sequence options after they were rearranged and made simpler.

To view the new presets, navigate to File > New Sequence or click the New Item  > New Sequence button on the Project panel. You'll now find a simplified list of presets, including:

- HD 1080p
- Social for 4x5, 9x16, and 1x1 timelines
- UHD (HDR) for 2160p timelines with an HDR color space
- UHD (4K) for 2160p timelines with an SDR color space
- Legacy for all previously included presets

These presets are meant to help you get started fast, but you can change them, delete them, or make new ones to make your process easier.

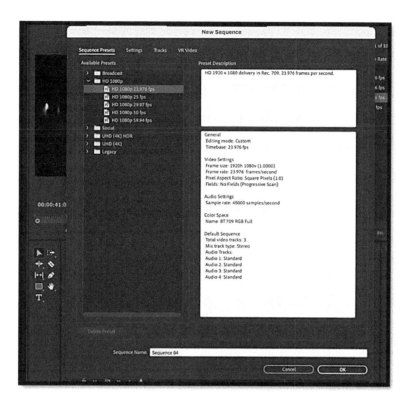

Easier access to Team Projects version history and auto-saves

If you click on the Team Project name in the Premiere Pro top bar, you can now see all of your versions and **Auto Save** records for that project. The new option in the top bar lets you choose from the following:

Team Project Settings

You can change the name, description, partners, and other settings for the Team Project, like the color, scratch files, and import settings.

Version History

Open the Premiere Pro Media Browser and make sure that the version of the Team Project you are working on is chosen from the list of saved versions.

Auto save History

Start up the Premiere Pro Media Browser and make sure that the most recent auto-save of the Team Project is chosen. From the auto-save, you can make a new Team Project or bring any version up to date.

Trimming and Multicam improvements

We're looking at feedback on the processes for features and episodes to make small changes that will make editing and cutting better. If you make a new sequence from a multicam clip, the audio mapping choices for that sequence will be more stable. There is now a new preference in the Trim menu called "**Ripple Trim**." This preference makes changes to keep both sides of the trim in sync. It is found under "**Shift clips that overlap trim points during ripple trimming.**" Premiere Pro will make changes to clips that cross a cut when this option is turned on. These new edit points will be cut along with the chosen edit points. This will keep any clips on either side of the edit from moving out of place while they are being cut.

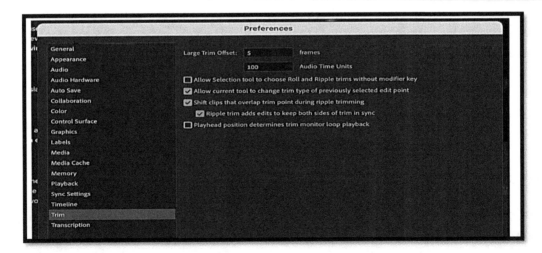

Browse Cloud Locations

It's easy to import media from Import mode or the Media Browser, just like you would from a local drive. The Media Browser panel will start to show any changes made to the files or media in the linked Dropbox or OneDrive folders. Locations that are currently linked to your system are shown automatically in the right column under Cloud when you are in **Import Mode**.

Additional updates

- Support for exporting 16-bit PNG files.
- In Export Mode, destination groups let you turn off parts that you don't need to keep your UI cleaner.
- Creative Cloud files that are synced are no longer being made. Adobe will stop running Creative Cloud Synced files for all free and paid personal users who aren't connected to a Creative Cloud for Enterprise or Creative Cloud for Teams business account on February 1, 2024.
- All Creative Cloud files will no longer have **Sync Settings**. Your personalized preset groups can be moved from an older version of Premiere Pro to a newer one on the same computer.

- As of Premiere Pro 24.0, the system needs have been changed. Adobe's video and music tools no longer work with Intel versions of Rosetta running on Apple M1/M2. Premiere Pro now needs CPUs that can handle AVX2 on AMD and Intel x86 systems.

Optimizing performance

This is very important for editing to go smoothly and quickly. A more powerful computer can make your artistic process much better by making edits go faster and more fun. The goal of Premiere Pro is to make the most of your computer's skills. Multicore processors and computers with multiple processors help it. It will be easier to edit if your processors are better and faster and if you have more CPU cores. It is necessary to have at least 8 GB of machine memory. It's best to have at least 16 GB of space to handle high-definition (HD) media, and 32 GB or more for ultra-high-definition (UHD or 4K) media. For playing videos, the speed of the file you use is also very important. It is suggested that you keep your files on a separate fast hard drive. If you have video files with better resolutions or RAW material, you should use a RAID disk stack or a fast solid-state disk. Putting media files and program files on the same hard drive could slow things down. For faster performance and easier handling, it's better to keep your media files on a separate disk. Using graphics technology or graphics processing unit (GPU) on your computer can make Premiere Pro play much faster. GPU acceleration is very helpful, and most video cards with at least 2 GB of specialized video memory (VRAM) will work well. However, it is suggested that they have 4 GB of VRAM or more. This improvement can make editing a lot easier, especially when you're working with high-quality video.

Installing Premiere Pro

On Windows:

1. **Download Premiere Elements 2024:**
    - Firstly, you need to download the installation file for Premiere Elements 2024 for Windows from the official Adobe website or a trusted source.
2. **Wait for the Download to Finish:**
    - Allow some time for the download to complete. The duration might vary depending on your internet speed and file size.
3. **Access the Downloads Folder:**
    - Once the download completes, locate your computer's 'Downloads' folder. Normally, this is where your browser saves downloaded files by default.
4. **Locate the Installation File:**
    - Look for a file named something like

"**PremiereElements_2024_LS31_win64.exe**" within your Downloads folder. This is the installer file you just downloaded.

5. **Initiate the Installation:**
   - Double-click on the "**PremiereElements_2024_LS31_win64.exe**" file to start the installation process. This action will launch the installer.

6. **Follow On-Screen Instructions:**
   - After double-clicking the file, an installation wizard will appear on your screen. Follow the prompts and on-screen instructions provided by the installer. This typically involves accepting terms and conditions, choosing the installation location, and specifying preferences.

7. **Internet Connection During Installation:**
   - Ensure that your computer remains connected to the internet throughout the installation process. This might be necessary for the installer to fetch additional files or updates required for the complete installation.

8. **Completion:**
   - Once the installation process finishes, you should have Premiere Elements 2024 successfully installed on your Windows system.

Remember, it's crucial to download software only from reputable sources to avoid potential security risks. Additionally, ensure that your system meets the requirements for running Premiere Elements 2024 to guarantee the smooth functioning of the software.

On Mac:
1. **Download Premiere Elements 2024:**
   - Begin by downloading the installation file for Premiere Elements 2024 designed for macOS from the official Adobe website or a trusted source.

2. **Wait for the Download to Finish:**
   - Allow sufficient time for the download to complete. The duration can vary based on your internet speed and the size of the file.

3. **Access the Downloads Folder:**
   - After the download is finished, locate your Mac's 'Downloads' folder. Typically, downloaded files are stored here by default.

4. **Locate the Installation File:**
   - Look for a file named something similar to "**PremiereElements_2024_MacLBS.dmg**" within your Downloads folder. This is the disk image file you just downloaded.

5. **Initiate the Installation:**
   - Double-click on the "**PremiereElements_2024_MacLBS.dmg**" file. This action

will mount the disk image and display its contents.

6. **Open Premiere Elements 2024 File:**
   - Inside the mounted disk image, you will likely see a file named "Premiere Elements 2024." Double-click on this file.

7. **Follow On-Screen Instructions:**
   - After double-clicking the "**Premiere Elements 2024**" file, an installation window or prompt should appear. Follow the instructions displayed on your screen to proceed with the installation. This usually involves agreeing to terms and conditions, choosing an installation location, and configuring preferences.

8. **Internet Connection During Installation:**
   - It's crucial to keep your Mac connected to the internet throughout the installation process. This might be necessary for the installer to fetch additional files or updates required for a successful installation.

9. **Completion:**
   - Once the installation process is finished, Premiere Elements 2024 should be installed on your macOS system and ready to use.

Uninstall Adobe Premiere Pro

1. **Access Add or Remove Programs:**
   - Go to the Windows search bar located typically at the bottom left corner of your screen. Type "**Add or Remove Programs**" and press **Enter** on your keyboard.

2. **Select Adobe Premiere Pro for Uninstallation:**
   - Once the "**Add or Remove Programs**" window opens, scroll through the list of installed applications to find "Adobe Premiere Pro." Click on it to select the program.

3. **Initiate the Uninstallation:**
   - After selecting Adobe Premiere Pro, you should see an option to "**Uninstall**." Click on this option to start the uninstallation process.

4. **Save Premiere Pro Settings (Optional):**
   - At this point, the Adobe Creative Cloud program might prompt you to save your Premiere Pro settings to your computer before uninstallation. You'll be asked if you want to save your settings. You can choose "**Yes" or "No**" based on your preference or skip this step if not prompted.

5. **Adobe Uninstall Wizard:**
   - The Adobe Uninstall Wizard will begin removing Premiere Pro from your

device. This process may take some time as it removes all related files, configurations, and registry entries associated with Premiere Pro.

6. **Completion of Uninstallation:**
   - Once the uninstallation process is finished, you should receive a confirmation message indicating that Adobe Premiere Pro has been successfully removed from your computer.

Performing nonlinear editing in Premiere Pro

NLE stands for nonlinear editor, and Premiere Pro is one. Premiere Pro is a program that functions similarly to a word processing program in that it enables you to position, change, and relocate video, audio, and graphics anywhere you like in the final edited work. Changes can be made to any component of your project at any time; this is the nonlinear aspect of an NLE. You are not required to make improvements in a certain sequence. You will build a sequence by combining some different bits of media, which are referred to as clips. You can alter any component of the sequence in any order, you can then change the contents of the sequence, or you can relocate clips so that they play sooner or later. Different layers of video can be blended, the picture size can be changed, the colors can be adjusted, special effects can be added, and the audio mix can be adjusted, among other things. In a video clip or sequence, you can mix various sequences and go to any point in the video without having to fast-forward or rewind the video. The process of arranging the clips you are working on within Premiere Pro is analogous to sorting through files on your computer. Premiere Pro is compatible with a wide variety of media file formats, such as XDCAM EX, XDCAMHD 422, XAVC, DPX, DVCProHD, QuickTime, AVCHD (including AVCCAM and NXCAM), AVC-Intra, DNxHR, ProRes, DSLR video, and Canon XF. RAW video formats are supported, including media from RED, ARRI, Sony, Canon, and Blackmagic cameras. Additionally, ProRes RAW and a variety of 360° video and phone camera formats are supported.

Expanding the workflow

Premiere Pro is a versatile tool that can be used alone, but it also functions well in collaboration with other programs. Because Premiere Pro is a component of Adobe Creative Cloud, you have access to a variety of additional specialist tools in addition to Premiere Pro. Your productivity will increase, and you will have more room for creative expression if you have a solid understanding of how various software components interact with one another.

Including other applications in the editing workflow

Premiere Pro is a sophisticated video and audio post-production tool; however, it is just one component of Adobe Creative Cloud, which is an all-encompassing environment for print, online, and video that contains video-focused tools for the following:

- High-end 3D motion effects creation
- Complex text animation generation
- Layered graphics production
- Vector artwork creation
- Audio Production
- Media management

Other components of Adobe Creative Cloud can be used to include one or more of these elements in a production. Every piece of software that you need to create sophisticated videos that are completed professionally is included in the collection.

Here's a brief description of the other components:

- **Premiere Rush:** To develop projects that are compatible with Premiere Pro (for sophisticated finishing), Premiere Rush is an intuitive video editing tool that can be used on both mobile devices and desktop computers.
- **Adobe After Effects:** Motion graphics, animation, and visual effects artists use Adobe After Effects as their tool of choice because of its widespread popularity.
- **Adobe Character Animator:** Using your camera to detect the movement of your face and body, Adobe Character Animator is a tool that allows you to create complex animations with genuine movement for 2D puppets.
- **Adobe Photoshop**: This is the product that is considered to be the industry standard for image editing and graphics creation. To get them ready for your project, you can work with pictures, videos, and even three-dimensional items.

- **Adobe Audition:** Audio editing, audio cleaning, and sweetening, music production and modification, and the development of multitrack mixes are all within the capabilities of Adobe Audition, which is a sophisticated and user-friendly system.
- **Adobe Illustrator**: This is a professional program for creating vector graphics that can be used for print, video, and the development of websites.
- **Adobe Media Encoder:** This is a tool that enables you to process files to make content for any screen straight from Premiere Pro, After Effects and Audition.
- **Adobe Dynamic Link**: This is a cross-product technique that gives you the ability to work in real-time with material, compositions, and sequences that are shared throughout After Effects, Audition, and Premiere Pro.

Exploring the Adobe Creative Cloud video workflow

The process that you use with Premiere Pro and Creative Cloud will change based on the requirements of each project. Just a few examples are as follows:

- The use of Photoshop allows for the editing and application of effects to layered picture compositions and still images that have been captured by a digital camera, a scanner, or a video clip. Premiere Pro should then be used to utilize them as source media. Adobe Photoshop was updated in Premiere Pro, and the changes were made.
- It is possible to send clips straight from the timeline of Premiere Pro to Adobe Audition for professional audio cleaning and enhancement. Premiere Pro's Audition upgrade has been updated with new features.
- Sending a full sequence from Premiere Pro to Adobe Audition allows you to finish a professional audio mix, which includes effects that are compatible with the session as well as modifications to the levels. Additionally, the session can include a video, which allows you to compose and alter the levels in the Audition depending on the action.
- It is possible to include video compositions created in After Effects into Premiere Pro projects by using **Dynamic Link**. Utilizing After Effects, you can apply special effects, include animation, and incorporate visual components. All of the modifications that are done in After Effects are instantly reflected in Premiere Pro.
- Create motion graphics templates that can be easily edited in Premiere Pro by using After Effects as your media creation tool. The original appearance and feel of the template can be preserved via the use of dedicated controls, which empower users to make particular sorts of modifications.

- Using Adobe Media Encoder, you can export video projects in a variety of resolutions and codecs, which can then be shown on websites, shared on social media platforms, or archived respectively. To upload content straight from Premiere Pro to social media networks, you can take advantage of the presets, effects, and social media support that are already incorporated into the program.

CHAPTER 1
GETTING STARTED WITH PREMIERE PRO

Understanding the Premiere Pro Interface

Adobe Premiere Pro uses a docked, panel-based interface. The whole of the interface setup is referred to as a workspace, and the program comes with five pre-built workspaces that are designed to fit a variety of working styles and the many activities that they need you to do. The majority of your editing work will be taken care of inside the many panels that are included within the program's user interface. Through the use of these panels, you will be able to import and organize your content, as well as preview your audio and video records. In addition to being a panel, the Timeline is also where the majority of the actual video editing will take place.

Understanding the Default Editing workspace

In the Premiere Pro interface, there are a total of 25 distinct panels that can be used. The panels that are included in the Default Editing workspace are discussed in the following paragraphs.

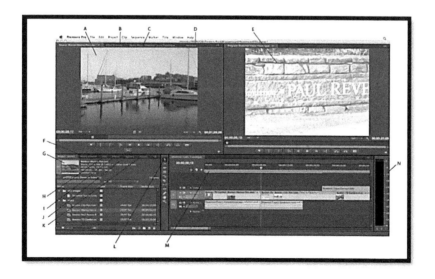

A. Source Monitor. B. Effect Control. C. Audio Mixer panel. D. Metadata panel. E. Program Monitor panel. F. Media Browsers panel. G. Project panel. H. Info Panel. I. Effects panel. J. Markers panel. K. History panel. L. Tools panel. M. Timeline panel. N. Audio Meters panel.

- **Source Monitor**: The Source Monitor functions similarly to a preview screen in that you can watch individual audio or video clips before adding them to your editing timeline. It gives you the ability to review, cut, and prepare clips by allowing you to specify start (In) and end (Out) points throughout the clip. Additionally, you can designate significant portions with markers, which will allow you to arrange the content more efficiently. You can add clips to this monitor by either dragging and dropping them into the Source panel or by double-clicking on the clips. Both of these methods are allowed.

- **Effect Controls Panel**: The Effect Controls panel is where you can manage and alter the effects that are applied to your audio and video clips that are included inside the timeline. Among these effects, you can find everything from simple color modifications to more complicated visual transformations. Through the use of this panel, you can fine-tune and modify the characteristics of these effects. When you choose a clip on the timeline, the Effect Controls panel will show the settings that are associated with the effects included inside that particular clip. Not only is this panel restricted to effects, but it also enables the modification of essential features such as **Motion, Opacity, and Audio** properties.

- **Audio Mixer**: The Audio Mixer is a tool that allows for the adjustment of audio settings while concurrently listening to audio tracks and seeing video tracks. It is a tool that aids the process of mixing audio. It is possible to find a track in the Timeline of the current sequence that matches each track in the Audio Mixer. You will be able to make adjustments to the loudness of tracks, add effects to audio tracks, and even record music straight into sequence tracks using this feature. You will find that this panel is very helpful when it comes to fine-tuning the audio parts of your project.

- **Metadata Panel**: The term "**metadata**" refers to a collection of information that specifies different aspects or features of a file. This information is included in the File Metadata Panel. It comprises information such as the **file size, format, creation date, and length**, and it can extend to more particular information such as the location, director, scene, or shot data. It is possible to inspect and make changes to these attributes via the use of the Metadata panel in Premiere Pro. It enables you to more effectively organize and classify your files, as well as communicate pertinent information with other Adobe products, improving the management and collaboration process as a whole.

- **Program Monitor**: The Program Monitor is a real-time representation of the media that you have altered located inside the timeline. The clips that have been assembled in your project timeline are the only ones that are played again and evaluated by this feature. You will be able to watch your altered sequence in the same manner that it will look to viewers thanks to this monitor, which displays the final product.

- **Project Panel:** In the process of video editing, the Project panel serves as a central hub that keeps references to all imported media assets (videos, audio, and photos), in addition to sequences, titles, and other types of supporting components that were developed inside Premiere Pro. It does not change the content of the files in their original state, but it does arrange references to those files, which makes the process of editing non-destructively easier.

- **Media Browser Panel:** Explore and preview files that are saved on your computer's hard drive with the assistance of the Media Browser panel, which is one of the features of the Media Browser. It offers a user interface that allows users to go through and examine a variety of files. While you are actively involved in the editing process, it is possible to have quick access to all of your assets if you have the Media Browser open and docked inside the workspace.

- **Info Panel**: The Info panel acts as a central information hub that provides information about the item that is presently chosen. This information can be either shown in the Project panel or inside the Timeline. Essential information about the element that has been picked is provided by it, which helps in the process of keeping track of certain qualities or features.

- **Effects Panel**: The Effects panel functions as a library that contains a variety of transitions, video and audio effects, and other transitions that are accessible in Premiere Pro. There are transitions available, such as Dissolves, Dip to Black, and Page Peels, that allow for a smooth transition from one clip to the next. Additionally, individual clips can be subjected to a variety of effects, including Black and White, Levels, and Balance, which can be used to change the visual or auditory qualities of the specific clips.

- **Marker Panel**: The Marker panel gives users the ability to both see and manipulate markers that are included inside a current clip or sequence. In addition to displaying information about markers, it also shows comments, color-coding tags, and in and out points. The use of this panel makes it easier to organize and navigate the indicated portions that are included in the project.

- **History Panel**: The History panel serves as a record of the activities that have been done throughout the editing session that you are now engaged in. The sequence of modifications that were made to your project is documented here. The Undo feature, which can be accessed by selecting Edit > Undo or by pressing Ctrl+Z/Cmd+Z, is an alternative to utilizing this panel, which gives you the ability to return to prior stages inside the current working session. It does not, however, preserve any changes that have been made to the program's layout, panels, windows, or overall preferences. Whenever Premiere Pro is closed and then reopened, the History panel is reset, which means that the ability to retrieve prior states is lost. This is an important feature.

- **Tools Panel:** An assortment of editing tools that are available inside the program are included under the Tools panel. As soon as they are enabled, these tools alter the look and behavior of the cursor in accordance with the tool that is now chosen and the content that it interacts with. This panel allows for easy access to a variety of tools, including selection, razor, text, pen, and others, which enables precise editing operations to be performed based on the tool that is now active.

- **Timeline panel**: This is the main workspace for carrying out editing operations. It is located in the middle of the timeline. Assembly of clips, arrangement of their location, and modification of their properties inside your project are all possible thanks to this feature. Another use of the Timeline is to act as a canvas on which effects and transitions can be applied to audio and video clips. In the course of the project, every sequence that was generated has its distinct timeline. Wherever there are numerous Timelines open, Premiere Pro will arrange them using tabbed displays, which are similar to those seen in web browsers. This will make it much simpler to navigate between the various sequences.

- **Audio Meters Panel**: The Audio Meters panel serves as a Volume Unit (VU) meter to show the volume levels of audio clips that are present in the Timeline. When evaluating video and audio clips inside the Timeline, this panel continues to be active. It provides visual representations of audio levels, ensuring that you have a clear grasp of the audio intensity while you are editing.

Using the Button Editor

The transport controls in Adobe Premiere are conveniently situated beneath the Source and Program monitors, offering various functionalities for navigating and examining video clips in detail. These controls include jogging options that allow frame-by-frame examination alongside regular playback options. Additionally, there's a marker placement button and a toggle switch to activate or deactivate the Comparison View feature, aiding in detailed editing and comparison tasks. In the Source monitor, alongside the set of transport controls, you'll find the **Insert and Overwrite buttons**. Conversely, in the Program panel, these buttons are replaced by the Lift and Extract buttons. Both displays also feature an Export Frame button, enabling users to capture a still image from the displayed footage if necessary, providing a convenient way to extract specific frames for various purposes.

To further customize the Premiere workspace, users can access the button editor by clicking on the small **"+"** symbol located in the lower right corner of the screen. This editor allows users to personalize their editing environment by utilizing various button options available, offering flexibility in tailoring the workspace to suit individual preferences and editing requirements. In Adobe Premiere, you have the ability to customize your workspace by adding buttons using a simple drag-and-drop method within the Button Editor. When the Button Editor is active, you can easily add buttons by dragging them directly into the button bar. This empowers you to include additional functionalities or tools that you frequently use for quicker access and a more personalized editing experience. Moreover, if there are default buttons that you don't require or prefer not to have displayed, you can remove them from the button bar by dragging those default buttons into the Button Editor's option panel. Once you've finished arranging and customizing your buttons to suit your preferences, you can click **"OK"** to confirm and continue with your editing session. This way, you can create a workspace that is tailored to your specific editing needs, optimizing efficiency and ease of access to the tools you use most frequently.

Premiere Buttons and Keyboard Shortcuts

Simply hovering over any of these buttons will show its name in a tool tip, with some having more obvious use than others. Most of us know what "Toggle Proxies" imply, but what are some of these other ones? What is "Play Around" supposed to be, after all? The following is a list of Premiere buttons, along with an explanation of their default keyboard shortcuts and sequence of appearance.

Here's a list of Premiere buttons explained in order of appearance, along with their default keyboard shortcuts:

1. **Mark In (I):** When you use the Mark in function, you're essentially setting the starting point for your editing or selection process on the timeline or clip. It's like setting the beginning marker for where you want an action or edit to commence.

2. **Mark Out (O):** This function serves as the counterpart to Mark In. It allows you to specify the endpoint or conclusion of your editing or selection process on the timeline or clip. It's similar to placing a marker at the point where you want an action or edit to stop.

3. **Clear In (Ctrl + Shift + I):** Clear In function works by removing the previously set starting point (In point) on your timeline or clip. It's like erasing the initial marker you placed, giving you the freedom to readjust or remove the starting point for your selections or edits.

4. **Clear Out (Ctrl + Shift + O):** Similar to Clear In, this function erases the previously set endpoint (Out point) on your timeline or clip. It's akin to removing the endpoint marker, allowing you to readjust or remove the endpoint for your selections or edits.

5. **Go to In (Shift + I):** This function swiftly moves the playhead (indicator) to the previously marked starting point (In point). It helps in quickly navigating to where you've set the beginning of your selection or edit.

6. **Go to Out (Shift + O):** In a similar manner, this function moves the playhead to the previously marked endpoint (Out point). It facilitates rapid navigation to where you've set the end of your selection or edit.

7. **Go to Next Edit Point (Down Arrow):** This feature enables the playhead to jump to the next break or change in the continuity of clips on your timeline. It allows for quick movement between different segments or cuts within your project.

8. **Go to Previous Edit Point (Up Arrow):** Conversely, this function moves the playhead back to the previous edit point or discontinuity in your timeline. It assists in swift backward navigation between different segments or cuts in your project, aiding in reviewing or refining your edits.

9. **Play Video In to Out:** This feature enables you to start playback from the designated In point and continue until the Out point. It provides a preview specifically focused on the segment you've marked, allowing you to review or assess that particular section of your project.

10. **Add Marker (M):** When you use the **Add Marker** function, you're essentially placing a visual reference point or annotation within your clip or on the timeline. These markers serve as notations for important moments or sections, making it easier to navigate or identify specific parts during the editing process.

11. **Go to Next Marker (Shift + M):** This function swiftly moves the playhead to the next marker located ahead of its current position on the timeline. It streamlines the process of jumping between marked points, allowing for efficient navigation during editing.

12. **Go to Previous Marker (Ctrl + Shift + M):** Contrary to the previous function, this command navigates the playhead to the marker immediately preceding its current position. It facilitates quick movement backward between markers, aiding in precise navigation through designated points in your project.

13. **Step Back One Frame (Left Arrow):** By using the Left Arrow key, you can move the playhead backward frame-by-frame. This meticulous navigation allows for precise adjustments at a granular level within your footage, facilitating detailed editing work.

14. **Step Forward One Frame (Right Arrow):** Similar to the previous function, the Right Arrow key advances the playhead forward frame-by-frame. This functionality assists in precise navigation through individual frames, enabling fine-tuning and precise editing adjustments.

15. **Play-Stop Toggle (Spacebar):** This feature provides a convenient way to control playback. Pressing the spacebar initiates playback, and pressing it again pauses the video. It offers a quick and accessible way to start and stop playback during editing, allowing for easy review and adjustments.

16. **Play Around (Shift + K):** Play Around encompasses a preroll and a postroll during playback, meaning it plays a specified number of frames before and after the

playhead's starting position. This setting allows you to preview a segment with a bit of context before and after the marked area. The number of frames for preroll and postroll can typically be adjusted in the software's Preferences under the Playback settings, giving you control over the playback range for this function.

17. **Loop Playback:** This function allows you to set a sequence to play continuously in a loop. It's particularly useful when you want to review specific segments, transitions, or effects repeatedly. Loop Playback helps in analyzing and fine-tuning these sections without having to manually restart the playback.

18. **Insert (Comma):** When you use the Insert function, the content from the Source monitor is inserted into the timeline, pushing any existing content beyond the insertion point further along the timeline. This function helps in adding new material without replacing or deleting existing content.

19. **Overwrite (Period):** Overwrite replaces the existing content on the timeline with the content from the Source monitor. When applied, it directly substitutes the material on the timeline with the new content, effectively overwriting the previous footage or audio.

20. **Lift (Semicolon):** Upon using the **Lift** function, the selected portion from the timeline is copied to the clipboard and simultaneously removed from the sequence. This offers a quick way to isolate and remove specific segments from the timeline while keeping them accessible in the clipboard for potential later use.

21. **Extract (Apostrophe):** Similar to the Lift function, Extract removes the selected section from the timeline but with a slight difference. It not only copies and removes the segment but also heals the gap created by the removal. This means that the adjacent clips are brought together seamlessly, closing the edit point.

22. **Safe Margins:** these feature overlays visual indicators on the monitor, delineating the title-safe areas. It ensures that critical content—such as text or important visual elements—remains within the safe viewing area, preventing any potential cropping on different display devices. Safe Margins are essential for guaranteeing that crucial content is always visible and not cut off, especially in television or screen displays where overscan may occur.

23. **Export Frame (Ctrl + Shift + E):** This function allows you to capture a still image of the current frame being displayed on the monitor. It provides the ability to extract a specific frame from the video for various purposes such as creating thumbnails, references, or for further analysis.

24. **Multi-Camera Record On/Off Toggle (0):** This feature enables or disables the recording of a multi-camera cut in real-time. It's particularly valuable for capturing

live events with multiple camera angles simultaneously. Toggling this function on allows for the recording of multi-camera sequences.

25. **Toggle Multi-Camera View (Shift + 0):** This command switches the multi-camera view on or off, providing the ability to swiftly alternate between different camera angles in a multi-camera setup. It's a convenient way to preview and select the desired camera angle during editing.

26. **Revert Trim Session:** Reverting a trim operation while the trimming handle is still active undoes the trimming adjustments made, offering flexibility in refining edit points. It allows editors to experiment with trims without committing to the changes immediately.

27. **Toggle Proxies:** This function switches between displaying proxies (lower-resolution versions of the original footage) and full-resolution original footage in the monitor. It helps in enhancing playback performance during editing, as proxies are easier to process, allowing for smoother playback, especially when working with high-resolution or resource-intensive media.

28. **Toggle VR Video Display:** This feature turns the VR (virtual reality) display on or off, facilitating the editing and viewing of VR video content. It provides a specific mode optimized for editing immersive VR content, allowing editors to work efficiently within a VR environment.

29. **Global FX Mute:** Temporarily bypassing all effects applied in the sequence, Global FX Mute is beneficial for improving playback performance. It helps alleviate performance issues during playback, allowing editors to review the footage without the effects, giving a smoother playback experience, especially when dealing with computationally intensive effects or when experiencing performance lags.

30. **Show Rulers (Ctrl + R):** Enabling rulers places guides along the edges of the frame, aiding in the creation of perpendicular guides for precise alignment and editing. These rulers act as visual aids, allowing editors to precisely position elements within the frame.

31. **Show Guides (Ctrl + Semicolon):** This function toggles guides on and off within the frame. Guides are visual markers that assist in aligning and arranging elements accurately. They're essential for maintaining consistency and precision when positioning elements in the video frame.

32. **Snap in Program Monitor (Ctrl + Shift + Semicolon):** When activated, this function enables objects in the monitor to snap to the center or to the guides, ensuring accurate positioning while moving them. This snapping feature enhances efficiency by automatically aligning elements with specific markers or guides, facilitating precise arrangement.

33. **Comparison View:** This feature allows for the comparison of the current frame under the playhead with a reference frame. It's particularly useful for tasks like color correction and grading, aiding editors in achieving visual consistency across frames. This side-by-side comparison assists in fine-tuning the visual aspects of the footage to maintain a consistent look throughout the video.

Regarding the mention of the Space entry: In certain editing interfaces, the Space entry serves as a placeholder or a space within the interface design. It allows users to adjust and refine the layout of their button bars or toolbars, providing a visual breathing space between groups of related buttons. It offers flexibility in organizing the user interface elements in a more structured and user-friendly manner. Each of these functions contributes significantly to the precision, efficiency, and visual consistency in video editing, empowering editors to achieve more accurate and refined results in their projects.

Setting Up Your Workspace

Adobe Premiere Pro has some standard workspaces that can be customized to meet a variety of editing requirements and processes. **An explanation of some of the general workspaces and the applications that are suggested for them is as follows:**

1. **Essentials**: The "Essentials" workspace has a well-organized structure that makes it simple to access all of the important panels and tools that are necessary for editing. The use of this workspace is particularly advantageous while working with a single monitor since it ensures a comfortable workflow.

2. **Vertical**: The "Vertical" workspace was developed with the express purpose of facilitating the work with vertical video formats. It makes it simple to switch between the Source Monitor and the Program Monitor inside the same panel, which improves the editing experience for information that is shown vertically.

3. **Learning**: The "Learning" workspace is perfect for users who wish to learn while working and take advantage of the in-app lessons that are available. The arrangement of this workspace has been designed to accommodate learning tools, offering an atmosphere that is beneficial to the development of editing abilities.

4. **Assembly**: The "Assembly" workspace is distinguished by its bigger Project panel, which makes it possible to do hover scrubbing with ease, establish In and Out points, and generate rough cuts in a short amount of time. When it comes to activities that need the rapid arrangement and organizing of film, this structure is perfect.

5. **Captions and Graphics**: This workspace is designed specifically to work with graphics or captions inside the editing undertaking. Text, graphics, and other components that are relevant to the layout are handled and manipulated more effectively because of this optimization.

6. **Review:** To conduct project reviews, the "**Review**" workspace is intended to be used for the utilization of external collaboration solutions such as Frame.io. It is likely to give a layout that is favorable to smooth integration with review platforms, which will make it easier to collaborate on editing and feedback procedures.

7. **Production**: The "**Production**" workspace is best suited for collaborative projects in which numerous members of a team are working on a production. This workspace probably has a well-organized structure that is designed for work that requires collaborative editing and for effectively managing a production pipeline.

These preconfigured workspaces in Adobe Premiere Pro are designed to simplify various editing chores, improve the user interface for specific workflows, and accommodate a variety of project requirements according to the unique needs of the project. To increase productivity and the efficiency of their workflow, users can transition between different workspaces according to their editing requirements.

Change Workspaces

1. **Dropdown Menu:**
   - To access workspaces via the dropdown menu:
     - Click on the "**Workspace**" menu located in the menu bar at the top of the Premiere Pro interface.
     - From the dropdown list, select the workspace name that corresponds to the specific layout you want to use. This action will switch the interface to that workspace configuration.

2. **Window Menu:**
   - Alternatively, you can open a workspace via the "Window" menu:
     - Open the project you want to work on in Premiere Pro.
     - Go to the "**Window**" menu located in the menu bar.
     - Choose "**Workspace**" and then select the desired workspace from the list provided.

3. **Keyboard Shortcuts:**
   - Premiere Pro offers keyboard shortcuts to quickly access workspaces:
     - With your project open, press *Alt + Shift + a number key (from 1 to 9)* to instantly open specific predefined workspaces.
     - For instance, pressing Alt + Shift + 1 would open the workspace assigned to that particular shortcut.

4. **Customization of Keyboard Shortcuts:**
   - **Premiere Pro allows users to customize keyboard shortcuts, including those for opening specific workspaces or custom workspaces:**
     - You can customize the keyboard shortcuts by going to the "Edit" menu, and selecting "**Keyboard Shortcuts**."
     - In the Keyboard Shortcuts panel, navigate to the "**Workspaces**" section to assign or modify keyboard shortcuts for different workspaces, including any custom workspaces you've created.

Import a workspace with a project

Premiere Pro typically opens projects within the currently active workspace, but it also provides the option to open a project in the last-used workspace associated with it. This particular feature proves handy for those who frequently rearrange their workspace set up for various projects. To access this functionality, before opening a project, navigate to the "**Window**" menu, then select "**Workspaces**," followed by "**Import Workspace From Projects**." It's important to note that if you import a project and find the workspace empty, the recommended steps are to close the project, unselect "**Import Workspace From Projects**," re-import the project, and this time, choose an existing workspace for the project.

Modify the order of workspaces

Managing the order of workspaces or concealing specific ones is also possible. Utilize the "Edit Workspaces" option found at the bottom of the Workspaces menu or directly through "Window > **Workspaces > Edit Workspaces**." This action triggers a dialog box where you can rearrange workspace orders, hide them, or delete any custom layouts. Should you decide to undo any changes made, a simple click on "**Cancel**" will revert the modifications.

Create Custom Workspaces

Crafting custom workspaces tailored to your preferences is another capability within Premiere Pro.

After adjusting panels and groups to your liking, there are two methods to save these setups:

1. Open the Workspaces dropdown menu and select "**Save as New Workspace**."
2. Alternatively, choose "**Window > Workspace > Save as New Workspace**."

These saved custom configurations will be accessible through the Workspace menu for future use. However, a crucial point to consider: if you make alterations to the default workspace and save these changes, the only way to revert to the original default settings is by deleting the workspace configuration file from your Layouts folder. This step is essential to restore the default layout if necessary.

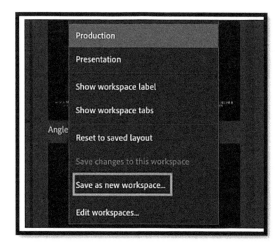

Reset a Workspace

Reset the current workspace to return to its original, saved layout of panels.

Do one of the following:

- Open the **Workspaces** dropdown menu and select **Reset to Saved Layout**. Or,
- Choose **Window** > **Workspace** > **Reset to Saved Layout**.

Creating a New Project

- Go to the top menu and choose **File > New > Project**. You can also click on the **New Project option** on the welcome screen.
- This will show the **'New Project'** box:

Create Project File

- **Pay Attention to Screen Fields**: First, look at the top part of the screen. Two important fields are waiting for your input.
- **Descriptive Project Name:** To start, type a name that describes and makes sense for your project into the "**Project name**" box. This name will help people find your project file, so it must match the material or goal of your project.
- **Picking a place for the project**: After that, click on the "**Project location**" box. When you click, choose the "**Choose Location**" option. When you click this button, a file

viewer will open, letting you look through your system's folders and find the perfect place to save your project file.

- **Getting around in the File Browser**: When the file reader starts up, you can go to your project folder or a more useful place, like your **Desktop or Documents** folder, and choose it. The goal is to pick a place that works well for your process and will make it easy to get to your project in the future.
- **Importance of Naming and Saving Location**: It's important to stress that this file will hold all of your hard work and effort on the project. So, take the time to give it a name that describes it and makes it easy to find. It will also be easier to find later if you save it in a place that makes sense and is easy to get to.

Importing Media Files

- **Finding Media Files**: Go to the left side of the screen and find the where your media files are saved. This could include places like your Desktop, the Downloads folder, or any other folder where your video files are stored.
- **Single File Selection**: Once you've found the folder that has your video files, click on a single file inside that folder to pick it. This step lets us know that you have picked this file to import.

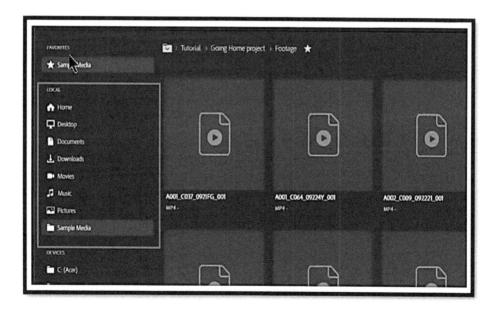

- **Picking out Multiple Files or a Range**: You can use a selection method to bring in multiple files or a continuous range of files from the folder. To begin, click on the first file in the list that you want to import. Hold down the "**Shift**" key on your computer and click on the last file in the group. This will show or pick all the files in this area at the same time, which will speed up the import process.

Turn Off Sequence Option

- Look on the right side of the screen for "**Import settings**."
- Make sure that the "**Create new sequence**" option is not selected. (It should look gray. If it's blue, click it to turn it off:

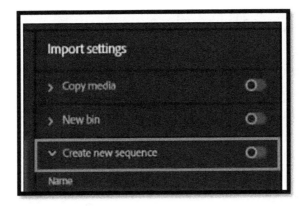

- If you turn this option on, all of your files will be added to the Timeline, which is not what we want right now.

Confirm

- Then, click the **Create option** in the bottom right area, and your project will be made.
- It will show up in the Project panel, and you can start changing.

Setting up a Sequence

The **'New Sequence'** window appears when you begin a new project and click the **'OK'** button. In this box, you are asked to make a basic order for your project. But it can be hard to choose because there are so many options, each one broken up into a different category. This can be scary, especially if you don't know what kind of movie you're making or how it should turn out in the end. You shouldn't worry though if you're not sure which settings to choose for your series. There is a program called Premiere Pro that can help you. It lets you use your video clips to make a series that fits your material automatically, so you don't have to worry about picking the right settings by hand. It is important to know that the values for each process in your project can be changed to fit its needs. To make sure the system doesn't have to work too hard, it's best to make sure that the settings of your sequence are as close as possible to the settings of the original video. This helps make the quality of real-time playing better and the general look better. Now, at the bottom of the Project screen, there is a useful "**New Item**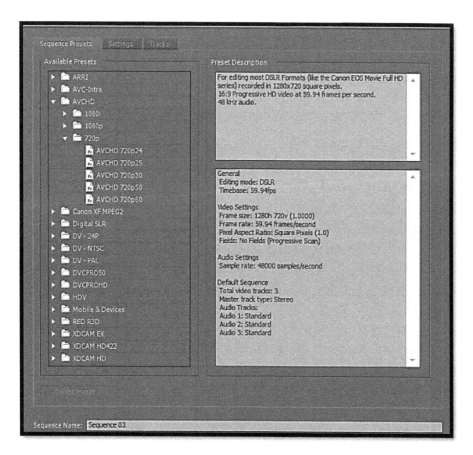" menu. You can make different parts of your project from this menu, like sequences, comments, and color mattes, which are full-screen colorful images used as backgrounds. If you drag a clip or several clips from the Project panel onto this "**New Item**" menu, it's easy to make a series that goes with your video. When you do this, Premiere Pro makes a new series immediately with format settings that work with your video. The new clip will have the same name as the first one you chose, and its frame size and frame rate will also be the same. Another option is to right-click on one or more clips and then chooses "**New Sequence From Clip**" from the context menu. So, your sequence settings will always be the same as your files. You can also directly drag a clip or clips onto the Timeline box if it is empty. This will make a series that fits the limits of your video. This method makes sure that the choices for your series will work with your files.

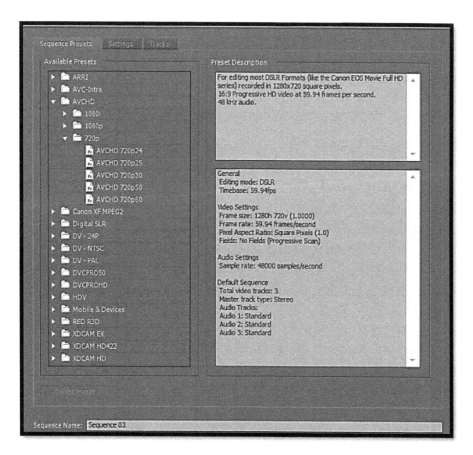

When working on a project that uses a lot of different types of media, you may need to choose which media to use so that your order settings are correct. Editing programs like Premiere Pro let you work with a variety of forms. For better playing, though, it's best to pick settings that work with most of your video files. This helps keep your system running at its best during playback since matching the clips to the order settings usually makes playback smoother and faster. In Premiere Pro, let's say the first clip you add to your sequence doesn't match the conditions that were already set for the sequence. When this happens, the software notices the difference and gives you the option of instantly changing the order settings to fit the features of the clip you're adding. This tool helps keep your project consistent by letting you work with different kinds of media without having to worry too much about the technical side of things. It's helpful to have this automated adjusting tool in Premiere Pro when you're adding different types of media. It keeps your editing process smooth by changing the order settings based on the qualities of the first clip you add.

Understanding the Makeup of Sequence Presets

It can be easier to choose the best sequence setting for your job if you know how they work. Adobe has simplified this and made it easy for people to start making movies right away by giving them three simple steps.

There are four main things that these sequence settings have in common:

1. **Mode**: In Adobe Premiere Pro, the editing mode includes frame size, pixel aspect ratio, field dominance, audio sample rate, and preview file, among other things.
2. **Frame Size:** The frame size tells you the aspect ratio of the pixels, which tells you whether the pixels are square or not.
3. **Audio Sample Rate:** This specifies the frequency, at which audio samples are captured, often common rates like 48000 Hz.
4. **Video Preview Files**: These are the preview files that are made while the video is being edited. They can also be used as render files in some cases.

The codec is missing from the list of features, which is noticeable for people who have used editing software before. No matter what kind of picture you're working on, Adobe Premiere Pro will handle files with the Mercury Playback Engine. This engine lets you mix different types smoothly within the same series, which has a small effect on speed. Another thing to keep in mind is that your list of sequence presets will grow as your editing system changes or grows. For example, if you add a third-party I/O (Input/Output) card, you might be able to access extra settings that are designed to work with that card. I/O cards could not be used with older versions of Adobe Premiere Pro before CS6. You could get MPE acceleration or output through your I/O card, but using it for video transfer didn't always mean better performance. However, these problems have been fixed to make the program work better and have more features when connecting to I/O cards.

The selection processes

It is easier to choose the right setting for your project if you know how Adobe Premiere Pro works with sequence presets. You need to know what kind of footage you'll be using for most of your scene. This will help you quickly set things like frame size and pixel aspect ratio. The fact that speeding is available in CS6 is because Adobe used Mercury Transmit technology. This technology brings MPE acceleration to the I/O card, which makes the system run faster overall.

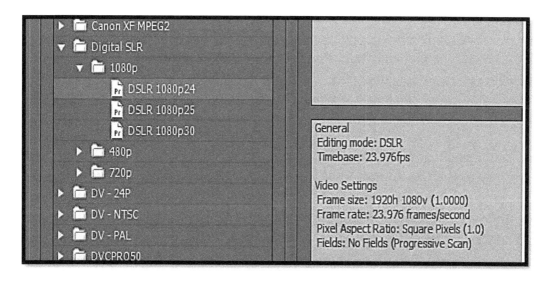

Here are steps you can follow to select a format from the presets:

1. **Choose the Main Type of Footage**: Choose the main type of footage you'll be using in your series. This could be XDCAM HD, DVCPROHD, RED R3D, or another format you want to work with most.
2. **Look through the categories**: You can find the file that works with the type of footage you want by scrolling down through the Category folders.
3. **Set the Frame Size**: Once you've found the style you want, pick the frame size that works best for you. In this case, you might have to choose whether the video is

progressive or interlaced. To make your choice, go through the box called "**frame size**."

4. **Pick a frame rate**. Based on the main sources you're using, pick the right frame rate.
5. **Name and Make Sequence**: Name your sequence and click **OK**. Based on the settings you chose; a new series will be added to the Project panel.

It's easy to use a setting, but you need to change it so that it works better with your routine. You can do this quickly by going back to the New Sequence window. Do these things:

- To open the **New Sequence** dialog box, go to the File menu and choose File > New Sequence.

Adjust the clip length

In Adobe Premiere Pro's Program screen, all you have to do is press the spacebar to see a sample of your work in progress. There is a Program Monitor that you can see if you go to **Window > Program Monitor** in the menu. To stop playing, press the spacebar again. To go back to the beginning of your video, you can also drag the blue playhead to the spot you want. When you play your sequence, the video clip that is shown on the Program screen might look too big or too small at times. To change this, all you have to do is right-click (Windows) or Control-click (macOS) on the clip in the Timeline panel.

After that, choose **Set to Frame Size** to make sure it fits correctly in the watching area. A popular way to edit clips to show only the part you want is to trim them. You can easily do this by dragging the clip's edge to shorten it and show only the parts you want to use in your video. After sorting and changing the locations and lengths of clips, it's important to look for and get rid of any breaks in your series. There might be a space between two clips. To show it, click on the space in the Timeline box. Then, press the Delete key on your computer to join the clips together and make sure your sequence flows smoothly. In your video sequence, this makes sure that there are no breaks or gaps between the clips.

Explore the Project Settings

After starting a new project and setting up a series in Adobe Premiere Pro, it's important to know what options are available in the Project settings, which you can get to at any point. Here's how to get to the Project Settings text box for your current project: Start by going to **File** > **Project Settings** > **General**.

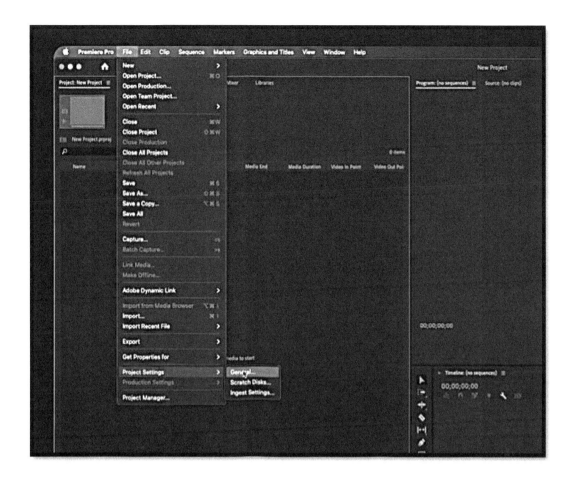

One of the most important decisions in these settings is how to display and play back videos. When you use visual effects to create change video clips within your scenes, some effects may start right away and change the way your original footage looks. When you press the Play button, you see this change happen in real-time. Seeing playback happen in real time is helpful because it lets you see right away how your artistic choices will turn out. However, if you add a lot of effects to a clip or use effects that aren't designed to work well with real-time viewing, your computer might have trouble keeping the full-frame rate steady. This is known as "**dropping frames**," and it happens when Premiere Pro tries to show video clips with effects but might not be able to show every frame every second. Along with producing the video, you should also change how Premiere Pro shows the time for your video and audio clips in the Project Settings dialog box. Under the General tab, you can change this in the **Video Display Format and Audio Display Format** parts.

Most of the time, it's best to leave things as they are: Select **Audio Samples** from the Audio Display **Format menu and Timecode** from the **Video Display Format** option. These settings don't change how Premiere Pro plays video or music clips; they change how time is shown visually in the program. These settings can be changed at any time during the writing process, though, so you can make them fit your needs.

The Video Display Format menu

In the Project Settings section of Adobe Premiere Pro, there is a section titled "**Video Display Format**." Within this area, there are four different options available. Whether you are working with video or celluloid film as your main source material for the project will determine which of these options you choose to go with.

Here's a breakdown of the options:

1. **Timecode:** First, the timecode option is the one that is selected by default. The term "timecode" refers to a standardized approach that is used all over the world to accurately count the hours, minutes, and seconds included in video footage. Cameras, professional video recorders, and nonlinear editing tools are all examples of devices that make extensive use of it.

2. **Feet + Frames 16mm or Feet + Frames 35mm:** These options are excellent if your source files come from celluloid film and you want to submit your editing selections to a lab to process the original negative and generate a final image. If you are interested in obtaining a finished picture, you should consider using one of these options. Specifically designed for celluloid film types such as 16mm or 35mm, this time measurement method is a standard approach to the measurement of seconds.

3. **Frames**: This is a simple option that simply counts the number of frames that are included inside a video. It is often used in animation projects, which are characterized by the need for exact frame counts for animation sequences.

4. **Project File**: The project file in Premiere Pro is where you will keep information about the sequences and assets that you include in your project. This information may include capture settings, transitions, audio mixing parameters, and other information. This file does not make any changes to the files that were initially imported, and it keeps a reference to each file. The reference to each file is determined by the filename and position at the time of import. It is possible that Premiere Pro will have difficulty locating a source file when you restart the project after you have moved, renamed, or deleted it at a later time. In situations like this, Premiere Pro causes the "**Where Is the File**" dialog box to appear.

There is a Project panel that is included in every project in Premiere Pro. This panel serves as a repository for any clips that are associated with the project. Media and sequences in the project can be more easily organized with the use of bins inside the Project panel. This means that a single project can have numerous sequences, each of which can have a distinct environment. Within the context of a project, segments can be altered as separate sequences, and then they can be layered together to produce a bigger sequence that will feature in the final program. Within the same project, you can also save multiple versions or revisions of a sequence as independent sequences, which provides you more versatility when it comes to handling your adjustments.

Using the standard digital video workflow

As you get more expertise in editing, you will develop your preferences on the order in which you should work on the various parts of your project. During the post-production process, each step calls for a certain sort of attention as well as a varied set of equipment. Additionally, many projects need a greater amount of time to be spent on one stage than another. Regardless matter whether you pass past certain phases with a fast mental check **or spend hours (or even days!) committed to polishing a component of your project, it is nearly inevitable that you will go through the following steps:**

- **Obtain your media**: This can include the recording of the original video, the creation of fresh animation content, the selection of stock media, or the collection of various assets for a project.
- **Ingest the video into your editing storage**: Media files, such as video files from a camera, can be read directly by Premiere Pro, and the process of conversion is often not required. Make sure that you have a backup of your contents stored in a different place since storage disks might occasionally fail unexpectedly due to physical issues. Take advantage of fast storage while you are editing videos so that your media files can be played back without any interruptions.
- **Reorganize your clips**: Your project may have a large amount of video footage from which to pick. Spend some time organizing clips in your project into bins, which are unique folders. Bins are another phrase that comes from the days when celluloid film was put through the editing process. It would be possible for the editor to quickly access the film strips that were organized and housed in huge bins that were lined with fabric. Metadata is extra information about the clips or media files, and you can add color labels and other information as metadata to help keep things organized. Metadata is also known as description information.
- **Create a sequence**: In the Timeline panel, choose the parts of the video and audio clips that you wish to combine into a sequence. This will cause the sequence to be created. You can think of a sequence as your finished edited video.
- **Adding transitions**: This involves adding specific transition effects between sequence clips, adding video effects, and creating composite graphics by putting clips on various levels, which are referred to as tracks in the Timeline panel.
- **Create titles, graphics, and captions, or import them**, and then add them to your sequence so that they may assist in telling the tale.

- **Make adjustments to the audio mix**: Make adjustments to the loudness of your audio clips to get the ideal mix, and make use of transitions and effects on your audio clips to do this.
- **Output**: Export your finished project to a file.

Through the use of industry-leading technologies, Premiere Pro can enable each of these phases. If you are interested in developing your skills as an editor, there is a big community of creative and technical experts who are eager to share their experiences and provide help.

CHAPTER 2
BASIC EDITING TECHNIQUES

The Timeline

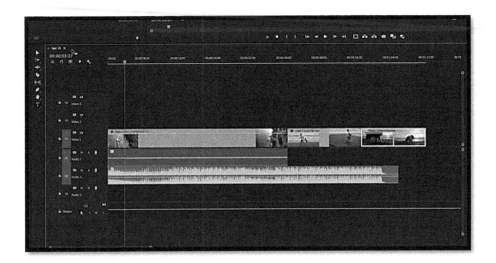

The Timeline Panel within Adobe Premiere Pro acts as the central workspace for all your video editing endeavors. Think of it as a visual canvas that encapsulates your entire project, enabling you to organize, manipulate, and refine video clips, audio segments, and graphics. Visualized as a horizontal layout, the Timeline Panel showcases your project's progression from start to finish. The left side denotes the beginning of your video, while the right side signifies its culmination. Within this panel, a multitude of editing functions can be performed. You can trim, slice, and relocate clips, incorporate transitions and effects, and fine-tune audio levels. Additionally, it offers the ability to manage numerous layers of video and audio tracks. Each track on the timeline aligns with a corresponding layer in the video—higher tracks correlate to higher layers in the video composition. Consider this panel as the hub of your editing journey, offering a bird's-eye view of your project's sequence. Its importance lies in providing a comprehensive overview and a hands-on space to refine and perfect every aspect of your video content.

Using the Timeline Panel

To utilize it effectively, start by importing your media files into the project. This can be done by accessing the "File" menu and selecting "Import," or simply dragging and dropping the files directly into the project panel. Once your media files are imported, you can then move them into the Timeline Panel. Within the Timeline Panel, you have the ability to organize and manipulate your clips. Trimming clips is achieved by dragging their edges to adjust duration, while splitting clips involves positioning the playhead at the desired point and using the razor tool to create a cut. Additionally, the Timeline Panel facilitates the incorporation of effects, transitions, and titles directly into your video. To apply effects or transitions, navigate to the effects panel, select the desired effect or transition, and then drag it onto the corresponding clip in the timeline. For transitions, you can place them at the beginning or end of a clip. Meanwhile, creating titles involves clicking on the "T" icon, typing your text, and dragging the title to the intended position in the timeline.

Customizing the Timeline Panel

To personalize the Timeline Panel in Adobe Premiere Pro, begin by launching the program and selecting your desired project. Once your project is open, locate the Timeline Panel, typically positioned at the bottom of the interface, although you can relocate it to better suit your workflow. To tailor the panel to your preferences, simply right-click anywhere within it. This action triggers a drop-down menu featuring a range of customization options. You can opt to add or remove different track types, like video or audio tracks, via selections such as "**Add Tracks" or "Delete Tracks**". Furthermore, you can modify the timeline's appearance by clicking "**Customize**" and selecting specific elements you wish to display.

Additionally, you can resize tracks by hovering over the border between two tracks and adjusting their height by dragging upwards or downwards. It's worth noting that Adobe Premiere Pro offers the ability to save your workspace layout. After customizing your Timeline Panel to your liking, you can preserve this layout by navigating to "**Window" > "Workspaces" > "Save as New Workspace**". This functionality enables easy access to your preferred layout configuration for future projects.

Basic Editing Tools and Functions

Understanding the tools

Eleven distinct tools are included in Premiere Pro, each of which was developed to carry out a certain function that is helpful throughout the editing process specifically.

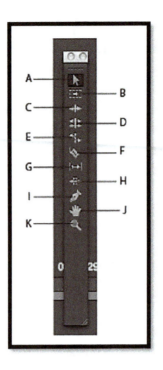

A. Selection tool. B. Track Selection tool. C. Ripple Edit tool. D. Rolling Edit tool. E. Rate Stretch tool. F. Razor tool. G. Slip tool. H. Slide tool. I. Pen tool. J. Hand tool. K. Zoom tool.

➢ **Selection Tool:** This multifunctional tool gives you the ability to choose a variety of objects that are included inside the user interface. These elements include buttons, menu items, and clips. Interacting with clips and navigating the UI are both made possible by this essential feature. After utilizing more advanced editing tools, it is recommended to make the Selection tool the default option. This is because the majority of interactions with clips and the interface often involve the use of this tool.

➢ **Track Selection Tool**: This is a tool that was developed expressly for track-based editing. Its purpose is to assist in picking clips that are located to the right of the cursor inside a sequence. When you use this tool to choose a clip, it will select not only the clip you have selected but also the clips that are located to the right on the same track. The ability to choose a clip and consecutive clips to the right across all tracks can be achieved by holding down the Shift key when clicking on a clip.

➢ **Ripple Edit Tool:** While the Selection tool can be used to trim the beginning or end of a clip in the Timeline, it may also result in gaps being created between clips. The Ripple Edit Tool is a tool that can remove these gaps. In this situation, the Ripple Edit tool is really helpful since it enables you to trim the In or Out point of a clip while

41

simultaneously sealing any gaps that are caused by the edit being performed. The integrity of the edits that were made on either side of the footage that was cut is preserved.

- ➤ **Rolling Edit tool:** Used for simultaneous edits to the In and Out points of adjacent clips on the Timeline. This tool allows for adjustments to be made without affecting the total time of the clips. Both the ***In point*** of one clip and the ***Out point*** of the other clip are trimmed, while the total length of the combined clips is maintained throughout the process.

- ➤ **Rate Stretch Tool**: The Rate Stretch tool is useful in situations when the goal is to modify the length of a clip in the Timeline without any changes being made to the clip's In and Out points. It gives you the ability to either shorten or lengthen a clip, which in turn allows you to change the playback speed of the clip without impacting its In and Out points.

- ➤ **Razor Tool**: Take use of the Razor tool to separate clips inside the Timeline in an accurate manner. Whenever you click on any point inside a clip, it will immediately split the clip at that specific spot for you. By holding down the Shift key while clicking on a clip, you can achieve the goal of dividing all clips among all tracks at a certain precise moment in time.

- ➤ **Slip Tool:** The Slip tool allows for simultaneous modifications to be made to the In and Out points of a clip inside the Timeline. These adjustments are made without affecting the total length of the clip.

- ➤ **Slide Tool**: The Slide tool is useful in situations when the goal is to move a clip to the right or left on the Timeline while simultaneously cutting clips that are next to it. Using this tool, you can be certain that the total length of the clips, as well as the position of the group inside the timeline, will not alter much.

- ➤ **Pen Tool:** Clips possess inherent properties that are customizable and can be animated using the Effect Controls panel. By selecting the Pen tool, you can set or select keyframes for these properties within the Timeline, enabling advanced control over clip attributes.

- ➤ **Hand tool**: This can be used as an alternative to the scroll bar that is situated at the bottom of the Timeline panel. It gives users the ability to shift the viewing area of the Timeline to the right or left, which makes it simpler for them to navigate inside the interface of the Timeline.

- ➤ **Zoom Tool**: When you use the Zoom tool, you will have the power to zoom in or out inside the Timeline viewing area according to your preferences. While working inside the Timeline interface, this tool helps alter the amount of depth and accuracy that is being shown.

Create a sequence of clips

The Editing workspace can be accessed by selecting Editing at the top of the screen or by selecting **Window > Workspaces > Editing**. Both of these options are available. It is now possible to see the footage that you imported in the Project panel. If you are unable to locate the Project panel, choose **Window > Project**. You can see a list of your files; if you want to see thumbnails instead, you can do so by clicking the thumbnail view icon that is located at the bottom of the panel. You have reached the point where you are prepared to construct a sequence, which is the location where you will arrange your audio and video clips along a timeline. From the Project panel, choose the first video clip that you want to show in your sequence, and then drag it from the Project panel to the Timeline panel, which is empty (if the Timeline panel is not visible, select **Window > Timeline**). Other clips can be added to this sequence by dragging each one from the Project panel to the Timeline panel and positioning them next to another clip that is already present in the Timeline panel. If you bring in a lengthy film that takes up the whole of the Timeline panel, you can zoom out and see more of your timeline by repeatedly pressing the **minus (–) key** on your keyboard. By repeatedly pressing the plus (+) key, you can zoom in on the area around the location of the playhead.

Adjust the clip length

To view what your video looks like up to this point in the Program panel, press the spacebar. To expose the Program Monitor, choose **Window > Program Monitor** from the menu bar. To halt the playing, press the **spacebar once** again. To begin playback, move the blue playhead to the location where you want it to begin. **Note**: If a certain video clip seems to be too big or too little in the Program panel when you are playing your sequence, you can easily adjust the size of the clip by right-clicking (Windows) or Control-clicking (macOS) the clip in the Timeline panel and selecting **Set to Frame Size**. This will ensure that the clip can properly fit the viewing area. The process of shortening a clip so that it displays exactly what you want (also known as trimming) is as simple as dragging the edge of the clip to the length that you want it to be. After you have experimented with adjusting the placements of the clips and the durations of the clips, check to see that your sequence does not include any gaps. If you come across one, you should first click the gap that exists between two clips to highlight it, and then use the Delete key on your keyboard to pull the clips together.

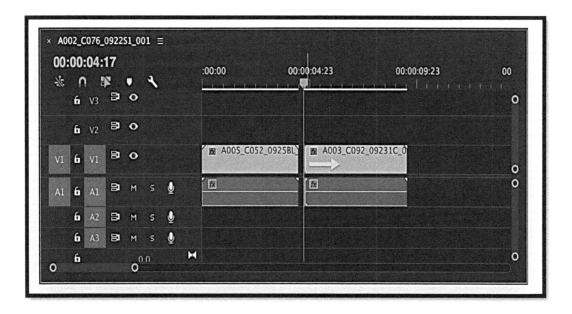

Add transitions between clips

Since your clips are now arranged in a sequence, you can experiment with creating transitions between them now that they are side by side. It is possible to access the Effects panel tab by selecting **Window > Effects** from the menu bar. This tab is located in the same panel group as the Project panel. When you want to view the several dissolve effects that are available, enter the Video Transitions folder first, and then open the **Dissolve** folder. Apply the **Cross Dissolve** effect by dragging it between two clips that you have already cut, and then play your sequence to see how the effect appears. Have a good time playing with different dissolve effects between two adjacent clips, such as making the transition from black to white or vice versa.

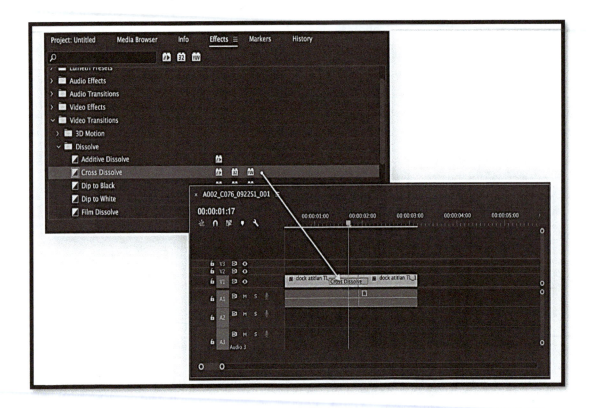

CHAPTER 3
IMPORTING MEDIA

You are not making a copy of the file when you add media to a Premiere Pro project. Instead, the process of importing sets up a reference, which is like making a tag or link in your project that, leads to the original media file. This connection lets Premiere Pro get to the media and work with it without making copies or changes to the source files.

There are four primary methods to import assets directly into Adobe Premiere Pro:

1. **Standard Importing:** This involves selecting **File > Import** within Premiere Pro and navigating to the files you want to bring into your project.
2. **Media Browser Panel:** Premiere Pro includes a **Media Browser** panel that allows you to browse through your local storage, external drives, or networked drives to locate and import media directly into your project.
3. **Adobe Prelude**: Another way to add images is to use Adobe Prelude, a tool made for adding and organizing video files. You can easily bring video from Adobe Prelude into Premiere Pro.
4. **Adobe Bridge**: You can connect media to Premiere Pro using Adobe Bridge, which is a tool for managing media. It lets you look through video files, organize them, and choose which ones to add to your projects.

Premiere Pro creates a connection to the media no matter what method is used. The media can be videos, photos, music files, or even interactive projects from other Adobe Creative Suite programs like After Effects. This linking method lets Premiere Pro work with the original media files while still letting you move, change, and rearrange these assets in your project without making copies or changing the source files.

Standard Importing

One of the easiest and most common ways to add media to your projects in Adobe Premiere Pro is to use the File menu to load standard files. This method has been around for a long time and includes using the tools to find your way around. **To perform a standard import:**

1. In Premiere Pro, go to the menu and select **File > Import**.
2. Find the files you want to add to your project and click on them.

On macOS, you can quickly get to the Import text box by pressing **Command+I**, and on Windows, you can press **Ctrl+I.** This way works best for items that can be used on their own, like music files, graphics, and popular video file types like MP4 (H.264) or MOV (QuickTime). It's especially helpful if you know exactly where the files are on your drive and can get to them quickly. But it's important to keep in mind that this normal way of importing media might not work for some types, like RAW media files or camera footage stored on a file.

This kind of footage usually comes with complicated folder structures that hold different audio and video files as well as important extra data, like information, that define the film. The **Media Browser** panel in Premiere Pro is the best way to work with media created by the camera or files with more complicated structures. This screen makes it easier to import, control, and work with video from cameras that use complicated folder systems. It makes sure that all the important parts of the video are treated correctly in Premiere Pro.

The Media Browser window

Many people think that Adobe Premiere Pro's Media Browser is one of the best and most flexible ways to load media because it can be used by pretty much anyone. It's better than the old file system import method in some ways, which makes it an essential tool for handling media assets and adding them to projects.

Here's why the Media Browser is highly regarded:

1. **Versatility and Information Display**: The Media Browser shows files in a list style and changes how they are shown based on the available information. You can see useful Information about each file or picture in this feature, which makes it easier to move through and choose them from a long list.
2. **Accessible Location**: The Media Browser panel is in the bottom left area of the screen by default, in the Editing workspace. You can get to it quickly by pressing Shift+8. Because Premiere Pro's workspace is its panel, you can save it and move it to a different part of the screen to make it fit your needs. You can also access it by clicking the two-sided arrow and select **Media Browser**.

3. **Automated Media Examination**: The Media Browser is a powerful tool that automatically looks at media assets, which speeds up the process of importing them into Premiere Pro. For example, if your camera records video that is made up of several broken files, the Media Browser will cleverly show them as whole clips. No matter how the files were originally organized, each clip shows up as a single thing with both video and music.

4. **Easier Navigation**: Using images and the information that goes with them in the Media Browser makes it easier to find the right clip. It's easy to find metadata like clip length, recording date, and file type, which makes it easier to search and find specific media assets in a big collection.

In the end, the Media Browser makes it easier to import and handle media files by showing them in a way that is easy to understand, especially when working with complicated camera folder structures or footage that is split into parts. The fact that it can show detailed information along with visual views makes finding and loading the right media files for your projects much faster and easier.

Ingest Options and Proxy Media

You have to take in the information before you can use Prelude. Adding things to your disks is called "**ingesting**." If you save it to the right place, like your video drive, it will be easy to set up for future edits. Premiere Pro is great at playing back and adding effects to a lot of different types of videos and clips. If it's ultra-high quality or RAW video, though, your system gear might not be able to play media all the time. You can choose to work more quickly with low-resolution copies of your material while editing and then switch to the full-resolution originals to check your effects and send your finished work. This is a proxy process, where you make "**proxy**" files with low quality to temporarily replace your original files. You can switch between the two types of files whenever you want. Premiere Pro might make proxy files for you while you load. This option is probably not something you'll use if you're happy with how your system works with the original video. Even so, it has big advantages when it comes to system speed and working together, especially when working with high-resolution pictures on a machine that isn't very powerful.

You can set up the options for importing media and making proxy files on the Ingest Settings tab of the Project Settings dialog box:

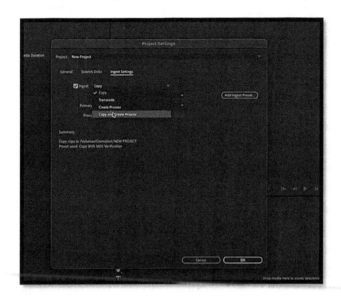

> **Copy**: Because you chose a different **Primary Destination** option below, Premiere Pro will send the source files to the location you specify. This is a good option if you want to import media files directly from your camera's storage since Premiere Pro needs to be able to view the files even if the cards aren't connected to the computer.
> **Transcode**: When you add media files, Premiere Pro will change them to a different format and codec based on the setting you pick and save them where you tell it to. This is helpful if you work in a post-production company that uses a mezzanine media file, which is a standard structure and codec for all projects.
> **Create Proxies**: Premiere Pro makes extra copies of your media files that are lower quality and easier to play on your system, depending on the setting you pick. What

you pick for the Proxy Destination option is where they are saved. Proxy servers are helpful if you're working on a computer that doesn't have a lot of power or if you need to save room when taking a copy of your project with you. You probably wouldn't want to use these files for your final release because the quality isn't very good, but they can help with working together on projects and setting up visual effects faster.

➢ **Copy and Create Proxies**: Premiere Pro copies original files to a place you choose in the Primary Destination menu and creates proxies that are saved in the Proxy Destination menu when you import media files.

It's easy to switch between showing your original, high-resolution media and your low-resolution proxy copies if your project has clips that need proxy media. To turn on proxies, go to **Edit > Preferences > Media (Windows) or Premiere Pro > Preferences > Media (macOS).**

Importing Still Images File

There are a few things you should do when adding still photos into Premiere Pro after you've made sure your picture meets the above requirements. Before you put anything in, go to the **Preferences** menu from the **Edit** dropdown. Click on Timeline.

If you change the **Still Image Default Duration** option, you can choose how long each still you bring into the software will be. It can save you a lot of time and trouble to avoid problems in the first place, especially if you want to import a picture sequence.

In Photoshop or Illustrator, you can make channel settings that you can then apply to the picture file you bring into Premiere Pro if you want alpha transparency. Keep in mind that alpha transparency can't be stored in JPEGs, no matter where the pictures come from. Also, make sure that the color space of any stills you want to use is compatible with video. sRBG and NTSC RGB are two common options.

So, how do you go about importing?

Right-click on one of your bins and choose Import from the Context menu, or press Ctrl + I to bring up the Import window. Pick the still picture you want to use and click "**Open**." It will be in the bin, and you can drag it right onto your timeline. You can change where the picture is, its size, its movement, and its transparency in the Effect Controls box. You can also give the picture different effects, just like you would with any other image.

CHAPTER 4
WORKING WITH AUDIO

Importing and Adjusting Audio

Accessing and Using the Premiere Pro Import Window

1. **Double-click in the Project Panel**: Doubling-clicking on a space in the Project Panel is one of the fastest ways to get to the Import window. When you do this, the Import window will appear, letting you choose which video files or images to import.

2. **Double-click in an Open Bin Panel:** If you have a separate Bin panel open, you can access the Import window by double-clicking on an empty area within that panel. Similar to the Project Panel method, this action triggers the **Import window** to appear, enabling you to import your desired files.

3. **File Menu Option**: You can also access the Import window by going to the File menu and choosing the "Import" option. If you click on this option, the Import window will open, letting you add files to your project.

4. **Keyboard Shortcut**: Keyboard shortcuts can help you get things done faster. On a Mac, press Command+i. On a PC, press Control+i. using this keyboard option starts the **Import window** right away, which makes adding media files or images to your project faster.

Now, find the sound file you want to add to Premiere Pro in the Import window. If you want to import multiple clips, you can pick them by pressing **Command/Control+click or Shift+click**. Then click Bring in. If you don't want to use the Import window, you can drag and drop the file into the Project panel from **Finder (Mac) or Computer (Windows).** But I like the Import box better and think you should use it. After you click "**Import**," a box will likely appear for a short time (***see picture below***). As soon as it goes away, you then add the music file(s)!

After the Audio is imported in Premiere Pro

Put the music file you just added in the right bin. First, double-click it to open it in the Source monitor and choose the In and Out Points. Then, drag it into your timeline to add it to your sequence. Most of the time, you'll be working with **MP3 (.mp3) and WAV** (.wav) files for audio tracks. You can add both types of files into Premiere Pro without any problems.

Basic Audio Editing

Set Up the Workspace

To work with audio in Premiere Pro, it is helpful to switch between workspaces. Premiere comes with a lot of built-in workspaces that make it easy to see all the tools you need for the job. To get to the view with the tools you need, click on **Audio** at the top of Premiere Pro. Now it helps to get a sense of where you are. You'll see a view with a few key screens that are only available in the Audio workspace by default. Essential Sound is to the right of your workspace, and the ***Audio Track Mixer*** is in the middle of the window. When we work with Premiere Pro audio, we mostly use these two screens.

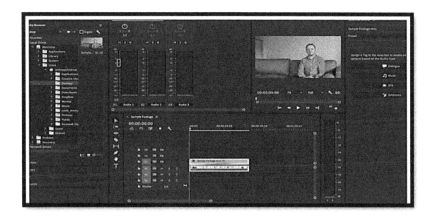

You will also see screens that you know from other Premiere workspaces. The timeline panel at the bottom of the app is the same one you were using before you went to Audio. It shows how the video and audio clips in your production are put together visually.

Adding audio files

The Media Browser is on the left side of the app. Click it to add audio to your project. This can be used to find more audio clips to add to your project and add them. You only need to find the files and drag and drop them onto the screen. You can click and drag clips on the timeline to put them in the right place on the video. You can have already done this in a different workspace, but you can click and drag your audio to make it line up with your video. Before we go any further with this process, it would be helpful to make the audio track bigger so that you can work with it more closely. You can see the pattern better if you pull down on the handle below the track.

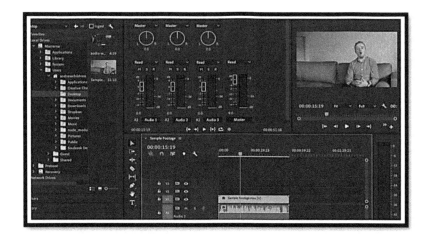

Let's learn more about the key panels in this view and how you can use them to change the audio now that we're familiar with where we are.

Changing the Audio Levels

One of the most usual things to do with audio in Premiere Pro is to change the volume. This is very important when you need to change more than one audio track separately while balancing them. Finding the sweet spot between **"loud enough"** and **"not too loud"** is the objective of audio levels. Decibels are used to measure sound levels, and the numbers to the left of the bars in the picture below show the amounts. The audio clip's goal should match its volume. The audio should be the most visible and loudest track if it's the main conversation track. The background music and sound effects need to be turned down so they don't get in the way of the other parts. Find the track on the **Audio Mixer** panel and change the audio levels for the whole clip. You can change the level by moving the button up or down. Make sure that the colored lines don't flash red as you play back the audio. This means that you've turned up the levels too much.

The audio levels can also be changed over time using keyframes. Holding Ctrl or Cmd on your keyboard and then clicking on the waveform on the timeline will allow you to adjust the audio levels in Premiere. Now, you can change the volume by grabbing the line that runs across the track and pulling it down.

Next, hold down Ctrl or Cmd and click on a different part of the screen. The timeline now has two points that hold it together. To change the audio over time, you can move them up and down separately. You can change audio to rise and fall throughout an audio clip, just like you can change visual effects over time.

Panning Audio

Watch how the sounds around you come from different speakers the next time you're in a movie theater. Pro audio engineers work very hard to bring sound to certain areas of the soundstage so that the experience is fully realistic. Yes, the person listening to you might be watching a video at the same time as listening on AirPods, so full sound isn't a given. However, working with shifting the tracks can help make things sound balanced, especially when you have more than one audio track to work with. To say it again, there are different ways to do this in Premiere. The Mixer panel at the top lets you change a track for the whole output. To do this, move the button to the left or right to change the audio.

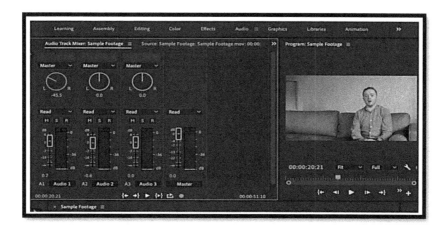

To change the audio mix throughout a movie, another option is to use keyframes. Similar to how we used keyframes to establish "anchor points" to change the audio mix as the clip went on. First, click on the **keyframe** button. Then select **track panner**. Finally, select **balance**. There you go! You can now use the keyframes on your clip to control and change the balance all over it. It will oscillate if you move it back and forth.

Editing Audio

Working with audio is pretty much the same as working with video on the timeline. You can change where it starts and stops by grabbing the handles on either end. You can also drag and drop clips into place and use the knife tool to split clips, as shown in the image below.

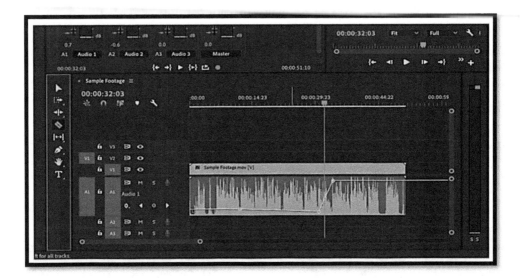

Keep an eye on the waveform when you're working with audio. It's easier to see as you make each track bigger. This can help you see where the best cut should be made. A few other changes will become clear as you work with Premiere Pro audio. The sound that you added to your video clips goes along with the video they are connected to. You can split the two audio clips by right-clicking on them and selecting "**Unlink.**" To sum up, Premiere's audio settings are mostly just drag-and-drop. Don't forget that you can find a clip in the **Media Browser** on the left and then drag and drop it onto the timeline. From there, you can also use drag-and-drop to move clips around. Don't forget that each project has more than one audio track. You can stack clips between those tracks to play more than one clip at the same time. Remember that balancing the levels can help you make the sound experience more realistic. You might also want to try adding audio effects that can change the way your sound sounds. Open the Audio Effects panel on the left side of the Audio workspace. Then, find an effect you want to use and click and drag it onto the audio clip on your timeline.

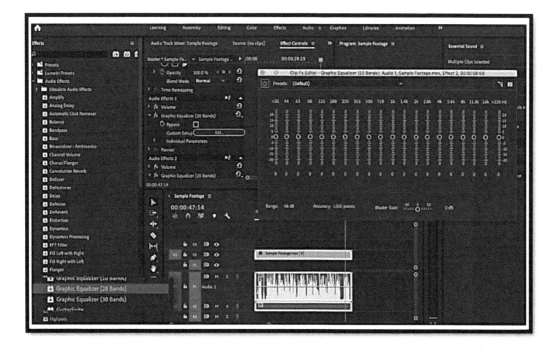

The Effects Control box will have more options now that the movie is chosen. For example, there will be a part with a Graphic Equalizer (20 Bands). A new adjustment box will appear where you can change the audio output after clicking on Edit on this effect. Each of these effects will have a different impact on the audio, but they all add something to the clip you already have and don't require any additional apps.

Using Adobe Stock

Adobe Stock is a flexible service that gives creatives access to a huge library with millions of high-quality, royalty-free assets like music, videos, Motion Graphics themes, and more. Customers can subscribe to a plan that gives them access to multiple assets.

Here is a guide on how to add Adobe Stock audio to your Premiere Pro projects for your reference:

1. **Accessing Adobe Stock Audio in Premiere Pro:**
   - Begin by selecting the "Audio" workspace within Premiere Pro. Then, navigate to the **"Essential Sound"** section and click on "**Browse**."
2. **Browsing and Selecting Tracks:**
   - Tracks can be explored based on mood or genre. Each genre often contains several sub-genres for more refined choices. You can navigate through sub-genres by using the **">"** arrow.
3. **Searching for Specific Tracks:**
   - If you have a particular track in mind, you can input its name into the Search box located at the top of the Essential Sound panel. This will display the relevant results, allowing you to select your desired track.
4. **Fine-Tuning Search Results:**
   - **After your initial selection, you can further refine your search results by applying filters based on specific criteria:**
     - **Tempo:** Adjust the pace of the music from as low as 30 beats per minute to as high as 250 beats per minute.
     - **Duration:** Set minimum and maximum durations for the tracks, ranging from 0:00 to 5:00.
     - **Vocals:** Choose between music with vocals, purely instrumental tracks, or a mix of both.
     - **Audio Partners:** There's a list of audio partners available from which you can select tracks.

You can effectively explore, discover, and choose the best music tracks that suit your project's requirements, mood, tempo, duration, and even vocal preferences by using these search and filtering options within Adobe Stock's audio library integrated into Premiere Pro's Essential Sound panel.

Recording a Voice-Over

You have the option to make a voice-over while your sequence is playing in Premiere Pro. Make sure you follow these step-by-step steps to get this done:

1. **Make Sure Microphone Is Set Up Correctly**: Check that your microphone is set up correctly and is set as the default input in Premiere Pro's audio hardware settings. Go to **Edit > Preferences > Audio Hardware > Default Input** on a Windows computer. If you're using a Mac, go to the Premiere Pro application menu, then click on Preferences, then Audio Hardware, and finally Default Input.

2. **Prepare for Recording**: Either put on headphones or stop the playing audio before you start recording the voice-over. By doing this, you make it less likely that microphone noise will affect the quality of your video.

3. **Start Recording Your Voice-Over**: When you're ready to begin recording your voice-over, find the "**Record Voice-Over**" button in Premiere Pro and press it. After you click this button, Premiere Pro will start recording audio from the exact spot where the Timeline playhead is.

4. **Stop the Recording**: When you're done with the voice-over, press the "Stop" button. After that, the newly recorded audio clip will show up in both the sequence area and the Project panel of Premiere Pro. This new sound file will be saved in the same place as your current project file by default. This will make it easy to find within your project structure.

Change the volume over time

You can change the volume or loudness of audio across a timeline dynamically by using keyframes. This lets you make a more complex and detailed sound mix. To change sound **levels successfully in Adobe Premiere Pro using keyframes, follow these step-by-step instructions:**

1. **Display Audio Keyframes**: First, make sure that the "Show Audio Keyframes" option is turned on in the Timeline panel's Settings menu. You can see keyframes on audio clips better by changing the height of the audio track.

2. **Choose the Pen Tool**: Go to the toolbox and pick out the Pen Tool. We will use this tool to make keyframes for the audio clips and change them.

3. **Making Keyframes**: To make a new keyframe marker at a certain point in time, click on the thin white line that appears on an audio clip. These keyframes are like marks that hold settings, like how loud or level the audio is.

4. **Raising or lowering the volume levels**: Drag the newly formed clip up or down to raise or lower the sound volume at that specific moment in time. You can exactly adjust the audio volume using this move in real time.

5. **Timing and Placement**: Drag the keyframe left or right along the timeline to change the time when the changes happen. With this manipulation, you can exactly set when the changed sound should happen in your audio clip.

6. **Keyframe Management**: To get rid of a keyframe, select it and press the Backspace (Windows) or Delete (Mac) key (in macOS). You can also use the Pen tool to select several keyframes at once and move or delete them all at once, which speeds up the editing process.

7. **Application to Clips and Tracks**: It's important to remember that keyframes are mostly used on single clips, but they can also be added to tracks to change the sound in a more general way.

8. **Switching Tools**: When you're done working with keyframes, go back to the toolbox and select the Selection tool. It's possible to change normally with this tool without changing keyframes.

Make the sound better.

➤ **Getting to the Audio Workspace**: Go to **Window > Workspaces > Audio** to get to the Audio Workspace. The Essential Sound box is located in this workspace and is a powerful tool for making the audio quality better.

➤ **Choosing a Clip to Change**: In the Timeline panel, pick out the clip you want to change using the Essential Sound panel. This choice is very important because it tells you which audio you'll be editing.

➤ **Finding the Audio Type in Essential Sound**: Find the type of audio you're working on within the Essential Sound area. For example, choose the right audio group if it's a conversation.

➤ **Using Essential Sound Settings**: To improve sound quality quickly and easily, turn on the settings in the Essential Sound box. For example, if you turn on Loudness, the volume of words will be automatically changed to meet normal values in the business. By raising certain tones with EQ, you can make speech clearer, and the Enhance Speech option makes even smaller changes to improve sound clarity.

➤ **Looking at More Options**: The Essential Sound box has more changes that can be made to fit different types of audio. You can better understand their effects if you look into these options while listening to the changes as they happen. This live method makes it easier to make precise changes that meet your audio needs.

➢ **Making Changes to the Audio**: Once you're done using the Essential Sound panel to improve your audio, you can return to the Editing workspace and continue your editing work. With the help of this shift, you can continue working on your project while also improving the audio.

How to Use the Essential Sound Panel

Every designer could use the Essential Sound panel, which has a bunch of the most useful audio tools in one place. There are four pre-set options on the right side of the Audio workspace after you choose a track. They are conversation, music, sound effects, and background. These are where you should begin changing audio that fits these groups. Premiere will show you the tools that work best with the type of audio you pick when you choose a setup like a conversation. Set Premiere to work on your audio by checking boxes like **Loudness, Repair, and Clarity.**

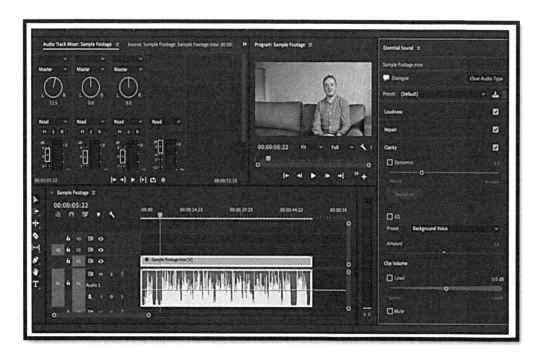

It's not always the goal to get your audio fixed and balanced. You can want to style and add effects to it sometimes. Using a setting from the list of options is helpful in this situation. To make the audio seem far away from the action, for instance, use a setting like **Make Distant**. It's simple to see how you could use this to experiment with audio in your upcoming project.

On the Essential Sound panel, make sure to use all of the effects to make your audio productions more interesting. Check out From the Radio for a retro look and Over the Intercom for the perfect "principal voice" in your next video.

Audio Track vs. Audio Clip Mixer

There are two approaches you can take to edit audio in Premiere Pro. Let's talk about what the changes are between the audio track mixer and the audio clip mixer before we start. The Audio Track Mixer is made to manage the whole track where each piece of audio is stored. When you edit in the track mixer, you change settings that affect the whole track. With the Audio Clip Mixer, on the other hand, you can change any clip that is under the playhead at any given time.

How to Use the Audio Clip Mixer

Let's look at the Audio Clip Mixer in more detail now. It's in the Workspace and can be reached from the top menu bar by clicking on the Audio tab. The Audio Clip Mixer can be found in this area. You can see it by going to **Window > Audio Clip Mixer**. You can see that the number of audio channels in the clip mixing part is the same as the number of audio tracks on your timeline. The number of channels in your clip mixer will grow as you add more audio tracks to your timeline. Also, keep this in mind! The audio clip mixer doesn't change the audio tracks; it changes the audio clips that are in those tracks. The tracks are all it does to tell you which clip you're working with. As the playhead moves over a track, the effects of the clip on that track are shown on each audio clip mixing channel. To be used properly and even figure out which piece of audio you will be dealing with, the audio clip mixer is completely dependent on the position of the playhead.

Improve Your Audio with the Audio Clip Mixer

If the audio is playing, the audio meters will go up and down to show how loud or quiet it is. If the audio is playing at all, they will stay flat. It is important to keep an eye on your audio levels and know that if they get Into the red area, you could clip the audio and lose sound. By moving this button up or down, you can change the volume of each of the audio clips that your playhead is currently on. When you move the tool to change the audio level, the clip on the timeline that goes with it shows that the level has been changed. Make sure that your audio track is tall enough and that your audio keyframes are turned on if you can't see the keyframe indicator. You can do this by right-clicking on the clip and choosing **Show Clip Keyframe > Volume > Level**. When you move the audio scale, you'll see that the blue number changes too. The amount of the number can also be changed to make things different. It means you can click and drag the number to enter a new amount when it's marked in blue. Alternatively, you can click and then type in a number.

Staying Organized

Half the fight is won when you know how to find the channel that controls which clip and how to change the volume of the clip. Also, organization is very important. However, it can be hard to keep things organized and easy to find. Putting similar things on the same tracks can help. You can see that all of your music tracks will be on the same channel in the audio clip mixer if you keep the music on one track. It would be helpful if you gave this track a name, like "Music" or something else that makes sense for it. When you are watching the audio change, this will help you remember what each channel does.

Mute, Solo, and Keyframes

There are a lot more ways to control your audio clips besides just changing the volume.

There are three icons at the top of the screen: an M, an S, and a diamond-shaped icon.

- **M** means "**mute**." The M will turn green when you click it, and the whole track will be muffled.
- **S** means "**solo**." If you click on the S, it will turn yellow and become the only thing playing. Everything else will be muffled.

- The diamond-shaped icon means that you can specify keyframes below the track's playhead.

Using the Write Keyframes Function

When you click this, it doesn't make a new keyframe like normal keyframes do. Instead, it starts making keyframes for the clip under the playhead for that track. An audio meter change will cause a keyframe to appear on your clip if you select the write keyframes marker. There is a new keyframe added when you move the playhead forward and make another change. The clip's level changes over time. If you pick the Pen Tool, click on the keyframes, and then press backspace or delete, you can quickly get rid of them. It's pretty much the same if you select the write keyframe feature and move the scale while the clip is playing. Your audio will change over time as a result of the plethora of keyframes that you will receive. There is a new clip under the playhead. If you move the playhead forward, you can see that when you make changes, they only affect that clip. It doesn't change anything about the previous clip that you can change. Between the Audio Clip Mixer and the Audio Track Mixer, this is one of the most important changes that can be found. The audio clip maker knows that each clip is special and treats them as such.

Controlling the Audio Panning

The shifting, or how much of the audio is outputted from the left or right, can be adjusted in the Audio Clip Mixer. This can be done in one of two ways: using knobs or sliders.

Using the Panel Knob

The audio panning can be changed by moving the knob at the top of the panel to the left or right. When you have a clip of ocean waves coming in from the right side of the frame and want to make sure the sound is coming from the same direction, this will affect the balance of where it sounds like the audio is coming from. While you do this, remember that you can tell the audio clip to move to the left or right over time as long as the write keyframe button is on that channel. You can change a few things about your clip player if you right-click on any of the tracks. You can mark the high and low parts of your audio, which are called **"peaks and valleys,"** and show them. Those marks can be static or move around. They will change every few seconds to match how the audio is right now, which is what we call dynamic. Unless the audio itself moves them up or down, they will stay where they are. If you turn on color gradient, it will only change whether your audio levels are shown as solid green, yellow, or red. Or, shown as a slow gradient of all the colors that are between those three.

Using the Sliders

You can also right-click and make sure that the **Show Channel volume** is chosen as a second way to change the left and right audio channels. On the audio channel itself, this will bring up two knobs that can be used to change the volume of either the left or right channel. Remember that this can also be keyframed if the write keyframe option is set to true.

Applying Audio Effects

Applying a Single Audio Effect

1. **Accessing Audio Tools:** Navigate to the Effects panel. You can either scroll through the Effects panel to locate the audio tools or use the search box to find a specific sound effect by typing its name.
2. **Selecting and Applying an Effect:**
   - Once you've found the desired audio effect, select its icon within the Effects panel.
   - Drag the chosen effect and drop it onto the audio clip in the Timeline panel. Alternatively, select the clip in the Timeline and double-click the sound effect within the Effect Controls panel to apply it.
3. **Adjusting Audio Settings:** Post-application, you can fine-tune and modify the audio settings of the effect within the Effect Controls panel according to your preferences.

Applying Multiple Effects to a Single Clip

1. **Selecting the Audio Clip:** Begin by selecting the audio clip in the Timeline to which you want to apply multiple effects.
2. **Group Selection of Effects:**
   - In the Effect Controls panel, select multiple effects by holding down the Control key in Windows or the Command key in Mac while clicking on the desired effects.
3. **Applying the Grouped Effects:**
   - After selecting the effects, drag the entire group of selected effects to the chosen audio clip in the Timeline panel.

How to Use Auto Ducking in Premiere Pro

Sound that is fighting with other sounds in your footage is called "audio ducking." You choose one of the sounds to "**duck down**" and let the other one take precedence. In your video, there's some conversation that you want to hear. When it's over, you want the music to get louder. After that, when the conversation comes back, you should turn down the music volume so that you can hear it again. Usually, this is done by adding keyframes and manually adjusting each one. The process shouldn't take too long if you only have a few shorts of this. If you have a 10-minute video with a lot of these kinds of moments, though, it can take a lot of time to do this for each version. Especially if you're making a project like a conversation with music in the background. There is a quick fix in Premiere Pro that makes the process a lot easier, though. The Essential Sound Panel is where you can find it all.

The steps:

1. Start by either opening an existing multitrack session containing the audio clip you wish to work on or create a new one within Premiere Pro.
2. Utilize the Essential Sound panel to categorize or tag the content according to its specific type. This tagging process allows Premiere Pro to recognize and apply appropriate adjustments. For instance, you can tag clips as music or ambience for effective management.
3. Within your timeline, select the background clip (e.g., music) and navigate to the Essential Sound panel. Here, assign the selected clip the appropriate audio type, such as 'Music.' This categorization informs Premiere Pro about the nature of the audio content.
4. Enable auto-ducking for the selected clip by checking the checkbox labeled 'Ducking.' When activated, Premiere Pro automatically incorporates an Amplify Effect onto the clip. This effect includes keyframes generated by the Auto Ducking algorithm, precisely adjusting the gain parameter. These keyframes are easily editable or removable without disrupting your overall sound design.

A critical aspect to ensure the smooth functioning of auto-ducking is assigning audio types to the other audio tracks. By categorizing these tracks (e.g., dialogue, sound effects) using the Essential Sound panel, Premiere Pro gains the necessary information to effectively implement the auto-ducking feature. This categorization guides the software in determining which tracks should drive the ducking process, facilitating seamless audio adjustments across your project.

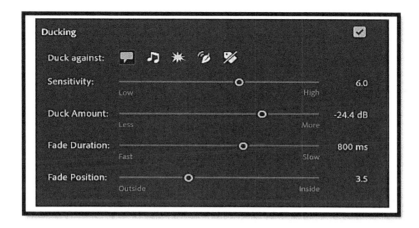

5. **Configuring Auto-Ducking Options:**
○ **Duck Against:** Choose the audio content types against which you want the auto-ducking to occur. You can select from various options such as Dialogue, Music, Sound Effects, Ambience, or un-tagged clips.
○ **Sensitivity:** This setting determines the threshold at which the auto-ducking activates. Higher or lower sensitivity settings result in fewer adjustments. Higher sensitivity prioritizes maintaining a lower volume for music, while lower sensitivity focuses on preserving louder music. Moderate sensitivity values trigger more adjustments, allowing music to quickly lower when speech pauses occur.
○ **Duck Amount:** Adjust this parameter to determine the extent of volume reduction applied to your music clip. Moving it towards the right reduces the volume more drastically, whereas moving it towards the left leads to subtler volume adjustments.
○ **Fade Duration:** Control how swiftly the volume adjustment occurs when triggered. Quick fades work well for rapidly changing music and speech, whereas slower fades are suitable for gradually lowering background music behind voice overs.
○ **Fade Position:** Choose where the background audio fades with the dialogue – either outside, inside, or in the middle of the dialogue segments.
6. **Generating Keyframes:**

After setting the desired auto-ducking parameters, click on the "Generate Keyframes" button. This action computes and sets keyframes for the Amplify effect, which was automatically added to the clip when enabling auto-ducking.

Note: While you can manually adjust the keyframes after their generation, clicking the "Generate Keyframes" button again will overwrite any manual changes made to the keyframes. Premiere Pro automatically includes keyframes and ducking adjustments on the effect's rubberband. Additionally, the Timeline clip's audio keyframe display switches automatically to show these keyframes on the Amplify effect for easier visualization and editing.

Add & End with Echo Effects in Premiere Pro (+5 Sound Effects)

A great way to create the world of your movie is to add echo to the audio. Where you are will change the sound of everything, from footsteps to traffic. Premiere Pro Echo Effects can help your foley sound effects feel like they belong in the scene. We will show you two ways to add an echo to your audio creations that you can change in any way you want.

Part 1: Create Quality Echo Effects (Surround Reverb) in Premiere Pro

When you add sound effects to your clips, you need to pay attention to how the camera moves and where it is in the scene. It can be hard to match the camera position, the sound source, and the size of the room, but it will get easier as you use more audio clips.

Option 1: Basic Echo Effect

When you use the Basic Echo Effect, all of your clips will have an echo. This kind of echo effect works great for sounds like footsteps, gunshots, slamming doors, and even talking.

- Make changes to the audio and video in the timeline until you're ready to add the reverb effect.
- Look for Surround Reverb in the Effects panel and add it to your audio clip.

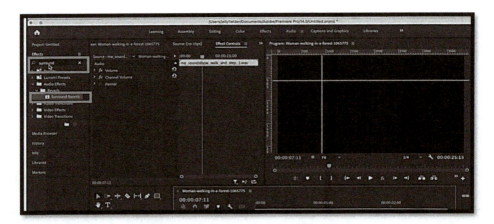

- Click the Edit button next to Custom Setup in the Effects Controls panel.

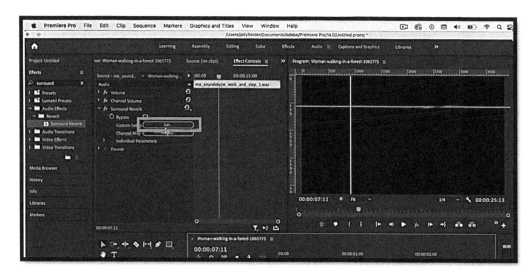

- Raise the **Gain** setting to set the amount of sound.
- Select **Audio Gain** from the menu that appears when you right-click on the audio clip.

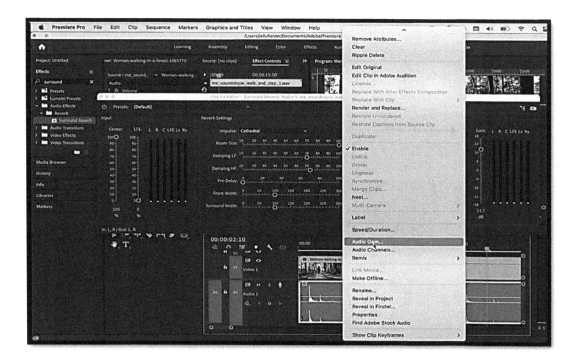

- Click on the **Adjust Gain by** option, enter 15, and then click OK.

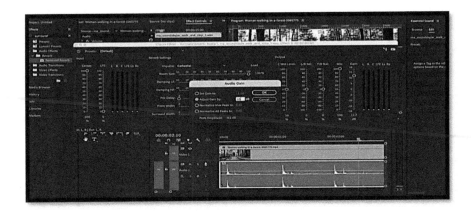

- Finally, make the room smaller so that your images can fit where you want them to be.

Option 2: End with Echo Effect

You can cut music tracks for your videos down by ending them with a fade-out. For something a little different, you can give your piece a cool echoey finish by adding some reverb.

- Use the Timeline to change your video and music. Cut the piece off where you want it to stop.
- Cut out the part of your audio clip that you want to repeat.
- Move the part of your Audio Clip that has the echo to a different Track.
- Click the "**New Item**" button after right-clicking in the project window and pick "Transparent Video."

- Move the Transparent Video to the end of your timeline to make room for the echo to go on after the audio clip ends.
- Under Window, choose Audio Track Mixer, and then pick the sequence you want to work in.

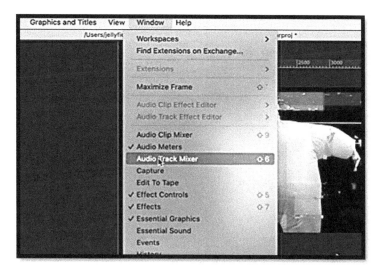

- In the Audio Track Mixer box, go to the end of the Audio Track 2 setting and click the down arrow. Then, go to Reverb > Studio Reverb.

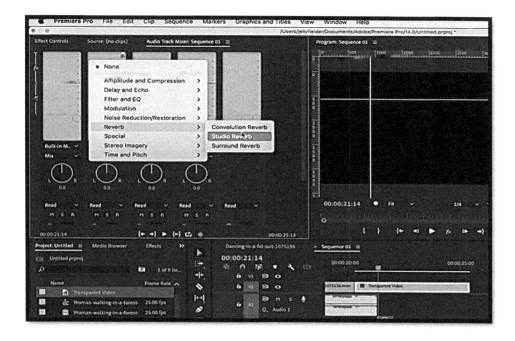

- In the Audio Track Mixer, double-click on the Studio Reverb effect that you just added.
- In the Studio Reverb Settings box, turn up the Decay and Wet settings until you like how the echo sounds.
- To make your echo effect fade out, go to the beginning of Audio Track 2 and click Show keyframes.
- Click the Keyframe settings and pick Track Keyframes > Volume from the menu that comes up.

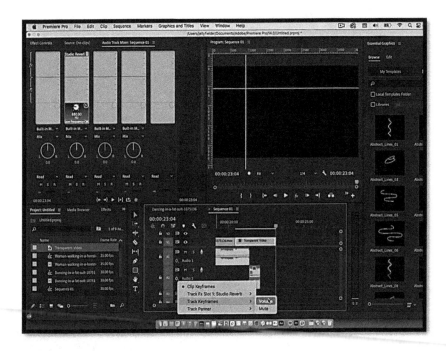

- Insert a Keyframe using the Pen Tool where you want to reduce the audio volume. Find the point in the music where you want the fade-out to end and turn down the volume.

Making changes to the media cache.

By making versions of video and audio files that it can quickly reach, Premiere Pro improves its speed. You can find these files in the Media Cache Files folder. They are called media cache files. Within the Media Cache area, there is also a database folder called Media Cache database files that contains URLs to these media cache files. Adobe Premiere Pro saves accelerator files like peak files (.pek) and compressed audio (.cfa) in the Media Cache. These files make playing smoother and make it easier to get to media faster while working.

Cleaning out old or useless media cache files can make a big difference in how well your system works. When the source media needs them, deleted cache files are automatically remade; making sure that access is smooth when it's needed. Clearing the Media Cache is a good way to get back storage space after you're done with a project. This action gets rid of any test image files that aren't needed, which frees up room on your hard drive.

To clear the Media Cache in Premiere Pro, do the following:

1. Getting to Media Cache Management: Go to the Preferences area in Premiere Pro. Click Edit > Preferences on Windows or go to the Premiere Pro Application Menu > Preferences on Mac to get to the Preferences menu.

2. Finding the Media Cache Settings: In the Preferences menu, look for the Media Cache settings.

3. Clearing media cache: Find the "**Erase Media Cache Files**" option and click on the "**Delete**" button that goes with it. This command tells Premiere Pro to get rid of the media cache files that it has saved. This frees up room on the disk that the cache data was taking up.

4. Getting to the Delete Media Cache Files Dialog Box: A dialogue box called "Delete Media Cache Files" will show up after you go to the Media Cache settings in Premiere Pro Preferences and start the process of clearing the cache.

5. **Options Available in the Dialog Box**: **You'll see three different options in this text box for how to delete media cache files:**

- **Delete Unnecessary Media Cache Files:** If you choose this option, media cache files that were made for source material that you can't get to or that your current projects don't need will be deleted. Getting rid of these cache files that aren't needed helps free up room without affecting the operation of the current project.

- **Delete All Media Cache Files from the System**: This option deletes all media cache files on the system from where they are now. By doing this, all of the stored files are deleted, leaving a blank page for managing the cache.
- **Rebuilding Cache Files When Source Media Demands**: When you remove cache files, it's important to know that Premiere Pro will automatically rebuild them whenever the source media needs them. It's best to restart Premiere Pro after getting rid of any cache files and before opening any projects so that this feature works properly. If you choose this option, any media cache files that are needed will be remade when they are needed.

6. **Finalizing the Selection**: Once you've chosen the best option for your needs, hit the "OK" button in the text box to start the delete process. This move confirms your choice and deletes the cache files you chose based on the option you chose.

What location should I save my Media Cache files?

Picking the right storage for your Media Cache is an important part of optimizing your Adobe Premiere Pro setup. For the best performance, you might want to use a fast SSD or NVMe drive that is only used to store your Media Cache files. The read and write speeds of these solid-state drives are faster than those of regular hard disk drives (HDDs). Their better speed makes it easier to get to Media Cache files, which makes editing better overall. Changing where your Media Cache files are saved by default in Premiere Pro is a simple process. All you have to do is go to Preferences and find the Media Cache settings. You can choose a folder or spot on your SSD or NVMe drive where you want to store the Media Cache files by hitting the "Browse" button. Being able to change where the data goes lets you make the setup work best for your needs and the tools you have.

Giving the Media Cache its SSD or NVMe drive is the best way to get the best speed. This method splits actions that use the cache from those that use other files, which makes handling data more efficient while writing. It is possible to store the video Cache on the same disk as your video files, though, if a separate drive isn't possible. Even though it's not as good as having a specialized drive, this setup is still faster than using a slower HDD. The performance of high-speed SSDs or NVMe drives can be greatly improved by changing where the Media Cache is stored in Premiere Pro and using these drives' features. This will also make the program respond faster when editing videos. In the end, this improvement makes the editing process go more smoothly and quickly.

Automatically manage your Media Cache files

In **Adobe Premiere Pro, you can change how the media cache works by changing a few settings that control how cache files are managed:**

- **Do Not Delete Cache Files Automatically**: Premiere Pro is set to keep certain types of cache files, like.pek,.cfa, and.ims files, in their subfolder folders, which are called Peak Files and Media Cache Files. These files are kept and won't be removed immediately unless you tell it to.
- **Automatically Delete Cache Files Older Than a Specified Period**: You have the option to set a specific period after which cache files will be instantly removed in the Media Cache Preferences. The number is usually set to 90 days, but you can change it to any length of time you want. This setting makes sure that cache files older than the given time are regularly deleted so that they don't build up for no reason.
- **Automatically Delete Oldest Cache Files When Cache Exceeds a Certain Volume Size**: Premiere Pro lets you delete the oldest cache files automatically when the total cache size exceeds a certain percentage of the volume where the media cache is stored. For example, the older cache files are deleted if the cache size gets too big— 10% of the total volume size is too big. This keeps the cache size below the level and stops too much cache from building up.

PART II
INTERMEDIATE TECHNIQUES

CHAPTER 5

ADVANCED EDITING TOOLS

Ripple and Roll Edits

Adobe Premiere Pro's Ripple and Roll Edits are basic tools that allow editors to fine-tune the time and pacing of their video scenes quickly and accurately. Let us take a closer look at these two editing tools and see how they can be used most effectively during the editing process. Ripple Change: In Premiere Pro, the "B" key controls the Ripple Edit tool, which lets you change the length of a clip while also changing the clips next to it on the timeline instantly. Using the wave Edit tool to cut or add to a clip has a wave effect that moves the clips next to it to make the change look natural. In the Tools window, click or press the B key to use Ripple Edit.

- The Ripple Edit tool is like a "ripple effect"—when you trim a clip, it moves all the other clips in your timeline to a new place.
- It cuts the layers in and out points and then slides all the clips that come after it over to meet the new out point.
- In this case, if you cut 10 frames off the end of the clip's back end, the clips that are left will move forward 10 frames.

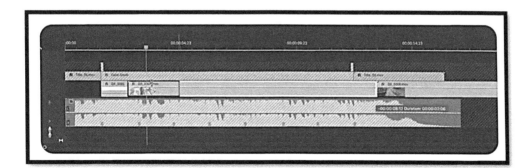

Note: The Ripple Edit will not change any locked video editing tracks. If you have more than one track of videos, make sure you check again to see what's locked and what's not.

How to Ripple Delete in Premiere Pro

The Ripple Edit tool can create gaps in your timeline. This is where Ripple Deleting comes in.

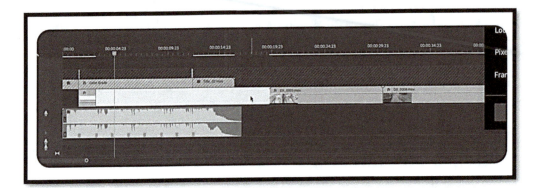

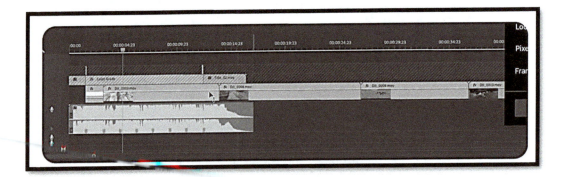

- Simply click the space between two clips to use Ripple Delete; this should turn the space white to show you which part you will be deleting.
- Then, press the backspace or delete key on your keyboard. This will move your clips so that they line up with the closest clip's endpoint in the timeline.
- Once more, make sure to lock any tracks that you don't want the Ripple Delete to change.

Roll Edit

The "N" key controls the Roll Edit tool, which is used to change the edit point between two clips that are next to each other on the timeline. When you use the Roll Edit tool instead of the Ripple Edit tool, you can change where the edit point is placed without changing how long the sequence lasts.

Click and drag the cut point, which is where the out and in points meet between two clips. This will change the in and out places without moving the clips. One clip will get shorter while the other gets longer.

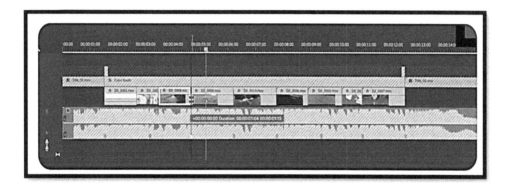

The Rate Stretch Tool

You can change the speed of a clip with the Rate Stretch tool, instead of having to right-click, go through the options, and guess by what percentage you need to speed up or slow down each clip. To use the Rate Stretch tool, press the R key on your computer or look for it in the Tools window, next to the Ripple Edit tool. With the Rate Stretch tool, you can change how fast your footage plays back by dragging the clip's beginning or ending point. This works the same way as changing the clip's length.

Slip and Slide Edits

You can fine-tune individual clips with the Slip tool, which is a powerful feature. Okay, so you have a clip in your timeline that fits perfectly between two other clips. But the part of the clip you used could be better. You can change a clip's In and Out points without having to delete it, choose new ones, and then add them to the timeline. The Slip tool lets you do this without having to move the clip or delete it first. To get to it, press the Y key on your keyboard or click on Slip Tool in the Tools box. The cursor on your mouse will change to arrows that point to vertical bars going in both directions.

The Slip tool is impressive for making fine adjustments to the portion of a clip the viewer sees; it can be super helpful when using **transitions** between your footage. Occasionally when you try to add a transition, you might be told there is not enough available clip; this is because the transition needs more frames than available. You can move the clips "In" and "Out" places with the Slip tool to add the transition without having to change the timeline or the clips around it.

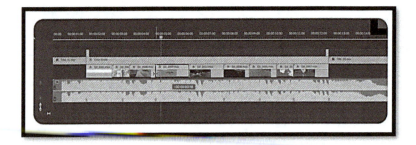

Slide Tool

You can use the Slide tool to change the order of clips on your timeline without cutting or rearranging all of your footage. The tool lets you move clips around on the timeline and change the clips around them to make them fit. The Slide tool looks at three clips: the one you want to slide, the one that comes before it, and the one that comes after it. In this case, if you wanted to move a clip up the timeline, you would change its place by cutting back on the clip before it and adding to the clip after it. Picture film that is split into two tracks. If you move a clip on the top track, it will change what you see of the clips below it. In the same way, the slide tool only lets you make changes in the same track. You can edit B Roll in your timeline very easily with the slide tool, which lets you change the order and placement of your clips to make room for talking-head footage.

Using the Razor Tool

There is a small razor blade icon in the menu of Premiere Pro that stands for the Razor Tool . Its main job is to cut clips or scenes at certain places, so producers can get rid of parts they don't want or split video for more work. You can choose the tool by hitting the "**C**" key on your computer. This makes it easy to switch between tools while you continue to write. One of the best things about the Razor Tool is that it makes precise cutting easy. Editors can get a better look at the timeline by zooming in. This lets them make cuts that are accurate to the pixel level. This feature comes in handy when making complex changes, like timing video to music beats or lining up certain visual elements. Using computer shortcuts can often make editing videos faster and easier. Users can speed up their work in Premiere Pro by changing the shortcut keys for the Razor Tool. Also, knowing how to use control keys like Alt (or Option on a Mac) can change how the Razor Tool works and let you do things like ripple deletes and lifts.

Ripple Edits and Trim Mode

The Razor Tool is often used with ripple edits, which change the timeline instantly when a cut is made. This keeps the time and flow of the video steady by preventing any breaks in the sequence. The Razor Tool and the Trim Mode can also be used together to fine-tune cuts by changing the in and out places of clips without breaking the flow.

- **Step 1:** Choose a video clip, then go to the Tool menu and choose the Razor tool. You can also press the "C" key to quickly get to this tool.

- **Step 2:** Now click on the part of the video clip that you want to cut. You can cut the video clip many times to make a new section.

- **Step 3:** Now, use the Selection Tool to pick out a part of the video that you want to delete. Then, press the "Delete" button to get rid of the part you chose.

CHAPTER 6
COLOR CORRECTION AND GRADING

Understanding Color Spaces

When it comes to digital video editing, color spaces are very important. Premiere Pro, which is one of the best video editing programs, lets users choose from different color spaces to get the look they want. It's crucial to understand the fundamentals of color science and how digital devices read and copy colors to appreciate the importance of color spaces in Premiere Pro.

What is a Color Space?

Some groups of colors are called "color spaces," and they control how colors are shown in pictures and videos. Color spaces describe the range and variety of colors that can be presented or saved in Premiere Pro's context text. RGB (Red, Green, and Blue) and YUV (Luma, Chroma) are the most popular color areas. Each has its role in the digital video process.

RGB Color Space

In digital media, RGB is the most common color system. In RGB, colors are shown as mixes of red, green, and blue. There are a huge number of colors possible because each channel (R, G, and B) can have a value between 0 and 255. Premiere Pro works with sRGB, Adobe RGB, ProPhoto RGB, and other RGB color schemes. When working with photos or videos that were taken in different places, it's important to know and choose the right RGB color space to keep the colors accurate and consistent.

YUV color space

YUV divides luminance (brightness) and chrominance (color information), which makes it better for compressing video. Many video broadcasts and streams use YUV. Users can work with YUV color spaces like 709 and 2020 in Premiere Pro, which supports a range of video standards. When working with streaming material or making videos for specific platforms, it's important to understand how YUV color areas work.

Working with Color Management

Premiere Pro has powerful color management tools that make sure that the colors look the same on all platforms and devices. Users can pick their own working color space and show color space in the Color Management settings. This is especially helpful when editing video from cameras that use different color spaces or when providing material for certain screen sizes.

Importing and Exporting Color Spaces

Premiere Pro lets users keep the original color space of imported video or change how it is interpreted. This function is very important when working with footage from different sources because it makes sure that the colors stay the same while the video is being edited. When uploading a video, users can also choose the right color space and bit level based on the device where the video will be sent.

HDR (High Dynamic Range) Color Spaces

Premiere Pro supports HDR color spaces like Hybrid Log-Gamma (HLG) and Perceptual Quantizer (PQ), which are becoming more popular as HDR video. HDR color areas support a wider range of brightness and color, making the watching experience more realistic and beautiful to look at. To get the best results when working with HDR video, you need to know how to set up and handle HDR color areas correctly.

Basic Color Correction

The color of your video content can have a big effect on the project's quality and mood. Coloring is an important part of the post-production process and can change mood and feeling. For example, Ex Machina used shades of red to show anger and violence, and The Matrix used shades of green to show new life and survival.

Coloring includes color grading, which is a way to improve the way your footage looks for creative reasons to get a certain look. The process usually takes place after color fixing and is done by a colorist. People often use the terms color grading and color correction to mean the same thing, but they're not at all the same. You can fix mistakes or make a picture look more natural by "balancing" the image by changing the brightness, contrast, and shadows. While you need to be skilled to do color grading, anyone can do simple color correction, which is a type of color grading. We will take you through all the steps you need to know to fix colors in Adobe Premiere Pro CC. Here's an example of a video that was recorded with the wrong color temperature. The video is also blue and not quite bright enough.

- **STEP 1:** Place the video into Premiere Pro and make a sequence. Next, open the Lumetri Color Panel window by clicking on Window at the top of the screen and then on Lumetri Color.

STEP 2: Open the Lumetri Color panel window and click on the Basic Correction tab. This will show you all of the main color correction options.

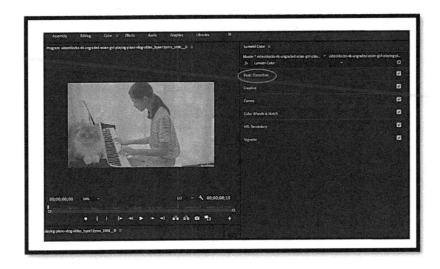

STEP 3: We will start by fixing the general color of this clip to fix the color. The video is blue, so we will use the WB Selector in the White Balance area to fix it. If you choose the part of the frame that is closest to white, Premiere will balance the picture for you.

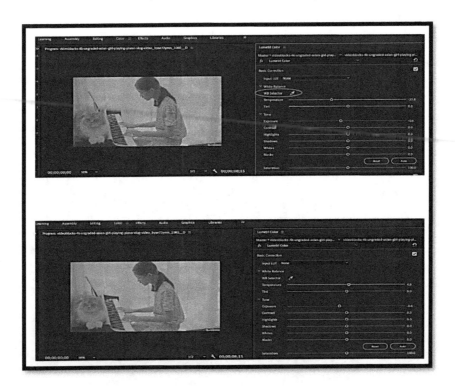

STEP 4: You can also fix the white balance with the Temperature tool, which is found under White Balance. You can move the Temperature tool to either the orange (warmer) or blue (cooler) side until the parts of your video that should be white become pure white.

STEP 5: Now that the image is balanced, let's change the Exposure to make the video brighter or darker overall. We'll raise the Exposure to 0.7 because this clip was too dark.

- The bright spots in the video are a little less clear now that the brightness has been fixed.

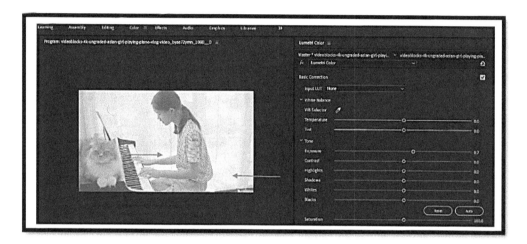

- To make up for it, let's move the Highlights scale down to -8.6.

STEP 6: We can change the brightness of the darker parts of the video without changing the brightness of the lighter parts by changing the Shadows setting. By moving the Shadows scale to about -20, we've made the shadows darker and the dark spots bigger.

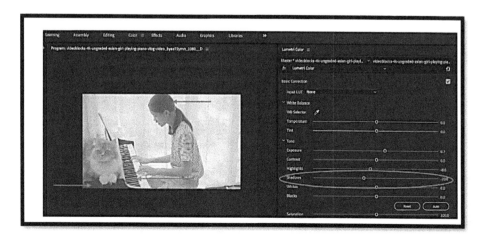

- It was suggested that you not move the Shadows setting past 30 or 40. If you do that, the video will have noise and grain in it.

STEP 7: The next thing we'll do is move the Contrast slider. Less contrast will wash out the video, making the darker parts much lighter. Increasing the contrast will make the whole picture darker.

- Set the contrast to 21 for this clip.

STEP 8: Move the Whites tool down to -13 to help keep the clarity in the curtains in the background.

STEP 9: Next, we'll move the Blacks scale down to -30 so that the darkest parts have a rich black level.

STEP 10: Finally, we'll adjust the saturation, which will greatly change how your video looks. There will be no color in the video when the Saturation is set to 0. It will look like black and white.

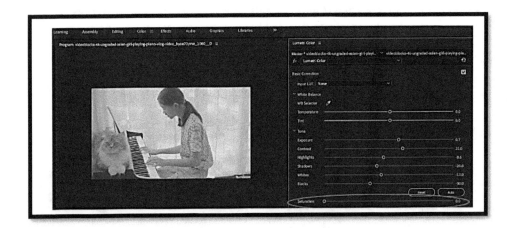

If you turn up the Saturation to 200, all of the colors will become more vivid. But keep in mind that raising the brightness level also adds noise to the video and can mess up the color adjustment that was already in place. With a brightness of 200, the clip now has a green tint, as you can see below.

- Set the Saturation to 137 for this clip. We're now done with a basic color adjustment.

Color Grading Techniques

Color can have a big effect on how we see a scene and how it makes us feel. In the early days of filmmaking, color, and lighting were carefully changed while shooting. To get the right lighting, directors used camera settings, natural light, and other methods. Thanks to plug-ins and effects that improve the color and lighting of your scenes, you can now get great results in post-production. You will learn the basic steps for color grading in Adobe Premiere Pro, which has some of the best tools for creating content and movies with new visual solutions. You can change the lighting, black and white, and color grade using the color wheel and curve settings. You can also find out more about the cutting-edge effects we created to make professional color grading results come to life.

The Importance of Color Grading

The process of adjusting color in post-production filmmaking involves two different concepts: color grading and color correction. Both of these concepts are related to color. First, let's examine these two different ideas. During the process of filming in several places with varying degrees of light and reflections, you could employ a variety of cameras, which might result in color discrepancies that you will need to address via the use of color correction procedures. Adjusting the white balance, temperature, saturation, highlights, and shadows so that they line up with the rest of the film is a necessary step in this process. Additionally, color grading can be used as a creative tool that employs the color palette to elicit feelings or even bodily sensations such as warmth or cold. This goes beyond the scope of simple color correction. Because Adobe Premiere Pro allows you to produce amazing effects in the desert, Tropical Island, or icy mountains, you can do so even if your camera is unable to adequately capture the actual spirit of the natural terrain when you are recording.

Preparing Your Color Grading Workflow

In the beginning, you will need to design your sequence and accomplish the fundamentals of video editing, such as cutting, trimming, and preparing your video clips. It is not necessary for you to be concerned about returning to edit a video clip at a later point in the post-production process via the use of this method.

- **Step 1. Create an Adjustment Layer**

Your first order of business should be to create an adjustment layer. This will enable you to make any color adjustments inside the adjustment layer without having any impact on the video that was originally captured.

Select **New Item** > **Adjustment Layer** from the dropdown menu that appears when you right-click in the Project area of your workspace. On the other hand, you can keep the video settings unchanged: These are the ones that are automatically used by Premiere Pro from your sequence. You will find your newly created adjustment layer in the Project panel after you click the **OK** button. It can be adjusted to the length of your sequence or to the clips that need color correction by dragging it to the timeline above your sequence and adjusting it to the appropriate length.

- **Step 2. Color Workspace: The Lumetri Color Panel and Lumetri Scopes Panel**

It is possible to switch between editing video, audio, or color tools inside the same program by using the many workspaces that are available in Adobe Premiere Pro. You will make use of the Lumetri Color panel, which is located inside the Color workspace, to grade and correct colors. Find Workspaces by going to the Window menu and searching for it. You can go from the Editing Workspace to the Color Workspace by selecting the Color option. For this particular workspace, the Lumetri Color panel will be located to your right, the Lumetri Scopes panel will be located to your left, and your video will be located in the center portion. The Lumetri Scopes panel is responsible for displaying and analyzing the waveform graphs that represent the color and brightness of your video. In addition, you can make use of it as a reference while you are modifying the color of your videos. **Changing the Scopes can be done by right-clicking on the area and choosing one of the following options:**

- **Vectorscope:** Measures and monitors saturation and hue in a circular pattern.
- **Histogram:** This shows a statistical breakdown of the pixel density for each degree of color intensity. It analyzes shadows, mid-tones, and highlights with precision to correct the tonal scale of the image.
- **Parade scope:** Displays individual waveforms for RGB values, making comparing and adjusting colors from the image quite simple.
- **Waveform:** Displays RGB, IRE, luminance, and chrominance from video clips.

On the Lumetri Color panel, you can find all of the tools that are used for color grading. In this section, you will discover a wide variety of tools, including curves, color wheels, HSL, and vignettes, in addition to fundamental color correction tools. You must take the time to get comfortable with the Lumetri Color Panel since it will serve as the focal point of your color-correcting procedure.

- **Step 3: Basic Color correcting**

However, before beginning the color grading process, we suggest beginning with the basic correction option. A look-up table, also known as a LUT, can be imported from this stage forward. LUTs are wonderful tools that can be used to add a particular style or to make rapid adjustments to the skin tone using its presets. Simply choose the "**Input LUT**" option and then search for the LUT that you want to import on your computer. You can begin by using LUTs as a starting point and then proceed to make more changes to the color, or you can begin from scratch and experiment with all of the adjusting options that basic color correction provides. You can use Auto Color to apply color correction to the whole sequence and get a baseline. After that, you can fine-tune each parameter to give your video more individuality. **Take, for example:**

- o **White Balance:** The whites in your video clip can be selected using the white balance feature, which also allows you to change the hue and temperature.
- o **Tone tools**: Transform the atmosphere of your picture. The exposure allows you to adjust the overall brightness, the contrast allows you to alter the range of colors from light to dark, and the highlights and shadows tools allow you to focus on parts that are bright and dark sections.
- o **Whites and Black sliders** Adjust the threshold lights and shadows, respectively, using the Whites and Black sliders.
- o **Saturation**: This setting determines how intense the colors are in the video clip you have. If you want a picture that has a greater number of gray tones, you can simply reduce the saturation.

To ensure that the color is consistent throughout, it is important to remember to utilize the Lumetri Scopes as a reference.

- • **Step 4. Advanced Color Grading Tools**

Creative Tab: To enhance the style of your video, you can apply looks by going to the Creative tab. Within the Effects menu of Premiere Pro, you will discover Lumetri Presets, which is where you will locate film stock and presets for camera looks. Using the intensity slider, you can make adjustments to the amount of the effect that is applied.

There are more modifications available under Creative, such as Faded Film, which will give your video an antique appearance, and Sharpen, which will boost the edge definition of your video. You can apply a blue or green tint to your inside film by playing with the Tint Wheels, Vibrance, and Saturation. You can also use these tools to create shadows and boost highlights.

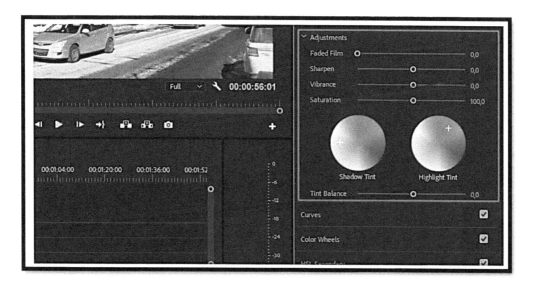

- **RGB and Hue Saturation Curves**

RGB curves and Hue Saturation curves are the two kinds of curves that are available in Adobe Premiere Pro. These curves allow for more exact color adjustments, which in turn produce more genuine tones. You can alter the Luma and tonal ranges of your video clips by using the RGB Curves. To add highlights, create a point in the upper-right corner of the screen and drag it to the left. To add shadows, use the lower-left corner of the screen. To make adjustments to the region with the curves, click on each color value. **To make more precise adjustments to the color, you can use the Hue Saturation curves, which include the following curves:**

- Through the use of the **Hue versus Saturation curve**, the saturation of any hue in the footage can be adjusted. For instance, to change the color of the sky or the skin tones to create scenarios that is colder.
- Through the use of the **Hue versus Hue curve**, you can alter the color of various components within the image, such as the plants, clothes, or furniture involved.
- On the other hand, the **Hue versus Luma curve** gives you the ability to modify the brightness of particular colors.
- The **Luma versus Saturation curve** adjusts the saturation level differently depending on the tonality of the image rather than the hue.

- The utilization of the saturation versus saturation curve allows for the selective modification of an image's saturation without affecting similar colors.

- **Using Color Wheels**

An easy-to-understand color wheel is better than a circle. There are three main color wheels, one for shadows, one for mid-tones, and one for highlights. You can change the colors in each of these places separately. Use a color match to look at two shots from the same sequence and make sure that the light and colors are the same in all of them. Pick out a scene, click the Comparison View button, and then use the playhead to pick out the reference clip from your sequence.

- **HSL Secondary**

You can have more control over certain colors on the HSL secondary tab. This is useful when you're using colors to tell a story because it helps the main color stand out. After basic fixing and other color-grading steps, this is usually the last thing that is done. Open the Key tab and pick a color from the frame with the eye dropper. Check the box next to Color/Gray, and then use the H, S, and L buttons to make the choices smaller. The Refine tab can also be used to get rid of noise and make the edges smoother. To change the color of the range you chose, uncheck **the Color/Gray** box and click on the Correction tab. As you change the adjustment controls, you can see what the changes will look like.

- **Add Vignettes**

Vignettes help draw attention to the scene's main subject by making it look like the edges are getting darker as you move toward the center, where it's brighter. The center, the size, and the amount of dark or bright fade out can all be changed.

- **Step 5. Finalizing and Exporting Your Video**

Color grade your video slowly until you get the look you want for your movie. The last and final step is to download your video so that you can share it online. Select "File" > "Export" > "Media." Change the name of your video, pick a place to save it, and click Export.

CHAPTER 7
TITLES AND GRAPHICS

Creating Basic Titles

You have to choose how the text should be presented when you're making the title. There are two ways to make text, and both can make text go in either a horizontal or vertical direction.

- **Point text**: This method makes a text box around you as you type. The text is on one line until you press Return or Enter. For example, if you change the shape and size of the box in the Effect Controls panel, the Scale property will also change.
- **Paragraph (Area) text**: The size and shape of a text box are set before any text is typed into it. Once you change the box size, the amount of text shown changes, but not the size of the text.

You can easily make titles right on your movie with Adobe Premiere Pro's Essential Graphics panel and the Type tool. Just follow the steps given below. In the Graphics workspace, choose the Enter tool and type your title into the Program Monitor's empty text. Press the Horizontal Center button in the Align and Transform tools to make your title center itself.

If you have the Selection tool open, click the gray square and drag its left side across the screen. You can move the layer down in the Essential Graphics panel if you don't like how it covers up your title. Right-click on the layer of a line and select "**Duplicate**." This will add another line. To change the name of a new layer, right-click it and choose "**Rename**." If you want to move a new part, change its Position or Rotation setting. Change the item's Opacity setting to make it see-through.

Zoom out in the Program Monitor. Find the spot where you want the motion to end and move the playhead there. You can change the position, transparency, size, and other features of each piece to get it exactly where you want it. Each time you change a setting, click its icon to set a keyframe to that number.

Go back to the beginning of the Timeline panel. You can change each element's position, transparency, size, and other settings until they are exactly where you want them to be. Use the Pen, Rectangle, or Ellipse tools to make a shape in the Program Monitor. This will add a border. The new shape will show up on top of the other shapes. Pick the Mask with Shape option to make the title image only show up inside the shape. (Click **Invert** if you only want it to show up outside the shape.)

Play the sequence and look at how the parts move inside the mask to finish your opening title design over the video background. If you only want to mask some levels, you can move the mask layer down in the panel or change its settings to make them move.

Create Title Graphics

You can add shapes, text, photos, and video to layers and you can change and rearrange them using tools you already know from other Adobe Creative Cloud products. After adding motion or effects, you can export your titles as Motion Graphics designs that you can then share through Creative Cloud Libraries. Just follow the steps given below.

Open the Graphics workspace

Choose **Window > Workspaces > Graphics** from the main menu, or click Graphics in the workspace bar at the top of the screen. Make sure your sequence is already open in the Timeline box.

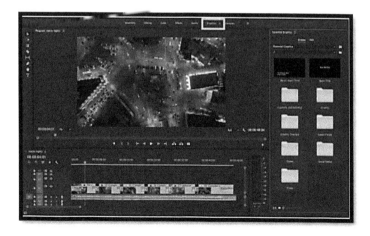

Choose a Motion Graphics template.

It is in the Essential Graphics panel. To open it, go there and double-click it. In the Timeline, drag the Film Presents Motion Graphics template to a video track. It will show up as a clip with the set time. Change the clip's time and length to make it fit your film. You might want to add a transition to the title to make it look better in your sequence. **Note**: Some themes use Adobe Typekit fonts that you might not already have loaded. To get it to work with your system, make sure you select the correct font in the Resolve Fonts box.

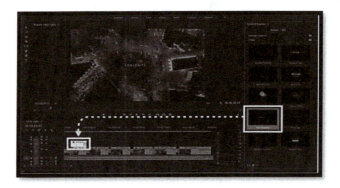

Make a copy of the motion graphic and use it throughout your project.

If you want to add thanks in the same way throughout your project, Alt-drag (Windows) or Option-drag (macOS) the clip to make a copy of it and place it somewhere else in your sequence.

Change the text in the template

Get a title clip and put it in your sequence. It will be shown in the Program Monitor. Choose the Type tool and click once on the sample text to see a red box around it. You can now change the text that is shown. You need to do this for all of your titles.

Change the template's style

Open the **Selection tool** and pick a title clip from your sequence. Click on the text in the Program Monitor once to see a blue box around it. It's easy to change the font in the Essential Graphics panel. Just go to the Edit tab and click on the Text area. You can change the size of the letter by moving the button up or down. You can change the text's other features as you like.

Create or apply a master style

Once you are pleased with your text style, select Create Master Text Style from the Master Styles drop-down menu. After giving the new master style a name, click OK. Now that you've made the master style in the Essential Graphics box, you can apply it to other title clips in the Program Monitor. You have to turn on the text in the Program Monitor before you can see its properties in the Essential Graphics panel.

Add motion with keyframes

You can change the position and size of an effect you apply to a title clip by animating the parameters of those effects using keyframes. You can also add a cross-dissolve effect to the beginning or end of a clip to make your title look better. In the models that come with Premiere Pro (Animated Diagonal Glow), the Fast Color Corrector (Blue Lens), Gaussian Blur, and Levels are all used in unique ways.

Export a Motion Graphics template

Get a title clip and put it in your sequence. Just go to the main page and select Graphics > Export as Motion Graphics Template. You can change the template's name and save it somewhere else, like the Essential Graphics panel, your hard drive, or the Creative Cloud Library. Press the OK button. You can now use the saved template in other projects and share it with other people through Creative Cloud Libraries. The Essential Graphics panel or your Library (under Motion Graphics Templates) is where you can find them after having saved the file.

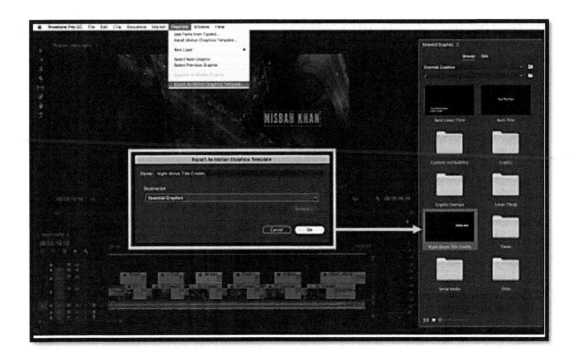

Working with Text Effects

Before you start working with effects, you should make sure you know how to work with text in Premiere Pro. With the Type Tool, users can add text, and the Essential Graphics panel lets them change how it looks. You can change the text, size, color, orientation, and more in this area. After the main text is written, it's time to add effects that make a difference.

Keyframing lets you make simple text movements in Premiere Pro. Editors can make smooth changes, transitions, and moves over time by turning on the Animation setting for the text layer. This can be very helpful for adding text to the screen, drawing attention to certain parts, or adding light movements to keep people interested.

Adding Text

Step 1: Click on the Type Tool (T) .

- The Type Tool, the Essential Graphics panel, or pressing Ctrl+T or Cmd+T at the same time will open a new text box where you can add text to a video clip. But if you want to change the text, it will be easier to do so in the Essential Graphics panel.

101

Step 2: Add a Text Box

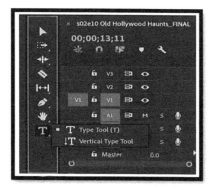

To add text with the type tool, go to the toolbar. If you can't find it, go to Windows > Tools and click and press the Type Tool for a moment. The Type Tool and Vertical Type Tool options will then appear. The option to start typing after choosing the Type Tool is to simply click anywhere in the program panel (on the viewer). You can also make the text box bigger by pulling it with the Type Tool after clicking on the window. The main difference is that if you make a real text box, your text will only fit inside that box, which is helpful if you're adding a lot of text.

Step 3: Customize the Text Shape, Size, and Color

- In the Essential Graphics panel, you can see all of your text's options for things like style, size, and color. Click on that to change your text. Before you can make any changes to a certain piece of text, you have to select that layer of text. From here, you can change the text to fit your project's needs.

Step 4: Consider Adding a Custom Font

There are a certain number of font styles that come with Adobe Premiere Pro, but you might want to use a different font in your project. Then you can add more fonts by clicking on the "Add Adobe Fonts" (formerly "Typekit") option in the drop-down font menu located in the upper right corner. In a new tab, this will open Adobe Fonts, which is the main font's library. When you get to Adobe Fonts, all you have to do is choose the font you want and turn it on. When you turn on fonts in Adobe Premiere, they will show up in the font options.

- Plus, you can go to **Graphics > Add Fonts from Adobe Fonts**.

If you want to use a font that Adobe Fonts doesn't provide, you'll have to download it and set it up on your computer first. If it works with Premiere, it will show up in the font menu in your options.

Note: The font may not show up right away and you may need to restart the app.

How to Create Text Templates

If you write some text that you want to use again, you can save it as a motion graphics file and repeat it later.

1. Choose the text and go to Graphics > Export as Motion Graphics Template. 2. Give your file a name and save it.
2. To use this template file again, go to File > Import and pick the design you want to use.

103

Add a Logo Intro in Adobe Premiere Pro from a Template

First, let's go over how to make a reveal that focuses on the brand. I'm going to use a template called Flat Logo Opener for this part. With ready-made themes, it's simple to add your logo. After getting the file, double-click it to open it in Adobe Premiere. Then, look for the part that says "Your Logo." This piece will open up when you double-click on it.

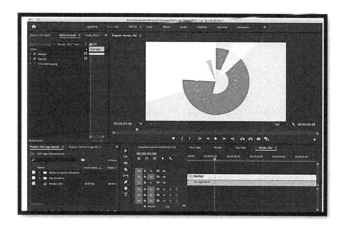

After going to "Your Logo," you need to add an image to the timeline. Pick out your image file, then drag and drop it on the timeline. To cover the template with the name, we need to grab the right handle and pull it to about the 10-second mark.

One tip: you might need to click on the logo and scale: click and drag the corner to resize it down.

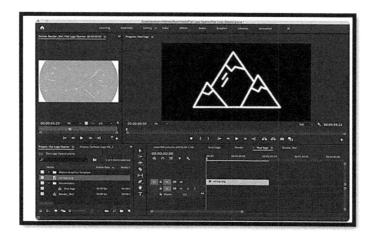

That's it! Jump back to the Render_Me! Layer and play the preview to see an updated animation that includes your logo.

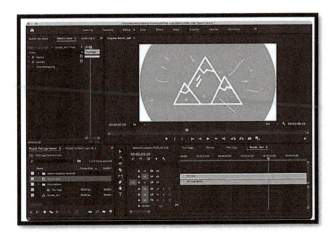

You could also make more changes by opening the layer called "**Flat Logo Opener**." You need a little more skill to change the shapes and colors at this point, so if you're just starting, it's best to pick a pattern that fits your style. Using a template is the best way to make a beginning that is all about an image. It keeps you from having to start from scratch with graphics that take too long.

How to Add a Logo Overlay

A logo layer stays on top of your video the whole time. This is great if all you want to do is add your logo. Make sure to put your brand on top of the video clip. This will cover the whole video. Then, move the logo's handle to the right on the timeline.

After you place your logo, you might notice that it's too large or out of position versus what you had in mind. Find the tab labeled **Effect Controls** near the upper left corner (when working in the **Editing** workspace).

Take the Effect Controls box and start by making the logo the right size. To make the size smaller or bigger, move the scale slider to the left or right. Then, move it around with the Position tools. Move the two numbers that show where pixels are on the screen by clicking and dragging them.

Overview of Text-Based Editing

An easier way to start editing videos is with text-based editing, which uses transcriptions of source media to make it easier to make a first edit, also known as a "rough cut." **Here are the steps you need to take to use Text-Based Editing correctly:**

1. Transcribe Source Media:
- Transcribing your source footage is the first thing you need to do. During this process, the spoken information is turned into text.
- The text will show up in the Transcript box of your writing program once the recording is done.

2. Add Clips:
- Use the text that has been copied in the Transcript box to find specific content in your source media. The text helps you find the parts you want.
- Pick out parts of the source transcripts that have text that matches the video content you want to use in your project.
- Use this selection to add the appropriate video clips to the Timeline, making sure that the recorded text lines up with the right visuals.

3. Change a Sequence:
- In your editing program, go to the sequence text view. This mode lets you work on putting together a rough cut or first sequence from the material that has been recorded.
- Put the video clips in order and make any necessary changes based on the text-based format you created. Based on the transcriptions, this step helps make a unified and sensible order of the clips.
- Once you've made a rough cut with the text-based instructions, switch to regular video editing tools and platforms to make your changes even better. At this stage, you'll fine-tune transitions, change times, add effects, and more.

Text-based editing uses transcriptions of source media to make the first step of a video editing project quick and easy. By recording text and using it as a visual guide, editors can quickly find the material they want and put together a rough sequence. This gives them an organized base that they can build on with traditional video editing tools to make the end product look great.

How to transcribe source media

1. **Launch Premiere Pro and Create a New Project:**

- Open Premiere Pro and start a new project where you'll organize and work with your video footage.

2. **Import Media with Automatic Transcription:**
   - As you import your media files into Premiere Pro, ensure that you enable the "Automatic transcription" feature in the Import settings.
   - This feature allows Premiere Pro to automatically transcribe the audio content of your imported media files.

3. **Customize Transcription Settings:**
   - While importing your media, you'll have the option to customize transcription settings.
   - You can select your preferred Language for transcription, choose Speaker labeling options if applicable, and set Transcription preferences for the selected imported media.
   - These preferences might include settings related to accuracy, timing, or specific transcription requirements based on your needs.

4. **Review Transcripts in Text-Based Editing Workspace:**
   - Once the transcription process is completed, and your transcripts are ready, navigate to the Text-Based Editing workspace in Premiere Pro.
   - In this workspace, you'll be able to review and access the transcribed text of your source footage.
   - The Text-Based Editing workspace provides an interface designed to work efficiently with transcribed text, allowing you to analyze, select, and work with the transcriptions to assemble your video edit.

How to transcribe individual source files

1. **Open Text-Based Editing Workspace:**
   - Launch Premiere Pro and access the Text-Based Editing workspace within the software.

2. **Transcribe Specific Clips:**
   - In the Project panel of Premiere Pro, locate and double-click on the specific video clips you want to transcribe.

3. **Access the Text Panel and Start Transcription:**
   - Within the selected clip, navigate to the Text panel.
   - Click on the blue "Transcribe" button available in the Text panel.

4. **Configure Transcription Settings:**
   - A dialogue box will appear where you can select your preferred language for transcription.

- Additionally, you can choose whether Premiere Pro should separate speakers if applicable to your video content.

5. **Transcription Process and Transcript Window:**
   - Premiere Pro will initiate the transcription process for the selected clips based on the configured settings.
   - Once the transcription is complete, the dialogue or spoken content from the video clips will appear in the Transcript window of the Text-Based Editing workspace.

How to edit transcripts

To fix the spelling of words or names that aren't used very often, use the built-in spell checker or the search and replace tool. If a source file has more than one person, choose **Speakers** to add their names to the text.

How to add clips to the Timeline

Text-based editing allows you to perform three-point edits to build a sequence on the Timeline.

- In the Transcript box, read the text or look for the parts you want to use.
- Select the text in the copy and press the "Insert" button to add it to the main sequence.
- Keep adding clips from the source media to the Timeline until it has all the clips you want to use.

How to change a sequence

When you add clips to the Timeline, Premiere Pro makes a new sequence transcript. You can make changes to your rough cut in this new file.

1. Switch to Sequence Transcript:
- In Premiere Pro, find and pick the Timeline panel to get to the sequence transcript, which shows your video sequence in text form.

2. Move Clips by Selecting Text:
- In the sequence transcript, pick out the text parts that match the clips you want to move.
- You can move these clips around in the text by pressing Ctrl+C or Command+C or Ctrl+V or Command+V. When you change text, the Timeline also changes right away.

3. Remove Clips Using Text Editing:
- To remove clips from the sequence, all you have to do is select and delete the corresponding text in the sequence transcript.
- Premiere Pro will then apply a Ripple Edit to the timeline, which will make sure that the sequence adjusts correctly by filling in any gaps left by the deleted clips.

4. Transition to Video Editing Tools:
- Once you've completed your rough cut using the sequence transcript, transition to conventional video editing tools available in Premiere Pro.
- Use these tools to further refine your edit by trimming, adjusting pacing, performing color grading, enhancing audio, and incorporating titles or graphics into your video cuts.

Filler Word Detection with bulk delete

Text-Based Editing lets you find filler words like "uh" and "umm" and delete them all at once from recordings.

1. Click on the ▼ icon in the list of transcripts.
2. Pick **Text, Filler words, or Pauses** to delete a lot of them at once.
3. After that, you can choose to remove a single instance or all the instances of the searched text, space, or breaks.

By clicking on the three dots in the upper right area of the Text panel and choosing Transcript View Options, you can change the shortest amount of time that Premiere Pro will wait to recognize a stop.

How to Use Your Logo as a Watermark

One twist on a logo overlay is a **watermark.** This is a more present but faded logo overlay style. Use a watermark when you want to protect your brand's intellectual property or for draft copies. Find the Opacity dropdown in the Effect Controls option while your image layer is chosen. Then lower the brightness to make it less clear. Watermarks should be easy to see without getting in the way.

Most of the time, label patches cover the whole area. The Scale and Position options were changed to make the logo bigger.

Animating Text and Graphics

I'll begin by selecting **Window > Essential Graphics** from the menu. My title will be crafted with the help of the **Text Tool (T).** In the panel that is located under the Edit tab, I will have a new text layer after it has been written out. The Text layer is the one that I will choose to access all of the properties and tools that belong to it.

I will utilize the tools that are included in the **Align and Transform** area to center my text. The Text area is where I can alter the font and style. If I go to the **Appearance** menu, I can change the color, add a responsive backdrop, drop a shadow, and even use numerous strokes. I'm going to make two new rectangle layers for the objects that are in the backdrop. The button labeled "New Layer" can be found at the very top of the panel, right next to the layers that are already there. Because I will be applying a mask to crop everything, I will make them a little bit larger than they are now. I'm going to make one of the shapes white and one of them red by using the Fill tool in the Appearance section to modify the color of each object. In conclusion, I will reorganize the layers by positioning the white background at the bottom, the red background above it, and the text at the top of the screen.

In the Essential Graphics panel, masking is one of the most recent features that have been included. To create a mask, I will first add a new layer that has a rectangular shape. After making the necessary adjustments to the size and location, I will go to the Appearance area and pick the Mask with Shape option. As the mask will apply to any layers that are behind it, I will need to place my layers in such a way that they are appropriate. When I am working on a very complicated project, I can also organize the layers.

Following the completion of all of the necessary assets, I am now prepared to bring the title to life. The text and the backgrounds both move in utilizing a simple Y Position change, as can be seen in the animation. I would want the opening two seconds of my animation to be dedicated to the events that take place. It will begin with the white background, then the red background will come shortly after that, and ultimately the text element will be shown. Beginning with the text layer, let's begin animating it. I must shift my Playhead to the two-second mark to animate the Y Position. This is the point at which I want the animation to conclude. After that, I will choose the Text layer, and then I will hit the Position symbol in the area that is devoted to align and Transform. A keyframe will be added at the position of the current time indication as a result of this action, which will turn animation on for the attribute. The icon will change to blue, thus I can determine that the animation is turned on.

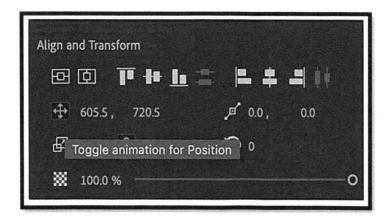

I will now move the Playhead to the one-second mark and make the necessary adjustments to the Y property to position the text according to its starting position. Every time I modify the attribute, a keyframe will be added to the location automatically. The next stage is for me to animate both of the background rectangles by following the identical processes, but I will offset the time that each object takes.

Using the Effect Controls tab, I can make minute adjustments to each keyframe to further fine-tune the timing of the animation. I will go to **Window > Effect Controls** to inspect the keyframes that are created by my animation. I can view all of the effects that I have altered in the Essential Graphics panel by using this panel. When you click on a graphic layer in the Essential Graphics panel, the layer will instantly reflect and highlight in the Effect Controls panel, and vice versa.

An ease-out will be applied to all of the initial keyframes, and an ease-in will be applied to all of the end keyframes. This will ensure that the animation is smooth for each element. Easing can be accessed by right-clicking or control-clicking on a keyframe, and it is located under **Temporal Interpolation** under that heading. To further fine-tune the time of each animation, I can alter the Speed Curve. Select the dropdown arrow that is located to the left of the Position property to have access to the curve. Manipulate each keyframe via a **Bézier** handle.

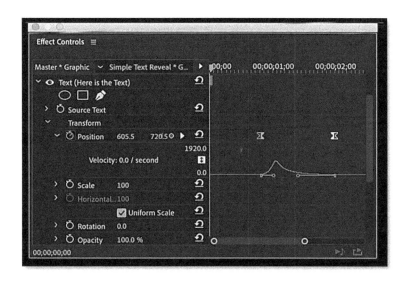

Understanding the Fundamentals of Typography

It is essential to have a solid understanding of how to properly use type when it comes to the creation of excellent video graphics. The text that you produce will nearly always be composited over moving pictures, which will make it much more challenging to read. When developing a typeface for a video, it is essential to strike a balance between readability and beauty. This involves packing as much information as possible onto the screen without making it seem cluttered. The combination of this practical purpose with a better sense of style and control can help you achieve a more professional appearance in the designs that you create. In the process of developing text for a video, it is advantageous to adhere to typeface norms. It is possible that developing a design that is easy to understand will be challenging when text is composited over a moving video background that has a variety of colors. You should strike a balance between readability and style, and you should also make sure that there is enough information shown on the screen. There is a correlation between the amount of text and the difficulty of reading it, particularly when the words are moving.

Choosing a Font

Because of the large number of fonts that are available on your computer, it can be challenging to choose a good one for use in video editing.

To simplify the process of selecting anything simpler, you could want to consider using a triage technique and taking into consideration the following factors:

- **Easily readable**: With the font size that you've selected, are you able to read it? Am I able to read about every one of the characters? After giving the text a cursory look and then closing your eyes, what do you remember of the text?
- **Style**: If you were to use just adjectives to describe the font that you have chosen, what would you include? Does the font effectively communicate the mood that is intended? In the same way that selecting the appropriate typeface is essential to the overall success of a design, type is comparable to the selection of clothes or a haircut.
- **Flexibility**: The degree to which the typeface blends in with other fonts is discussed. Does it come in a variety of weights, such as bold, italic, and semi-bold, so that it is easier to draw attention to the significance of the information? Is it possible to create a hierarchy of information for the lower-third name graphic of a speaker that conveys different sorts of information, such as the speaker's name and title?
- **Language compatibility**: Do you have access to all of the characters that you will need in the font? Certain fonts have limited character sets.

It is expected that the replies to these guiding principles will take you in the direction of titles that provide a more appealing appearance. To find the font that works best for your needs, you will probably need to experiment. To do a side-by-side comparison, it is simple to make changes to an existing title, or you can duplicate it and customize the copy. In the process of creating text for a movie, you will often find yourself placing it on top of a background that has some different colors. As a consequence of this, it will be difficult to create the appropriate contrast, which is needed to maintain legibility. To get a contrasting edge in this situation, you can either add a stroke or a shadow.

Selecting a Color

The process of selecting the appropriate colors to use in a design can be surprisingly challenging, although there is an almost infinite number of color combinations that can be generated. This is because only a select few colors are suitable for text while still allowing the viewer to see it. This process gets much more difficult if you are editing your video for broadcast television or if your design has to conform to the aesthetic and branding of a certain show, product, or company. The text may need some adjustment when it is placed over a busy shifting background. When it comes to text in the video, the most common options are black and white, which may seem to be a little conservative. Colors are either very light or very dark tones, or they have a thick, highly colored stroke if they are used at all. If they are used at all, colors are frequently used. Because the color you choose must be able to stand out against its background, you will need to evaluate the best colors frequently, taking into consideration factors such as the requirements of your brand and the necessity to maintain a color palette that is constant throughout your sequence.

Adjusting the kerning

It is usual practice to modify the space between the letters in a title to enhance the look of the text and to assist it in matching the design of the backdrop. The operation in question is referred to as kerneling. Because it makes faulty kerning more evident, the requirement to manually fix text grows as the font size increases. This is because the font size will increase. Creating a visual flow while simultaneously increasing the appearance and readability of your material is the focus of this endeavor. Products that have been professionally manufactured, such as journals and posters, have the potential to teach you a great deal about kerning. Application of kerning is done letter by letter, which enables creative spacing to be created.

Setting the tracking

Another essential text characteristic is tracking, which is comparable to kerning in its function. In situations when a large number of letters are selected, this is the general control of letter spacing. On a global scale, tracking can be used to either reduce the size of a text selection or increase its size.

It's often used in the following situations:

- **Tighter tracking**: If a line of text is overly long (for instance, a lengthy title for a speaker's lower third), you can significantly tighten the tracking. The font size has not changed, but there is now a greater amount of content packed into the available space.
- **Looser tracking**: Readability can be improved by spreading out the letters, particularly when using a font that is more difficult or when using all capital letters.

Frequently, it is used to create gigantic headlines, as well as when text is utilized as a component of design or motion graphics.

Changing the tracking for a particular layer (or item in the Program Monitor) is something that can be done in the Text section of the Essential Graphics panel.

Setting the alignment

When it comes to aligning text for video, there are no hard-and-fast rules to follow, even if you are used to seeing it left justified for things like newspapers. It is common practice to align the text for a lower-third title either to the left or to the right. The text that is centered in a rolling title sequence or segment bumper is something that you will notice rather regularly. Included in the Essential Graphics panel are buttons that allow you to align and justify the text you are working with. The alignment buttons allow you to shift the text that you have selected to the left, center, or right about the anchor point of the text. By dragging the Type tool in the Program Monitor, you can create a text box instead of clicking on it. This is an alternative to clicking. You can make the text contained inside a box fill the width of the box that it is enclosing by using the justification buttons. If you are dealing with text that is contained inside a box, you can use the vertical alignment buttons to align the text with the top, middle, or bottom boundary of the box. It is not necessary to worry about remembering which alignment option is which; it is quite acceptable to investigate and make use of the Undo option if it is necessary.

CHAPTER 8
MAKING USE OF ESSENTIAL EDITING COMMANDS

In comparison to other nonlinear editing systems, Adobe Premiere Pro provides conventional editing features that are comparable to those offered in other products.

You can edit your project in two main ways, depending on which material you want to utilize and which portions you want to include:

- **Overwrite Edit:** In Adobe Premiere Pro, the overwrite edit is the editing approach that is used by default throughout the editing process. When an overwrite edit is performed, the frames from the chosen clip are inserted directly into the frames of the sequence, either replacing the content that is already there or filling in the vacant gaps. This technique is often used to replace video in the timeline in an easy manner.
- **Insert Edit:** This is an alternative method of editing, which includes inserting a clip into the sequence. This causes the information that is already there to move to the right, which is later in the sequence. By using this strategy, it is possible to include fresh material while still maintaining the continuity of the information that is already there.

There are more specialist editing methods accessible inside Premiere Pro, such as the replace edit, and there are also other ways to edit within the program. However, the overwrite and insert edit commands serve as basic tools that meet the bulk of the conventional editing demands. The management of footage and the arrangement of sequences in your project timeline can be accomplished in an effective manner using these two strategies. By gaining an understanding of these essential editing methods, editors can alter videos, make corrections, and structure sequences inside Adobe Premiere Pro in a seamless manner. Even if there are extra specialized editing techniques available, it is essential to have a solid understanding of the fundamentals of overwrite and insert edits to be able to handle the majority of the editing chores in your video projects.

Performing an overwrite edit

1. **Selecting the Source Footage:** Open the desired shot, for instance, "HS Suit," in the Source Monitor within Adobe Premiere Pro.

2. **Preparing the Timeline Panel**: Before beginning the edit, make sure that the Timeline panel is correctly configured. To do this, the playhead of the Timeline must be positioned at the desired starting point. For example, setting it to 00:00:04:00 can be considered.

3. **Changing the Position of the Playhead:** You have the option of manually entering the required timecode into the timecode display of the Source Monitor, or you can use the keyboard shortcut to relocate the playhead in a precise manner. Working with camera logs or attempting to pinpoint certain portions in a short amount of time are two situations in which this strategy is very helpful.

4. **Understanding Playhead and Editing Behavior:** Know that while editing using the keyboard or on-screen controls, the location of the playhead decides where new clips are inserted, unless particular In or Out points have been established on the Timeline. When dragging a clip into a sequence, the previously established In or Out points take precedence over the location of the playhead.

5. **Managing Audio Tracks:** In the process of making the overwrite edit, you may wish to keep the audio that is currently present on the timeline. This is true even if the new clip has audio. Deactivating the audio track can be accomplished by clicking the A1 source track selection indication and making it gray. This will allow you to omit the extra audio.

6. **Configuring Track Headers:** Check that the track headers in the Timeline panel are appropriately configured before proceeding with the configuration of the track headers. To activate or disable the tracks in accordance with the requirements of the edit, click the track targeting buttons. Since there are no clips on any of the other tracks, the only track markers that are important in this case are the Source A1 and V1 track markers.

7. **Performing the Overwrite Edit:** In the Source Monitor, click on the Overwrite button to execute the Overwrite edit. This action adds the clip to the Video 1 track in the sequence.

8. **Playing the Edited Sequence:** This involves positioning the playhead at the beginning of the Timeline panel or the Program Monitor, clicking the Play button on the Program Monitor, or simply using the spacebar to start playback. This allows you to see the results of your edit.

It is important to keep in mind that when you drag a clip into a sequence, an overwrite edit is immediately performed. Holding down the Command (macOS) or Ctrl (Windows) key while dragging allows you to do an insert edit while you are dragging. Through the use of the Source Monitor in Adobe Premiere Pro, this comprehensive procedure guarantees that the Timeline panel is appropriately prepared, that appropriate track management is carried out and that an overwrite edit is carried out. To successfully manage and manipulate clips inside your editing project, you must get acquainted with these processes.

Performing an insert edit

Insert editing is a basic method in video editing that enables the inclusion of a new clip at a specific location within the timeline. This approach allows for the addition of a new clip. Through the usage of this operation, other clips will move ahead in the timeline by the same amount of time as the length of the clip that is being added. As a consequence of this, it modifies the total length of the sequence shown in the timeline without altering the duration of any of the other clips that are already present inside it. However, it is essential to keep in mind that insert editing runs the risk of causing significant problems, such as the audio and video tracks being out of sync with one another. The successive clips in the sequence can be out of sync throughout the length of the sequence if an additional clip that comprises either video or only audio breaks the sync that is already in place.

Performing an insert edit can be done using different methods:

1. **Dragging Clips into the Timeline:**
   - Create a sequence using your media.
   - Select another clip in the Source Monitor or Project Panel.
   - Press and hold the Control (Command) key, drag the clip to the desired location and track within the Timeline.
   - Release the pointer to execute the insert, which will shift subsequent clips on the same track and any other track where Sync Lock was not disabled.
2. **Using Insert Button Controls:**
   - Create a sequence from the media.
   - Select another clip in the Source Monitor and adjust the in and out points.
   - Move the playhead precisely to the intersection point between the two clips in the Timeline.
   - Click the **Insert button** in the Source Monitor's Tools panel to perform the insert, effectively increasing the timeline's total duration after the clip insertion.

Whenever an insert edit is being performed, the pointer will transform into an insert pointer, which will indicate the insertion operation. This procedure is shown by the picture that is supplied as an example of an insert edit. The graphic demonstrates how the overall length of the timeline grows when the clip is inserted.

Performing Storyboard – Style Editing

The process of bringing a tale to life on the big screen begins with the creation of storyboards, which are visual representations of a screenplay. As part of the pre-visualization process, they are used in a wide variety of media, ranging from Disney cartoons to live-action blockbusters for example. According to Mellon, "***Storyboards are a tool that helps the filmmaker to convey what's in their brain to a hundred other individuals on site***." Storyboards are often a collection of drawings that represent the intended camera angles and action sequences for a film.

The term "storyboard" is commonly used. Storyboards have a look that is similar to that of comic strips; nevertheless, they often include significant amounts of technical information, such as planned camera motions, lines of speech, and sound effects. Video clip thumbnails stored in a bin can be used as visuals for storyboards. By selecting the in and out points of some clips that are stored in a bin, arranging the clips in the appropriate order, and then constructing a sequence from those clips based on their in and out points, a storyboard edit is a method that allows for the rapid assembly of a sequence. It is possible to rapidly generate the basic assembly of a scene by using a storyboard edit, which is a great method.

Let's start by making a Storyboard Edit.

The clips that you will require for each scene should be separated into their bins or folders before you begin the process of editing the storyboard. The bin can be opened in its window by double-clicking it, and then it can be expanded out to provide you with a large number of workspaces. If you're familiar with Final Cut Pro 7, you'll recall that you used to be able to drag icons around in Windows and they'd just 'float around freely.' Although Premiere's more ordered interface, which locks the positioning of clips into tidy rows, makes storyboard modifications a bit more visually responsive, you can still accomplish the same objectives with Premiere's more orderly interface.

The **new bin window** should have the Thumbnail view turned on, the icon size should be adjusted to your satisfaction, and **the sort icons' drop-down box** should have the **'User Order'** option selected. The implication of this is that you will be able to move the clips around rather than having them arranged in order of their names.

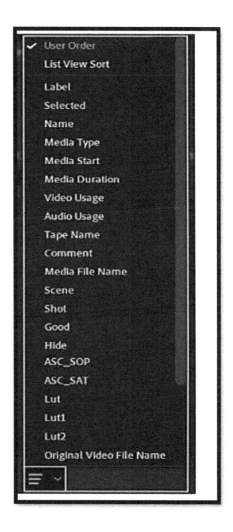

Following that, organize the clips in the appropriate sequence so that the scene can be edited. Drag a clip around in the sorting order by clicking and dragging it. This will accomplish the desired result. As soon as you let go of the clip, the icon that represents the cursor will change into a hand, and white bars will appear to show the location where the clip will fall. The in-point and the out-point of each clip can be specified by using the following keyboard keys: I for the in-point and O for the out-point per clip. You can either use the keyboard keys **J, K, and L** to **play forward (L), pause (K), and play backward (L), respectively (J),** or you can click on a clip and utilize the shortcuts to search through your clips using the hover-scrub feature. In addition, you can use the spacebar to play and stop the video you are watching. As you click on a clip in the trash window, a little blue bar that has a miniature playhead will emerge. You can check which portion of the clip has been chosen by using the In and Out points. To select all of your clips, use the CMD+A key combination. Choose **'New Sequence from Clip'** from the context menu that appears when you right-click on one of them.

This will result in the creation of a new timeline that is identical to the format and frame rate of the clip that you have selected, as well as an edit of your clips in the order that you choose. In a short amount of time, you can organize your clips and create a basic first edit using this method.

Three-Point Editing

A three-point edit is the most precise adjustment that editorial professionals who are educated can make. It is now possible to specify the three-point edit by making use of three marks in both the Timeline (or Program Monitor) and the Source Monitor. Two in points and one out point are the options available to you. Alternatively, you might have two out points and one in point. You do not need to provide any specifics on the fourth point since Adobe Premiere Pro will figure it out for you. To define the edit's range, you will make use of an In point and an Out point. Establishing these places inside a source clip is the option that is most often preferred. Nevertheless, there are circumstances in which you would want to make use of the Timeline to define that range (for example, if you have a sound bite that you want to cover with a B-roll). Following that, you will be required to outline the precise placement of the third point. This can occur on both the program and the source side. Positioning the point is the most popular strategy that is used to determine where the beginning of a clip should be considered. Additionally, the end of a clip can be defined by utilizing nothing more than an Out point.

As an example of how to take advantage of a three-point edit, consider the following:

- You should open the sequence that you wish to edit after selecting it.
- After opening the Source Monitor, put a clip into it. The time that you would want to utilize should be written down.
- By clicking on the headers of the tracks where you want the alteration to take place, you can choose the tracks where you want the insert or overwrite to take place.
- The source clip track indications should be dragged to the headers of the tracks where the material should be overwritten.
- The Source and Program Monitors can be configured with any combination of three In and Out points by the user.
- To insert or overwrite data, use the buttons shown on the Source Monitor display.

CHAPTER 9
ADDING TRANSITIONS

A transition is a crucial narrative tool in video editing, similar to conventions in screenwriting. It helps viewers perceive and follow the tale by providing them with a sense of continuity and continuity. To portray changes in place, passage of time, or alterations in character viewpoint within a movie, effective transitions make a significant contribution. The use of methods such as animated transitions fades to black, or dissolves can be used to accomplish a variety of tasks, including transitioning from scenes that take place indoors to scenes that take place outside or signaling the passage of time. The audience is better able to comprehend changes in surroundings, the passage of time, or variations in character emphasis to grasp these visual clues. Through the use of transitions in Adobe Premiere Pro, editors can enhance the level of professionalism of their works in a variety of simple but significant ways. Even though simple cuts between clips are an effective way to convey the story, transitions are an extremely important part of a film since they help to reinforce the narrative components and emotional themes that are being presented. As an example, the use of gradual crossfades is a method that is often utilized to imply the smooth passage of time. It is possible to get significant insights into the strategic use of transitions by seeing how they are used in the movies, television episodes, and music videos that you like watching the most. When it comes to diverse settings, paying attention to when, where, and how transitions are used can provide both inspiration and knowledge. By analyzing these examples, editors can get the knowledge necessary to include transitions in a strategic manner, which will allow them to improve their narrative efforts and elicit certain emotional reactions from the audience.

What are Transition Effects?

A multitude of special effects and preset animations are available in Adobe Premiere Pro. These animations and effects are meant to integrate clips within a sequence in a seamless manner. These tools make it possible to create seamless transitions between scenes visually. They include anything from traditional dissolves to page wipes, color dips, and a variety of transitions. The use of transitions serves several functions, including highlighting significant changes in the narrative and providing seamless transitions between different portions of a video. In its most basic form, a transition is a visual effect that is used between two pieces of material to manufacture a link that is both fluid and dynamic. The program provides a broad variety of effects for users to choose from, ranging from the straightforward Cross Dissolve effect to more complex effects such as glitches and whips. By making use of the fundamental transitions that are available in Premiere Pro, you can dramatically improve the visual attractiveness of your project. The incorporation of transitions is an art form that contributes to the overall narrative of a video. The execution of these transitions is a simple process: from the Effects panel, just drag the transition that you want to use between two clips in the sequence timeline. The effectiveness of transitions is affected by a variety of elements, including their location, length, and the conditions in which they are implemented, which include direction, motion, start/end positions, and other aspects. When it comes to obtaining the intended effect, fine-tuning these factors is necessary. Some transition parameters can be altered directly in the Timeline panel; however, it is often more useful to tweak them in the Effect Controls panel. This is because the changes are more precise. In the Effect Controls panel, editors can access and adjust the parameters of a transition effect by choosing it inside a sequence. This allows for exact control over the transition's look and behavior.

Importance of a Clip Handle

The extra information that is present before and after the in-point and out-points of a clip is referred to as the clip handles. These handles serve as essential supplemental content that is used for modifying transitions on the clip. The application of a transition to a clip in Adobe Premiere Pro results in the transition being shown as a colored overlay on the timeline at the location where it is inserted. It is important to note that the transition does not truncate or shorten the clip to fit the overlapping information. Instead, it makes use of the content that comes before the in-point and after the out-point of the clip. It is the portion of the clip that extends beyond the in and out points that is referred to as the Clip Handle.

When it comes to establishing transitions between two clips, this portion is quite necessary. To create a smooth transition, it is vital to make sure that there is a sufficient Clip Handle after the first clip and the introduction of the second clip. If the source material does not include an adequate number of frames, however, Clip Handles may not be seen. Under these circumstances, there is no additional video material that can be made accessible to make the transition easier. Premiere Pro alerts users when there is insufficient material included in the transition and when there is a possibility that repeated frames will be included in the transition. Premiere Pro can construct Clip Handles automatically by reproducing the end frames, which results in the creation of a freeze-frame of the clip. This has been done to compensate for the shortfall. Regarding the Timeline panel, this circumstance is represented by warning bars that are diagonally positioned above the transition.

For editors to efficiently apply transitions without any interruptions or repetitions in the video, they need to guarantee that their source material has a suitable number of Clip Handles.

Using a Transition to Connect Two Clips

To begin, you should begin by making adjustments to your movie in the timeline until you are pleased with the final product. Click the Effects tab at the top of the screen to transition between displays. Within the Effects Panel, you will discover a folder that is categorized as Video Transitions. The transitions that are pre-installed in Adobe Premiere are stored in this folder, along with any transitions that you add to the program yourself. Find the point in the timeline that connects the two clips that you want to transition between, and then choose the transition you want to use in the Effects Panel. Then, when it has been selected, drag it to the link that exists between the two clips. If your Clip Handles are sufficiently lengthy, the transition will be carried out. The duration of the transition can be altered with relative ease. Simply dragging the effect across the timeline will allow you to utilize it. This may increase the time in both directions, provided that you have Clip Handles that are sufficiently long.

Adding Video Transition Effects

Cross Dissolve is the default transition for video tracks in Adobe Premiere Pro, while Constant Power Crossfade is the default transition for audio tracks. Both of these transitions are available for each track. The symbol for these preset transitions, which is underlined in blue, makes it simple to identify them inside the Effects panel. If, on the other hand, you regularly use a different transition and would rather have it set as your default, you can do so. The ability to change the default transition option gives you the ability to make a different transition from your default choice for all of your projects. Changing the default transition does not have any impact on transitions that have already been applied to sequences, which is a crucial point to keep in mind. The "**Automate to Sequence**" tool is a crucial command in Premiere Pro that enables users to quickly apply the default transition across many clips that are included inside a sequence. When this command is executed, the default transitions for both video and audio are applied to all of the clips that are included in the process. Because it enables the quick inclusion of transitions between sequences of many clips, this feature has the potential to save a significant amount of time. The editing process is simplified as a result of this functionality, which enables editors to simply adjust their default transition choice and apply transitions across sequences in an effective manner by using the Automate to Sequence command.

Create a standard transition

1. **Access the Transitions:**
   - Go to Window > Effects to open the Effects group.
   - Expand either the Video Transitions or Audio Transitions container, based on which one you want to be the default.
2. **Pick the transition you want:**
   - Look through the different changes and pick the one you want to use for all of your projects.
3. **Set as default transition:**
   - Either right-click on the transition you want to use in the Effects panel or press the Menu button in the Effects panel.
   - When the drop-down menu comes up, choose "**Set Selected As Default Transition.**"

Set the default transition's duration.

Method 1: Using the Edit Menu (Windows) or Premiere Pro Menu (Mac)

1. **Access Preferences:**
   - Navigate to the Edit menu (Windows) or Premiere Pro menu (Mac).
2. **Select Timeline Preferences:**

- Choose Edit > Preferences > Timeline (Windows) or Premiere Pro > Preferences > Timeline (Mac).

3. **Adjust Transition Duration:**
   - Look for options related to transition duration within the Timeline preferences.
   - Modify the value for Video Transition Default Duration or Audio Transition Default Duration based on your preference.

4. **Confirm Changes:**
   - Once you've adjusted the duration to your liking, click OK to confirm and apply the changes.

Method 2: Using the Effects Panel

1. **Access the Effects Panel:**
   - Open the Effects panel from the navigation bar within Adobe Premiere Pro.

2. **Navigate to Default Transition Duration:**
   - Within the Effects panel, access the drop-down menu.

3. **Choose Set Default Transition Duration:**
   - Select Set Default Transition Duration from the drop-down menu options.

4. **Adjust Duration Values:**
   - Modify the value for Video Transition Default Duration or Audio Transition Default Duration as desired.

5. **Apply Changes:**
   - After adjusting the duration values, click OK to confirm and implement the changes.

Apply default transitions between selected clips

The basic audio and video changes can be used with any mix of two or more clips. The fixed transitions are applied at every edit point where two chosen clips touch. The arrangement is the same no matter where the current time indicator is or whether the clips are on certain tracks. The preset transitions are not used when a chosen clip touches a non-selected clip or no clip at all.

- ❖ Pick out at least two clips from the Timeline. To choose clips, either shift-click them or make a box around them.
- ❖ Choose the sequence you want to use for default transitions.

Copy and paste transitions

Copying a Transition

1. **Select the Transition:**
   - Within your sequence, choose the transition you want to copy. Click on it to select.
2. **Copy the Transition:**
   - Use one of the following methods:
     - Go to Edit > Copy from the menu bar.
     - Press Ctrl+C (Windows) or Cmd+C (Mac) on your keyboard to copy the transition.

Pasting a Transition to a Single Clip

1. **Place Current-Time Indicator:**
   - Position the current-time indicator (playhead) on the cut line where you intend to paste the transition.
2. **Paste the Transition:**
   - Use one of the following methods:
     - Go to Edit > Paste from the menu bar.
     - Press Ctrl+V (Windows) or Cmd+V (Mac) on your keyboard to paste the transition.

Pasting a Transition to Multiple Clips

1. **Select Multiple Edit Points:**
   - To copy the transition to several clips, you can:
     - Drag a marquee around the edit points in the sequence to select multiple edit points.
     - Use the Shift key along with any trim tool to select multiple edit points in the sequence.
2. **Paste the Transition:**
   - **Once the desired edit points are selected:**
     - **Use one of the following methods to paste the transition:**
       - Go to Edit > Paste from the menu bar.
       - Press Ctrl+V (Windows) or Cmd+V (Mac) on your keyboard to paste the transition.

These steps allow you to copy transitions within a sequence in Adobe Premiere Pro and paste them onto specific cut lines, whether it's for a single clip or multiple clips simultaneously. This functionality streamlines the editing process by enabling quick application of transitions across various parts of your sequence.

Replace a transition

You can change a video or audio transition in the sequence by dragging a new one from the Effects panel over an old one. When you change a transition, its length and orientation stay the same. This, however, gets rid of the parameters for the previous transition and sets them to the default parameters for the new transition.

Using A/B Mode to Fine-Tune a Transition

The A/B editing mode in Adobe Premiere Pro lets you test the settings for transition effects by splitting a single video track into two separate tracks in the timeline. In this mode, two clips that would normally play one after the other on the same track are split into two different tracks so that a transition can be made between them. When writers use the A/B editing mode, they can see more details and change different transition settings in the Effect Controls panel. This includes changing the head and tail frames, which are also called handles, as well as other transition settings. This gives you more control and freedom to finetune the transition effect. By separating the transition's parts, this method makes it easier for editors to break them down and fine-tune them. This is because each part can be changed separately. This method works especially well when exact changes or tweaks need to be made to transition effects to make the final video project look smooth and professional.

Audio Transitions Effects

When you want to switch between audio clips, you can use crossfades. An audio fade is the same thing as a video change. For a crossfade, you add an audio shift between two audio clips that are next to each other on the same track. To fade in or out, a crossfade transition is added to both ends of a single clip. You can use three different types of crossfades in Premiere Pro: Constant Gain, Constant Power, and Exponential Fade.

Choose a preset audio transition

❖ In the Effects panel, right-click (Windows) or control-click (Mac OS) Constant Gain or Constant Power.

❖ From the context menu, choose Set Selected As Default Transition

Set the length of audio transitions to their default value

❖ Go to the Edit menu on macOS and choose Timeline from the list of options. On Windows, do the same thing but in Premiere Pro.
❖ In the Preferences box, enter a number for the Audio Transition Default Duration.

Crossfade Audio in Adobe Premiere Pro

Want to sync two audio tracks in Adobe Premiere Pro by crossfading them? Maybe you've added background music to your video and want it to crossfade into the following piece gradually. You want your audio tracks to flow as smoothly as possible as a video editor, with no sudden cuts or transitions. You should always pay special attention to the audio tracks, since poorly processed or out-of-sync audio may severely degrade your viewer's experience. Let's look at how to crossfade audio in Adobe Premiere Pro so that different audio tracks are indistinguishable.

Using the Crossfade Audio Effects

To crossfade audio in Adobe Premiere Pro, first use the Selection tool to select the two audio tracks. Then, on Windows, use Ctrl + Shift + D, and on macOS, press Cmd + Shift + D to apply the default crossfade effect.

The Constant Power effect is applied to the beginning and finish (including cuts) of the specified audio tracks using this keyboard shortcut. If you don't want the additional effects

at the start and finish, select them and press Delete. To apply the effect solely at a certain point (for example, between cuts), manually select the effect from the Effects > Crossfade tab and drag & drop it to the appropriate location.

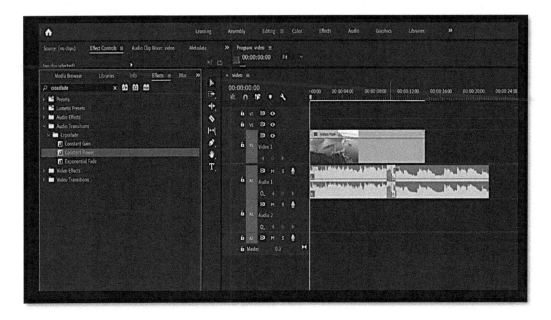

To change the duration of the effect, click and drag either of the two ends of the effect box. If you know how to deal with effects in Adobe Premiere Pro, you can do a lot more with the crossfade effect.

Aside from Constant Power, Adobe Premiere Pro provides various built-in effects for crossfade audio tracks. Expanding the Crossfade area under Effects reveals three options: Constant Gain, Constant Power, and Exponential Fade.

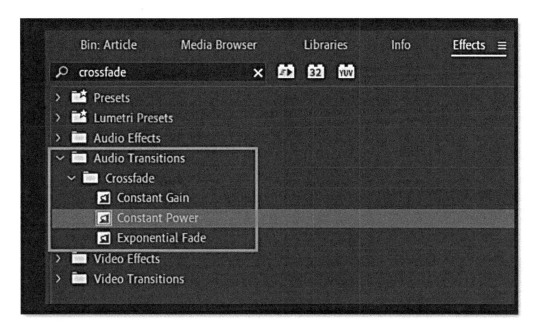

Exponential Gain vs. Constant Gain vs. Constant Power

Constant Power is the default effect that appears when you press Ctrl + Shift + D on Windows or Cmd + Shift + D on Mac. Constant Gain, on the other hand, is the simplest of the three crossfade effects since it generates a fading audio effect by adding two keyframes to each audio track and increasing/decreasing the audio levels at a regular pace. All three effects accomplish the same purpose, which is to crossfade audio; the difference is in how the audio levels are faded in and out.

The effects of Constant Power and Exponential Gain are significantly smoother and less sudden than Constant Gain. This is because the volume reduction in those effects is gradual, as opposed to Constant Gain, where the audio level increases/decreases at a constant rate. For a better crossfade effect, choose the other two effects from the Effects menu. It's great to experiment with all three effects and determine which one works best for you. Expand the **Effects > Crossfade** menu, right-click an audio effect, and select **Set Selected as Default** Transition to alter the default audio effect.

The new default effect will then be applied to the clips by pressing Ctrl + Shift + D (or Cmd + Shift + D).

Overlapping Tracks and Crossfading Audio Manually

If you want more control over the effect, manually crossfade the audio clips using keyframes or the Pen tool. This approach is preferable for professionals since it enables you to alter the volume level at each timestamp, giving you granular control over the audio tracks.

Making Use of the Pen Tool

When you want to experiment with audio levels or video opacity, the Pen tool is your best friend. To create a crossfade effect using the Pen tool, overlap the two audio tracks and apply a fade-out effect to the first audio track while fading in the second. To begin, relocate the two audio files to separate audio tracks and overlap them. The overlap duration is determined by the intended effect duration. Double-click the audio tracks to expand them; the volume bar should be visible within the tracks.

Select the Pen tool from the tools panel (or press P) after you are finished. Take note of the timestamp at which the second audio starts to play, and then click on the volume bar to make a new point at that timestamp in the first audio. Make another point near the end of the first audio and drag it down. Create two points in the second audio file in the same way, but this time, silence the first point by dragging it down.

Using Keyframes to Crossfade Audio in Premiere Pro

Generating a crossfade effect using keyframes is comparable to generating one with the Pen tool, except it takes longer. To begin, overlap the two audio files and set the crossfade time. Then, under the Effect Controls menu, expand the Volume option and select the first audio file. Set the marker to the timestamp where you want the crossfade to begin, and then click the Stopwatch button next to Level to create a new keyframe.

Once the marker is generated, place it to the end of the audio and adjust the Level value to -999 dB. When you update the value, the keyframe is automatically produced. Likewise, expand the Volume option and select the second audio track. To create a new keyframe, place the marker at the beginning of the audio and click the Stopwatch button next to the Level choice. Then, set the value to -999 dB.

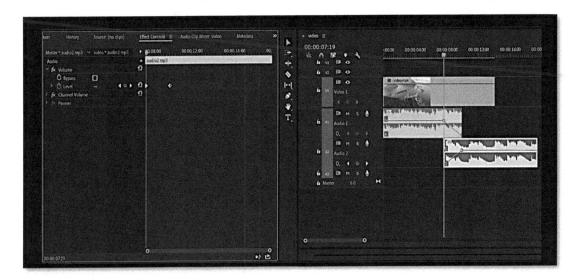

Finally, position the marker at the timestamp where the effect will terminate, and then create a new keyframe by clicking the Stopwatch button once again. To make things simpler, indicate timestamps ahead using markers. When you play the video, you'll hear a crossfade audio effect that was generated by hand. You may now edit the remainder of the video in peace and export it when you're finished. It takes longer to create a crossfade effect using keyframes, so utilize the Ctrl + Shift + D or Cmd + Shift + D keyboard shortcuts or apply the Constant Gain effect using the preset.

Why Crossfade Audio Tracks in a Video?

If you want the viewer to have a nice watching experience, crossfading two or more audio tracks is essential. Carefully editing the audio eliminates any sudden cuts or transitions in the video that move the viewer's attention away from the video and toward the audio. If you're creating a podcast, it's best to process the audio with Adobe Audition rather than directly in Premiere Pro. Adobe Audition is a digital audio workstation that allows you to edit and improve the quality of your audio tracks.

Audio clip fade in or fade out

Make sure the audio track is bigger in the Timeline panel. If you need to, click the triangle to the left of the track name to make the audio tracks you want to crossfade bigger.

Do at least one of these things:

❖ To fade in the sound, drag an audio transition from the Effects panel to the Timeline panel. This will make it stick to the beginning of the audio clip. You can also pick the change in the Timeline box. After that, go to the Effect Controls box and choose Start at Cut from the Alignment menu.

❖ To fade out the sound, drag an audio transition from the Effects panel to the Timeline panel. This will make it stick to the Out point of the audio clip. You can also pick the change that will be used in a Timeline. When you get to the Effect Controls box, go to the Alignment menu and pick End At Cut.

Adjust or customize an audio transition

1. **Access the Timeline Panel:**
   - Open your project in Adobe Premiere Pro.
2. **Double-Click an Audio Transition:**
   - Locate an audio transition in the Timeline panel.
   - Double-click on the transition to modify it.
3. **Adjust the Transition in the Effect Controls Panel:**
   - After double-clicking the transition, the Effect Controls panel should display the transition's settings.
   - Make desired alterations to the transition parameters in the Effect Controls panel to refine or modify the audio transition's behavior.

Adjusting Audio Volume Keyframe Graph for Fade or Crossfade

1. **Select the Clip with Audio:**
   - Identify the audio clip in the Timeline panel that you want to adjust.
2. **Modify Volume Keyframes:**
   - Instead of applying a traditional transition, adjust the audio volume keyframe graph.
   - **To create a fade or crossfade effect:**
     - Click on the audio clip to reveal the volume keyframes in the Effect Controls panel.

- Modify the volume keyframes graph to control the pace of the audio fade or crossfade.
- Adjusting the keyframes will alter the volume levels at specific points in the audio clip, allowing you to create a customized fade or crossfade effect.

These actions give you different ways to change audio transitions and directly control the speed of audio fades or crossfades in Adobe Premiere Pro using volume keyframes. This gives you more options for changing audio transitions and makes your project sound better overall.

Professional Transitions and Effects

Premiere Pro has more than 40 video transitions that make going from one video clip to the next smooth. You can either use a transition tool or make your transition in Adobe after Effect and add it to the Creative Cloud library if you think you'll need more. To use transitions, just drag and drop them where you want them. Click on the Effects menu to the left of your timeline and open the Transition Effect folder. After that, all you have to do is drag the file to the beginning or end of the clip. The clip can be played and seen in the video sample to see how the change works.

Premiere Pro comes with all the video effects you need to fix problems with the lighting, change the colors, and make your footage look great. In the most recent version, Adobe added Warp Stabilize to After Effects to fix video footage that is shaking. There are several options when fixing videos, such as cutting the video, choosing how smooth you want it to be, and letting the software automatically adjust the edges.

CHAPTER 10
ADVANCED AUDIO EDITING

Audio Mixing and Effects

Create an audio mix

Premiere Pro will need to know what each of your conversation, music, sound effects, and background noise clips are after you've put them on their audio tracks. In the Audio workspace (**Window > Workspaces > Audio),** select all the clips in a certain track. Then, in the Essential Sound box, click the right audio type from the list.

By naming the audio track's type in this way, you can change levels and add effects much more quickly and easily than if you had to change each clip individually. For instance, click Auto-Match in the Loudness area to quickly match all the clips on the track to a normal amount of volume.

One great thing about labeling audio types is that it lets you change how one track works with another. "**Ducking**" is one way to make an audio track stand out from the background sound. Click Generate Keyframes once you know which tracks to duck against. You can later fine-tune those keyframes to make sure they perfectly fit the background music and speech clips in terms of time and volume.

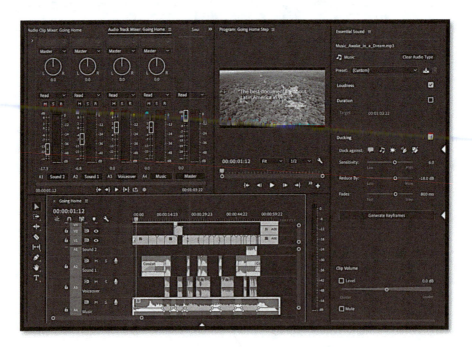

Music can also be made more interesting with EQ settings. You can drag the Amount scale to change how strong the effect is, just like you can with the other choices. You can also change the vertical bars in the Audio Track Mixer screen as you play your sequence. Like, move a tool down to soften all the clips on a certain track.

Adjustments are nondestructive, so play around and experiment. Click Clear Audio Type at the top of the Essential Sound panel to undo your changes and bring things back to their original state.

Working with Multichannel Audio

Multichannel audio refers to recordings of sound that have more than two audio channels, which is what stereo audio usually has. Up to eight audio channels can be recorded by professional-grade cameras, even if some of those channels are blank or not used in the final file. Premiere Pro is software for editing videos. It can handle clips and sequences with up to 32 audio channels, which lets you edit and change audio in complex ways.

To interact with multichannel audio in Premiere Pro, users can perform various actions:

1. **Review Audio Clips in Source Monitor:**
   - Open an audio clip in the Source Monitor within Premiere Pro.

- Utilize the "Drag Audio Only" button to swiftly switch to a view focusing on the audio waveform.

2. **Modify Clips:**
   - When adding multichannel clips to sequences in Premiere Pro, all audio channels within those clips are included.
   - Access channel selection settings:
     - Select one or more clips in the Project panel.
     - Right-click on the selected clip(s) and navigate to Modify > Audio Channels.

3. **Choose Audio Channel Settings:**
   - Options include using the file's settings (Use File in the Preset menu), selecting presets for channel configuration, choosing clip channel format (mono, stereo, 5.1, or Adaptive), and determining the number of clips added when editing into sequences.

4. **Match Source Channels to Clips:**
   - Checkbox options allow for assigning source audio channels to clips.

5. **Non-Destructive Changes:**
   - Modifications made to clip interpretation settings are non-destructive and can be adjusted at any time.

6. **Review Audio Channels:**
   - Any adjustments made to the audio channels of a clip reflect in the waveform when reviewing the clip in the Source Monitor.

7. **Appropriate Audio Track Types:**
   - Premiere Pro ensures that audio clips are restricted to suitable track types to maintain accurate mixing controls.
   - If an appropriate track type isn't available when editing a clip into a sequence, Premiere Pro automatically generates a new track with the required channel format.

In effect, Premiere Pro makes it easier to manage and change multichannel audio by giving you the tools and options you need to deal with complicated audio setups while still letting you change and adapt individual channel settings within the editing environment.

View audio waveforms

When an audio clip is played in the Source Monitor, the audio waveforms immediately show up. We can see the sound waves when we open a clip in the Source Monitor that has more than one audio channel. The wrench tool on the timeline screen is called **Timeline Display**

Settings. Click it to change the style of the audio track. If you choose Show Audio Waveform, the audio will be shown on the timeline as waves.

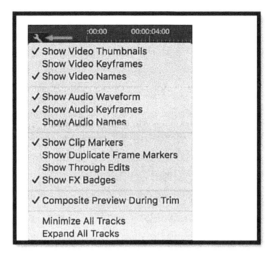

Scrub the audio waveform

Moving the playhead over a part of an audio pattern is called "**scrubbing**." It's an easy way to move quickly through an audio clip. If you double-click on a clip in the timeline, it will open in the Source Monitor. The playhead shows up when you click on the audio clip. To move through the video or clear it, click on it and drag your mouse forward or backward. By selecting **Edit > Preferences > Audio** and unchecking the option Play audio when cleaning, scraping will be turned off.

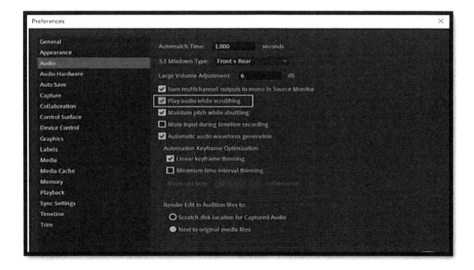

Zoom in or out on an audio waveform in the Source Monitor

In the Source Monitor, you can zoom into an audio waveform to better identify markers, In points, and Out points.

1. **Opening an Audio Clip in the Source Monitor:** First, double-click on one in either the project or timeline panel. The chosen audio clip can then be looked at and edited more closely in the Source Monitor after this move.

2. To **zoom in and out horizontally on audio waveforms**, find the zoom sliding bar below the time bar in the Source Monitor. You can zoom in or out by dragging either end of this bar horizontally. This changes how the waveform is shown across the timeline. The pattern for all channels gets longer as you zoom in horizontally, giving you a better look at the audio data.

3. **Vertical Zooming for Audio Channels**: To zoom in vertically on a single channel, find the up and down zoom bar on the right side of the Source Monitor, next to the decibel scale. You can zoom in on a specific channel's waveform by dragging either end of this bar vertically. This gives you a clear picture of marks and other audio features on that channel.

4. **Simultaneous Vertical Zooming for All Channels**: You can also hold down the Shift key and drag either end of the vertical zoom bar to zoom in on all channels at the same time. This move zooms in vertically on the waves of all channels in the same way. Because of this, the decibel scale and the pattern of each channel grow or shrink at the same time.

What is an Alpha Channel?

The Alpha channel is very important for keeping data about parts of a picture that are partially or fully transparent. This channel is an important part of Premiere Pro, especially in titles. It can also be found in some photos and videos. But if the content doesn't have an Alpha channel, certain effects can be used to make parts of the content see-through. It is also possible to combine photos without changing the clarity of any of the individual parts. By using Premiere Pro's Blending modes or different Channel effects, you can combine picture data from different clips into a single collage. When changing software layers, clips on higher tracks appear on top of clips on lower tracks unless the alpha channels show that the clips are see-through. Premiere Pro makes a collage by putting together clips from the bottom track to the top. As a result, black shows up where all the tracks are either empty or see-through. Particularly in the context of how opacity works with visual effects, understanding the processing order is important. In Premiere Pro, the Video Effects list is shown first, then geometric effects like Motion, and finally changes to the alpha channel. In each effects group, effects are worked on from the top down. The Fixed Effects list is where opacity lives, so it is displayed after the Video Effects list. The Alpha Adjust video effect can be used to handle extra opacity options or to control the output sequence of opacity for particular effects. There is also an option in the Interpret Footage text box to choose how to read the alpha channel in a file. For example, picking "**Invert Alpha Channel**" swaps opaque areas for transparent ones, while choosing "**Ignore Alpha Channel**" doesn't care about the alpha channel at all, which changes how transparency is treated in the movie. This feature lets you fine-tune the choices for transparency based on the needs of the project.

Mattes and alpha channels

Digital pictures usually keep color data in three channels, which are red, green, and blue. These channels are often called RGB. There is, however, a fourth channel that is often not seen. It is called the alpha channel, and it holds transparency information. Along with the color channels, the alpha channel is a key part that lets you store both picture data and information about how transparent it is in the same file. You can think of it as an unseen map that tells each pixel in a picture how transparent it is. It is very important to understand how transparency is shown in an alpha channel. When looking at the alpha channel in tools like the After Effects Composition panel or a Premiere Pro Monitor panel, white means nothing at all, black means nothing at all, and different shades of gray show different amounts of partial transparency. Within this context, a matte is a layer or a unique channel within a layer that makes parts of another layer see-through. In this case, white lines show unclear areas and black lines show clear areas. The alpha channel is usually used as a matte, but there are times when a different matte, like one from a different channel or layer, might better define the clear areas that are wanted, or when the source picture doesn't have an alpha channel at all.

Many file types can include an alpha channel, which gives you more options for saving transparent information. Some file types that might have an alpha channel are Adobe Photoshop, ElectricImage, TGA, TIFF, EPS, PDF, and Adobe Illustrator. Depending on the codecs used to make these file types, alpha channels may also be present in AVI and QuickTime files, especially when saved with a bit level of Millions of Colors+. Different file types include and use alpha channels, which make it possible to handle and preserve transparency information well. This makes picture and video editing processes more flexible.

About straight and premultiplied channels

Digital files usually store transparency data in one of two ways: as straight alpha channels or as premultiplied alpha channels. The only thing that might be different about the alpha channels is how they work with the color channels. When using files with straight (or unmatted) channels, transparency data is kept only in the alpha channel, separate from any information in the viewable color channels (like RGB). If you are watching pictures with straight channels, the effects of transparency might not be obvious unless the program you are using supports this format. On the other hand, pre-multiplied (or flattened) channels store information about transparency in both the alpha channel and the viewable RGB channels. The RGB numbers are increased by background color, and the amounts of transparency are used to mix them. This mixing is especially clear in partly see-through areas, like soft edges, where the colors are changed to match the background color in a way that depends on how see-through they are.

In some applications, users can choose the background color that is used for premultiplication. If not, black or white is generally used by default. When it comes to clarity, color information in straight channels is better than information in premultiplied channels. However, premultiplied channels work better with more programs, such as Apple QuickTime Player. Before sending things to be edited and put together, it's often decided whether to use pictures with straight or premultiplied channels. Premiere Pro and After Effects can find both straight and premultiplied channels in files with multiple alpha channels, but they usually only find the first alpha channel they come across. Adobe Flash, on the other hand, can identify premultiplied alpha channels. This difference between straight and premultiplied alpha channels is very important for how transparency information is treated and shown on different editing and watching platforms. This shows how important it is to know these types when changing photos and videos.

Making Compositing Part of Your Project

You can take your post-production work to a whole new level with compositing effects and settings. You'll find new ways to shoot and organize your edits when you start using Premiere Pro's blending effects. This will make it easier to combine pictures. Getting ready for production, following the shooting process, and setting up the effects correctly will all work together to make the best composite results. You can make moods with a lot of different textures by putting together still photos of places with interesting, complicated designs. Instead, you can cut out and re-add parts of a picture that don't fit. Compositing in

Premiere Pro is one of the most creative, versatile, and enjoyable aspects of nonlinear editing.

When compositing clips and tracks, keep the following rules in mind:

❖ To make the whole clip transparent, all you have to do is change the color of a clip in the Effect Controls box.

❖ To make areas see-through, importing a source file with an alpha channel is often the best option. When the file is used as a clip, Premiere Pro keeps the transparency information with the file and shows the clip with its transparency in all sequences.

❖ If the clip's source file doesn't have an alpha channel, you have to add transparency to each clip instance by hand if you want it to be transparent. You can add transparency to a video clip in a sequence by changing how opaque the clip is or by adding effects.

As long as the file is saved in a format that allows alpha channels, programs like Adobe After Effects, Adobe Photoshop, and Adobe Illustrator can save clips with or without alpha channels.

Audio channel mapping

You can send different audio channels from a clip to different tracks in the timeline using audio channel mapping. This can be helpful for audio clips with more than one channel, like those made with a surround sound microphone or a multi-track audio device. Premiere Pro makes a sequence with the right number of audio tracks to fit all channels when you load a clip with more than one audio channel. It's set so that each audio channel in the clip is linked to the right audio track in the sequence.

But you can change how the audio channels are mapped. You can do this during import, or you can right-click the audio in the Project box and choose **Modify > Audio Channels**. When you load, map the audio channels from the source. You can tell Premiere Pro how to automatically map audio channels in clips to audio tracks and the Mix Track when you import or record.

1. Go to Preferences and click on Timeline.

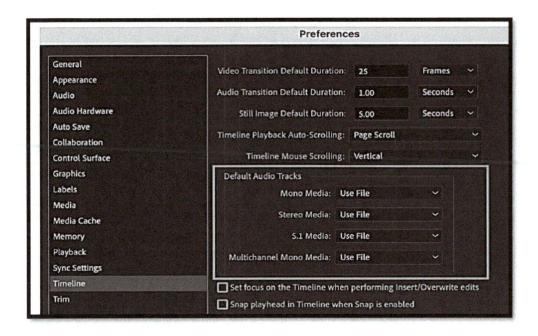

2. Pick a file from the list of Default Audio Tracks, and then click OK.

Change the source audio channel mapping

1. Select one or more clips containing audio in the Project panel and choose **Clip** > **Modify** > **Audio Channels**.

Be sure that all of the audio clips you choose have the same track format if you choose more than one. If you need to change the source clips using Modify Audio Channels, don't use proxies in Premiere Pro. If you do that, strange things will happen.

2. In the Audio Channels box, there is a grid with the source channels at the top and the clip channels on the left. To connect a clip channel to a source channel, choose the cell in the matrix that map to it. If there is a tick, it means that the clip channel is linked to the source channel.
3. Pick the source channel, press the Play button, or use the slider to listen to the audio in a channel.
4. Click "OK."

Note: You can't change the audio tracks of a clip that has been joined. For starters, they have to be mono. You can still change the order of the audio channels and turn them on and off from the component clips, though.

Map sequence audio channels to audio output device hardware channels

For each channel in a sequence Mix track, you can choose which channel to use in a target hardware audio device. In the Preferences dialog box, select the Audio Output Mapping pane and then map the channels. Premiere Pro plays each channel in a sequence through the hardware channel you choose. For instance, your project might have a 5.1-channel sequence, but the hardware in your system might only be able to handle two channels. You could choose which of the two hardware channels each of the six sequence channels goes through. But 16-channel sequences will still be mapped to 16 output channels even if the hardware device chosen doesn't have that many channels. One example is that the chosen gadget might only have two channels. Then, you could set up the two hardware channels to play only the first two channels of a 16-channel sequence.

Note: You can map sequence channels to any supported hardware device on your computer in the Audio Output Mapping pane, not just the device that is currently switched on. You can see and hear the channel mapping you set up for a device, though, only when that device is turned on. When you map sequence audio channels to the device, the device does not turn on. In the Audio Hardware preferences, choose the device you want to use to play audio.

First, you choose the hardware device in the Map Output For menu. Then, you map sequence channels to that device. The lists below the Map Output For menu show the channels that the device you chose can use. Then, you use channel tiles to connect each sequence channel to a hardware channel. In this case, if you pick a third-party 16-channel audio device, the list will show 16 hardware channels. If you pick a stereo, the list will only show you two hardware channels. The list has three tiles to the right of each channel name that show the three types of sequence channels you can connect to that hardware channel. These are stereo, 5.1, and 16-channel.

- ❖ Select **Edit > Preferences > Audio Hardware.**
- ❖ From the **Map Output For** menu in the **Audio Hardware** tab, pick the driver for the device you want to use. By default, Premiere Pro chooses **Desktop Audio** for Windows or **Built-In** for macOS.
- ❖ Move the tile for the sequence channel you want to the right place in the list for the hardware channel you want.
- ❖ Click "**OK**."

Extract audio from clips

In a project, you can take audio from clips and make new audio source clips. The original source clips have been kept. Any changes made to the original source clips, like gain, speed, duration, and interpret footage, are carried over to the new audio clips that were extracted.

1. In the Project panel, pick out one or more audio clips.
2. Select "**Clip**" and then "**Audio Options**" and "**Extract Audio**."

The word "**Extracted**" is added to the end of the filenames of the new audio files that Premiere Pro makes that contain the extracted audio.

Break a stereo track into mono tracks

If you use the Breakout to Mono command, you can turn a clip's stereo or 5.1 surround audio channels into mono audio source clips. When you separate a stereo clip, you get two mono audio source clips, one for each channel. When you separate a 5.1 surround clip, you get six mono audio source clips, one for each channel. The original source clip is kept by Premiere Pro. The Breakout To Mono command doesn't make new files; it only makes new source clips that have the right source channel mapping.

1. Choose a clip with 5.1 or stereo surround audio in the Project panel.
2. Go to **Clip > Audio Options > Breakout to Mono**.

The audio source clips that are made have filenames that start with the name of the original clip and then list the channel names. When Premiere Pro splits a stereo audio clip called Zoom into two audio source clips, it calls them Zoom Left and Zoom Right. Keep in mind that the Breakout To Mono command does not link clips together. Use the Source Channel

Mappings command to connect mono clips. In the Timeline panel, the Breakout To Mono command only works on clips that are part of a sequence. It does not work on items in the Project panel.

Break all stereo tracks into mono tracks

Premiere Pro can automatically separate stereo and surround channels into separate mono audio clips as they are imported or captured.

1. Go to Preferences and select Audio.
2. Pick Mono from the Stereo Media menu in the Source Channel Mapping area.
3. Click the OK button.

Use a mono clip as a stereo

There are times when it can be helpful to use a mono audio clip as a stereo clip. You can add a mono clip to a pair of left and right stereo channels using the Modify Clip message box.

1. Pick out a mono clip in the Project panel.
2. Go to Clip > Edit > Audio Channels.
3. In the Modify Clip box, choose Clip Channel Format > Stereo. Finally, click OK to finish.

Note: The Modify Clip command can only be used on a mono clip in the Project panel before it shows up in the Timeline panel. You can't change a clip instance to stereo when it's in a mono audio track. There are three audio filters that you can use: source clip channel mapping, the Fill Left audio filter, and the Fill Right audio filter. These filters let you replace the sound in one channel of a stereo clip with sound from the other channel.

Link multiple audio clips

A video clip can be linked to more than one audio clip and audio clips can be linked to each other. Whenever you link audio clips in a sequence, you only link the copies of the master clips. The Project panel's original raw audio clips have not been changed in any way. When you move or trim linked clips in a Timeline panel, they stay in sync. You can add audio effects to all channels in the linked clips, such as Volume and Panning effects. Out-of-sync signs show if you make an edit that only moves one of the linked clips. In the Source Monitor, you can see and cut a multi-clip link. That's all you can see and play in the Source Monitor at once. If the linked clips have markers, the Source Monitor timeline will only show marks for the track that is being shown. The Source Monitor can show a multi-clip link from the Project panel. To add the linked clips to different tracks in a Timeline panel, use the Overwrite or Insert buttons. The Effect Controls box shows all the video and audio tracks in a multi-clip link. The effects that have been applied are grouped by track. In the Effect Controls panel, you can choose which group to add effects from the Effects panel to.

Link audio clips

All of the audio clips must be on different tracks and have the same channel type. If clips are already linked, like an audio clip that is linked to a video clip, you have to disconnect them before you can link more than one clip.

1. If you need to, pick each video and audio clip that is linked, or select several clips at once, and go to Clip > Unlink.
2. Hold down the Shift key and click on each audio clip on its track in the Timeline gallery. To choose a video clip, you can also shift-click.

Take note that all of the audio clips must have the same track format, which can be mono, stereo, or 5.1 surround.

3. Go to **Clip > Link**.

Change a link between multiple clips in the Source Monitor

1. Click twice on a related file in the Timeline panel.
2. Choose a track from the Track menu to see a certain channel.
3. If you want to, you can set the In and Out points for a track.

When you set the In and Out points for a track, the cutting is applied to the other related tracks' In and Out points as well. When two joined tracks have different lengths, their "In" and "Out" points will be different. When two clips are connected, their "In" and "Out" points are only the same if their lengths are the same.

Keying

When you key in a picture, you set the transparency to a certain color value (with a color key or chroma key) or brightness value (with a luminance key). When you put in a value, all dots with similar brightness or color values become see-through. When working with things that are too involved to hide easily, keying makes it easy to switch out a background that stays the same color or brightness for a different image. Bluescreening or greenscreening is the process of keying out a background that stays the same color. You don't have to use blue or green, though; you can use any solid color as a background. One way to define transparency to a certain background picture is to use difference keying. Instead of a single-color screen, you can key out any background you want.

Color Keying a Greenscreen Shot

What color is the screen? When making live-action shows with unique backgrounds or mixing in Hollywood-style special effects, video shoots could be a game-changer. A green screen is used to film someone or add visual effects in front of a solid color. After that, you can "key out" or digitally remove that color in post-production and drop the scene into any background you want. The method of getting rid of the colored background is called "chroma keying." What does the green background mean? It's easy to take off without touching the person in the center because it doesn't match their real skin tone or hair color. A blue screen is the best option, though, if you need to match a background with less light or have a green object in your project.

It might save you time and money to shoot on a green screen, but if you do it wrong, it can make your work more difficult. First, make sure that your green screen is as flat and smooth as it can be. Then pay attention to how well you light your green screen. As much as possible, shoot in good quality.

Guidelines for lighting your green screen

Preparing your subject for the green screen

It will help you figure out how to light the things or people in front of your green screen better if you know what kind of film you'll be using for the background. "What kills a green screen composite is if there's sunshine from the left in the backdrop image, and you lit them from the opposite side," says cameraman Gerry Holtz. Those two things will not look good together at all."

Allow as much distance as possible between the person and the green screen.

Keeping a safe distance between your subject and the green screen can help you make sure that the lighting in your new background-clip is right. It will also help keep green tones from going off the screen and onto the edges of your subject. Make sure there are 10 to 15 feet between the person and the screen.

Don't forget that anything green will go away.

The Ultra Key tool in the video editing software will rip a hole in someone's chest if they show up with a green tie. Also, look out for colors that have a hint of green. "I've seen folks arrive wearing somewhat greenish khakis." "What happens is that they look kind of clear," Apley says. Things that are reversed or reflected could also be a problem. Powder can be used to take away shine from the head or face.

Add a picture to the background of your green screen video.

Once you're done filming your green or blue screen video, use green screen software or a video editing tool to get rid of the background color and add your new scene. Follow these steps to make sure that your edit in Adobe Premiere Pro goes smoothly.

Make sure you lock in your contents before you key out the picture.

Do a rough edit of your picture before you spend time cutting off the green screen background or even color-correcting it. Because these jobs are hard, you don't want to waste time on frames that won't be used in the final edit.

Use what the Ultra Key can do.

Use Adobe Premiere Pro's Ultra Key tool to key out the background after you've cut down your picture. The Effects menu has an Ultra Key tab that you can choose. To choose your key color, use the Eyedropper tool to point to a spot on the green or blue screen. You might be lucky and this will finish most of the job. As needed, move the sliders for Matte Generation, Matte Cleanup, Spill Suppression, and Color Correction. Because of these changes, the way your key is taken away will be different.

Change anything you need to about your new background.

Edit the new video background as needed. To improve the depth of field when shooting a close-up conversation, soften the background a bit. "Think about what that background would have looked like if it had been there when I took the picture. How am I going to make up for that?" Holtz is curious.

To take it a step further, use fancy green screens.

You should look for small, foldable background pieces that look like a sphere on the green screen. These can be used to quickly record keyable films. Keep the pop-up screen in front of the thing or person you want to shoot. In your video editor, place a basic matte (also called a "trash matte") between the person and the edge of the green area. Then, get rid of the background that goes past the line of the matte.

Advanced Audio Keyframing

An audio keyframe in Premiere Pro records a change to the sound at a certain point in time, just like any other animated keyframe. Sound effects can be keyframed the same way video effects can. Clip-level keyframes are one of the most popular ways that audio keyframes are used. You can use these to lessen audio spikes, play music below speech, lower the volume of a section of audio, and so on. One important thing to learn from this part is that the **Show Audio Keyframes** setting in the Timeline panel (wrench icon) needs to be turned on.

The "rubber band" is a white line that runs through the middle of all of your audio clips in the Timeline. This is where you can make keyframes for audio clips. There is an audio change at that point in the clip marked by a keyframe on the rubber band.

As a fun fact, the rubber band in the Timeline does the same thing as the one in the Effect Controls panel. On the other hand, the Effect Controls panel lets you see and change all audio factors, while the rubber band can only show one at a time. For example, Maxim suggests that instead of using the Pen tool to make keyframes, you can use the CMD/CTRL computer control. When you hold down the CMD or CTRL keys and click on the rubber band, Premiere Pro will make keyframes. In the picture below, the Pen tool is not selected.

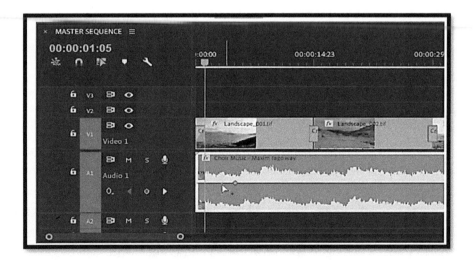

What Are Audio Track Keyframes?

Keyframes for audio tracks come in handy here. In Premiere Pro, audio track keyframes are added to the track (not the music track, but the audio track), and they don't change when audio clips are put on it. Yes, you can move or swap audio clips on the track and the keyframes for that track will still work. If you want to see the audio track settings and keyframes, double-click the audio track heading to make it bigger. To change the volume, click the **Show Keyframes** button and then choose Audio Track Keyframes ». Keep in mind that any audio effects that you added to the track in the Audio Track Mixer will also show up here. From now on, the rubber band's keyframes will be "**pinned**" to the track instead of to a single audio clip.

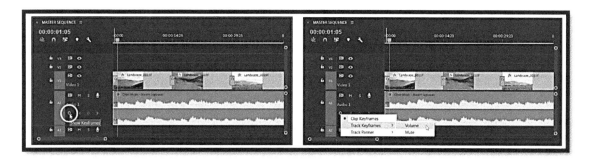

Maxim points out that when you change the view to display audio track keyframes, the keyframe rubber band will go past the clip and down the timeline. (When working with clip keyframes, the rubber band can only go around the clips.)

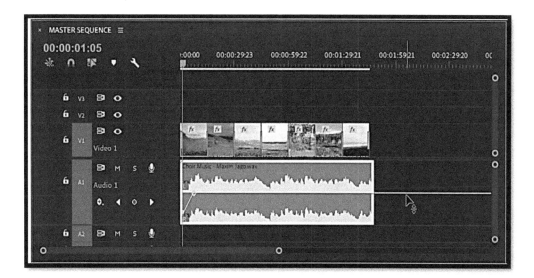

View autosaves and versions of Team Project

View versions of a Team Project

Team Project makes and saves a new version of the project every time a team member posts a change. You can easily see or go back to a version that was already released. Versions are an easy and lasting way to keep track of Team Project's written past.

There are several ways to get to and look at different versions of your Team Project.

❖ In Premiere Pro, go to the menu bar and click on the name of the Team Project. Then, choose **Auto Save History** from the dropdown menu.

❖ Go to **Edit > Team Project > Browse Versions** and find the most recent version of the project in the Media Browser.

❖ In the Media Browser panel, right-click on Team Project and choose Team Project Versions. This will bring up a box with a list of all the versions and details about them, like shared notes that have already been made.

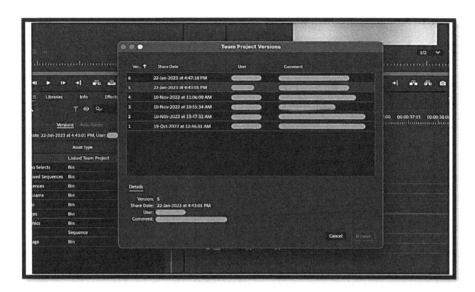

❖ In the Media Browser panel, choose the Team Project. Then, use the vertical scale under the Versions tab to see the different versions.

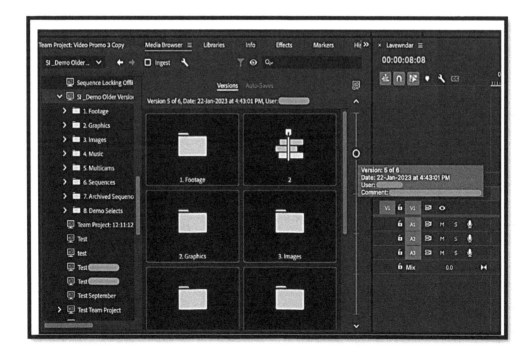

Create a new Team Project from a version

1. Use any of the previously mentioned methods to access the versions in the **Media Browser** panel.
2. Use the vertical slider for versions to get to the latest version of the project in the Media Browser. This slider lets you see all versions.
3. In the Media Browser box, right-click on the Team Project that is listed under Creative Cloud and choose "**New Team Project From Version**." This will make a new Team Project from a shared version that was already there.

A dialog box with the following characteristics opens up:

- Pre-populate the name of the current **Team Project** and append a copy to it.
- Queue up the same list of collaborators as the original Team Project.

2. Select **OK** to create a Team Project.

Specify Auto Save cache location

Every edit you make in the project while working on a Team Project is saved locally. It also instantly syncs with Adobe Cloud. As an option, you can choose where on your local machine to save the Team Project Auto Save store. Team Project saves itself to this place in the background as you work and make changes. Note: In local projects, your project is saved automatically every so often based on the times set in the Automatically Save box. Team Project saves every option under Preferences with each edit. There is no need to physically save your Team Project after every edit, and you don't have to worry about your changes not being saved.

1. In the menu bar, go to Premiere Pro and select Settings (macOS) or Preferences (Windows). Then, select Auto Save.
2. In the **Team Projects** area, click **Browse** and choose the place on your computer where you want to save the project.

3. When you're done, the changes you made will be made to the next Team Project you make.

View auto-saves

You can view all auto saves, see when your changes were saved automatically, go back to an earlier auto save, and even make a Team Project from an auto-saved edit with the Auto Saves tool.

1. Open the Team Project you want to look through your auto-saves by going to Edit > **Team Project > Browse Auto-Saves**.

You can also choose the "Team Project" name from the Premiere Pro menu bar and then "Version History" from the drop-down menu.

2. Another way is to right-click on Team Project in Creative Cloud and choose "Team Project Auto-Saves..." from the menu that comes up. This will show you a list of all the Team Project auto-saves that you have made. You can also move through auto-saves with the Team Project Auto-Saves vertical tool.

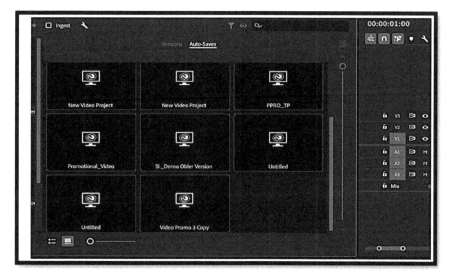

3. Choose "**Make Auto-Save the Latest**" to undo the most recent change and make the last one automatically save.

4. Right-click on the Team Project in Creative Cloud, choose "**New Team Project From Auto-Save,**" and then click "OK." This will make a new Team Project from an auto-save. A window pops up and:

   - Pre-populates the name of the current Team Project.
   - Appends an auto-saved copy to it.

- Queues up the same list of collaborators as the original Team Project.

Set Trim preferences

Large Trim Offset

There are Large Trim Offset buttons on the Trim Monitor. When you click on one of these buttons, the trim point goes forward or backward. You can choose how many frames the Large Trim Offset buttons move trim points in the Trim pane of the Preferences dialog box.

Allow the Selection tool to choose Roll and Ripple trims without the modifier key

Turn this option on if you want to edit in Ripple and rolling mode without pressing a control key.

Shift clips that overlap trim point during ripple trimming

If you turn this option on, the overlapping track items will be moved during a ripple removal.

Ripple trim adds edits to keep both sides of trim in sync

To edit clips that cross a cut, turn on this option. After you add edit points, they will be cut along with the edit points you chose to trim. This keeps clips from moving out of place on either side of the edit.

Playhead position determines trim monitor loop playback

If you turn this option on, a replay will loop around the playhead position instead of the whole edit point selection.

Set transcription preferences

When you use Premiere Pro to transcribe audio clips, the options and setups for transcription taste are what you see.

- **Automatically Transcribe Clips:** Check this box for the automatic transcription of clips.
- **Transcription Preferences:** Choose between Auto-transcribe all imported clips or Auto-transcribe only clips in sequence based on your specific needs.
- **Speaker Labeling:** Opt for "Yes, separate speakers" if you want distinctive labeling for individual speakers, or choose "No" to avoid separating speakers in the labeling.
- **Enable Language Auto-Detection:** Activate this checkbox to enable automatic language detection during the transcription of clips.
- **Default Language:** Select the desired language for transcribing clips from the available options.

Noise Reduction and Restoration

Noise reduction is the process of fixing parts of the shot that are fuzzy. The noise in the camera (CCD) comes from the electronic sensor, which counts the light for each pixel in your picture. The monitor will measure the information based on how you set up your camera. If you shoot in low light, the camera might not get enough information to record the full depth and clarity of the picture. The camera records the amount of light, so the darker parts of your shot are affected the most. By adding more light to your shot, you can get rid of video noise the best. Also, remember that making your movie darker is easier than editing out any noise. When you try these ways to get rid of noise in your video, it will become less obvious. Premiere Pro comes with a tool that cancels out noise. You won't need any other tools or apps to do it! It's quick and easy to do this. Getting rid of noise in Premiere Pro should be an important part of your daily work.

Let's get started!

1. Add Audio to your Premiere Pro Project

Adding audio to your project is the first thing you need to do to get rid of noise in Premiere Pro videos. Once Premiere Pro is open, take a quick look at the layout. To be more specific, you need to find the Timeline panel. There is a Timeline at the very bottom of Premiere Pro. It should be the focal point of your project. You can add a video to the Timeline and then sequence it however you see fit. It tells the video and audio when to start, stop, and work together. In Adobe Premiere Pro, you can edit audio by dragging and dropping it on the Timeline.

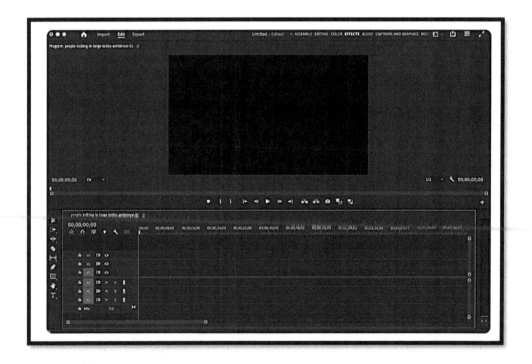

Let us look at how. Start by going to a computer file on your computer that has an audio file. To choose it, find it and click on it. You can drop it on your Timeline after dragging it there. Because it's the main audio track in Premiere, the A1 track is a good choice. This will be written on the Timeline's left side.

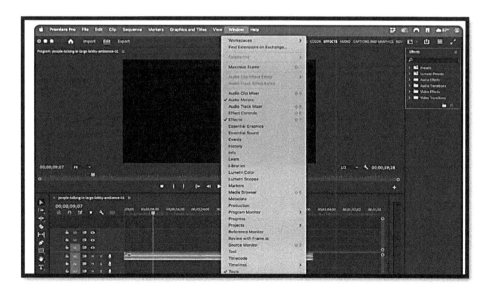

The audio you picked will be brought in by Premiere Pro. You are now ready to learn about all of Premiere Pro's noise reduction tools. Today you will learn how to get rid of background noise in Premiere Pro audio. **Note**: If you have a video with sound, the sound will already be on a track called "audio."

2. Open the Effects and Effect Controls

We will use two important choices to show you how to get rid of background noise in Premiere. These are the Effects and the controls for them. They are linked directly. In Premiere, you can add effects to clips using the Effects panel. You can change how strong these effects are in the Effect Controls panel. That is, you will add a DeNoise effect to the screen. Then, use the Effect Controls to decide how much noise to get rid of. You can find both of these areas in Adobe Premiere Pro. They're not instantly seen, though. They will need to be opened. To do this, go to the top of Premiere Pro and find the Window dropdown. When you click on it, the dropdown menu will show you a list of options. Click on Effects when you find it.

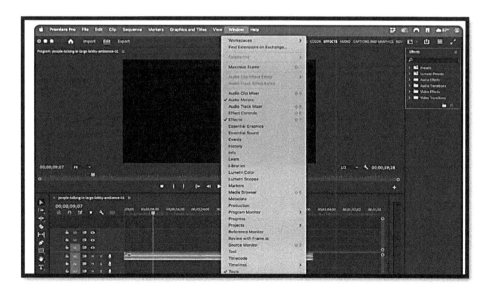

There will be an open Effects panel when you do that. It's on the right side of Premiere Pro, next to the Timeline. Let us open the Effect Controls now. Go back to the Window menu another time. Pick Effect Controls from the list that's close to the top this time. It will open in the top left corner of your Premiere Pro window this time.

We can now start working in Premiere Pro to get rid of the background noise!

3. Apply a DeNoise Effect in Premiere

DeNoise is an effect for Premiere Pro, as was already said. We'll need to use it on our audio first before we can do anything else. To begin, look in the Timeline for the audio clip. It looks like a green bar in this case. To choose it, click on it once. After that, go to the Effects panel on the right side of the screen that we opened. There are some subfolders inside the Effects panel. Sound Effects is the one to use. Open it, and then open the folder called Noise Reduction/Restoration. There are some effects written inside. It comes with the one we need, DeNoise.

169

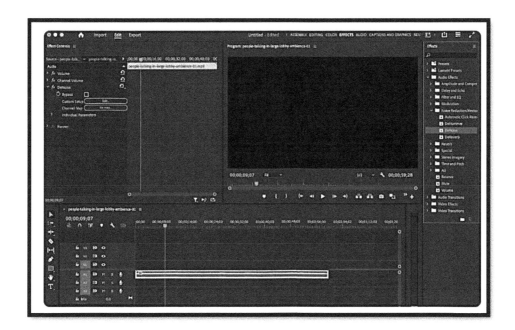

In Premiere Pro, click and drag on the DeNoise effect to do noise canceling. Place it on top of the audio track you chose in the Timeline. When you let go of the mouse, it will fall into place. There you have it! You now know how to move background noise from audio in Premiere Pro.

4. Adjust the Effect

Keep an eye on the Effect Controls box in the upper left when you add the DeNoise effect. It will fill up with new menu options. One of these is the DeNoise dropdown tool. The Effect Controls are where you change how strong the DeNoise effect is, as the name suggests.

Open the **DeNoise** menu. Click the Edit button in the Custom Setup group. Premiere Pro will then open the Clip Fx Editor. The audio will start playing if you press the Spacebar on your computer. In the Clip Fx Editor's sample box, you can listen to the sound waves as they play.

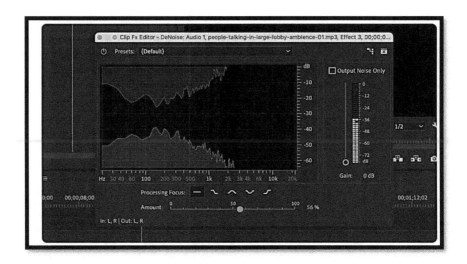

You have multiple options here. You can choose from presets, for example. On the **Presets** dropdown, you'll see that the **Default** settings are active. But by clicking, you can choose the **Light** or **Heavy Noise Reduction** options. In Premiere Pro, you can also fully decide how to reduce background noise at the bottom of the Clip Fx Editor. The Amount scale is used for this. You can move it to the left or right to change how much noise is blocked. There's no one setting that works every time. It's important to listen to your audio and make changes as you hear them. You can change how strong the noise reduction is while you work. This way, you can keep the sounds you want and get rid of the noise in the background. It doesn't take long at all. Get out of the Clip Fx Editor when you're done. The noise reduction features you set up in Premiere Pro are now added to your clip.

More Options: The Essential Sound Panel

You learned how to get rid of noise in Premiere Pro videos. The Effects and Effect Controls were used in that way. You have more options with Premiere, though. There is another screen that you can use that is called *Essential Sound*. The changes you've already made can be improved with this. You can also skip the Effects and use these other options instead.

Let's briefly look at how to denoise in Premiere using the Essential Sound panel.

1. Open up the Essential Sound Panel
Let's open Premiere Pro and go to the Essential Sound gallery. To do this, go back to the top of your screen and click on the Window dropdown. When you click it, a list of options will appear. Find Essential Sound. Press on Essential Sound.

The Essential Sound panel will open when you click. When you first open Premiere Pro, it will show up on the right side of the screen, on top of the Effects panel we were using earlier.

2. Reduce Noise with Essential Sound

With the new Essential Sound menu, you can now use Premiere Pro to get rid of noise. Click on your audio track in the Timeline to start. After that, go to the Key Sound panel. To work on Essential Sound, make sure you're on the Edit tab. You can see some subsections less than this. Pick out the one that says "**Repair**" and click on it. You will see new settings and options after you do that.

Reducing noise is the first thing you should do. Click the tick next to it to make it work. To start playing your audio, simply press the Spacebar as you did before. Slide the bar left and right as the music plays. Again, this sets the amount or strength of the noise reduction. You can also use the **Reduce Rumble setting** if you want to. When you record something and hear a rumble in the background, this can help. It makes sense this time too. Check the box next to Reduce Rumble to turn it on, and then change the volume as you playback the audio. You now know how to get rid of background noise in Premiere Pro with this set of tools! Because you have a lot of powerful options on your hands, you can save audio and make it sound great for your next project. Every time you edit, make sure that background noise reduction Premiere Pro effects are part of your process. Making videos this way will make them look and sound great!

CHAPTER 11
MOTION GRAPHICS AND ANIMATION

Introduction to Motion Graphics

Motion Graphics models (.mogrt) are special kinds of files that can be made in either After Effects or Premiere Pro. These themes are very useful for Premiere Pro editors because they include all of After Effects motion graphics features. They are easy to reach and have settings that can be changed right in Premiere Pro. Premiere Pro has its own Type and Shape tools that can be used to make new titles and graphics. Once these are made, users can export them as Motion Graphics designs to use or share with others. Premiere Pro also comes with examples of Motion Graphics designs that were made in both After Effects and Premiere Pro. These can be used right away as models.

Even better, Premiere Pro lets you load Motion Graphics models from different places, giving editors even more freedom and options:

❖ **Local Templates Folder**: Editors can store and access Motion Graphics templates locally, which makes them easy to find and use in Premiere Pro.
❖ **Creative Cloud Libraries**: Templates saved in Creative Cloud Libraries can be used right away in different projects, making sure they are always ready and consistent.
❖ **Adobe Stock**: A rich collection of designs for editors to use in their projects can be found in Adobe Stock, which offers access to a wide variety of expertly made Motion Graphics themes.

These import options greatly increase the number of Motion Graphics models that Premiere Pro editors can use. They make it easier to use motion graphics tools from After Effects and open up more creative options in Premiere Pro's editing environment.

Install templates for motion graphics.

In the Essential Graphics panel, you can add a Motion Graphics design from your computer to the Local Templates folder. **You can't find Motion Graphics designs in the Project panel like you can with video.**

1. To add templates to the Local Templates folder, drag and drop one or more templates onto the Essential Graphics viewer. You can also click the "Install" button in the bottom right area to put your MOGRTs in place.

2. Navigate to a folder where the Motion Graphics template is saved, and select **Open**.

The template is moved to the Local Templates Folder and can be found in the Graphics panel. **Note**: If there is already a Motion Graphics template with the same name, a box will show up asking you to either replace the existing one or stop the installation of the new one. Premiere Pro will tell you if you try to run a Motion Graphics template that doesn't work with your project version. If you made a Motion graphics file with a later version of After Effects, it won't work with the older version.

The Local Templates folder

The Local Templates folder is the default folder when installing MOGRTs or licensing them from Adobe Stock through the Essential Graphics panel. The folder is located at:

- macOS: **username/Library/Application Support/Adobe/Common/Motion Graphics Templates/**
- Windows: **root://Users/username/AppData/Roaming/Adobe/Common/Motion Graphics Templates/**

- **Note**: On macOS, the AppData directory is private, as is the Local Templates folder directory. On Windows, it is the same. To see these files, you need to make them visible again.
- **Note**: If you try to load a Motion Graphics template that has the same name as one that is already in Premiere Pro's Local Templates folder, you will see a message box. It gives you the option to either replace the current template or you can stop the download.

Premiere Pro will let users know if they try to install a Motion Graphics template that doesn't work with the current project. When a Motion Graphics template is made with a newer version of After Effects than the version used in the Premiere Pro project, problems can happen. Premiere Pro will tell you that the Motion Graphics template is not suitable if it was made using features or functions that are not allowed by the current version of the project.

Organize Motion Graphics templates

Create a library

Think of your computer as a huge library. Your files, photos, and videos are the books and other things that are spread out on the shelves. Just like putting books in a library so they are easy to find, Premiere Pro, software for making videos, lets you set up your own "libraries" to organize and keep track of your videos. Let's start by picturing Premiere Pro's Libraries panel as a special shelf on your bookshelf that holds all the libraries you've made.

To order your videos, you can make a new "library" or area in this panel by following these steps:

1. Make sure you can see the **Libraries** panel by going to Premiere Pro and picking on "**Windows**" and then "**Libraries.**" This move opens the **Libraries** panel, which is like putting your books on your shelf and going to the library area.

2. To do this, click on the three-lined ▦ "hamburger" icon next to "**Libraries.**" It will show a menu. Choose "**Create New Library**" from that menu. It's kind of like giving a new shelf on your library a name.

3. The screen will show a text box that asks you to name your new library. Type in the name and then click "**Create.**" There you have it! In the Libraries box, you've just added a new area. This is like adding a new shelf to your computer for your videos.

Now, let's say you have an important picture or graphic that you want to keep in this newly created library. Here's how you can add it:

1. Open Premiere Pro and go to the Essential Graphics Panel. This is like a drawer where you can store your important graphics.

2. Right-click on the picture you want to add to your library. This is similar to taking a special picture or item out of a box.

3. Click "**Copy to Library**" and pick the library where you want to save the picture. It's like putting that picture or thing in the new space you made on your shelves.

In this case, you've moved or saved the picture into your newly organized Premiere Pro library. Think of the Essential Graphics part as a gallery where you can see different Motion Graphics styles. It's like browsing a collection of cool things you can use in your videos.

In this part, you can do the following:

- If you want to find certain Motion Graphics templates, you can type buzzwords into the search field, just like you would in a book.
- When you move your mouse over these templates, an image appears, just like when you look through a catalog and see what each item looks like.
- Like putting things away by name or how often you use them, you can sort these files by title or by "recently used."

- If you like a template, you can make it easier to find later by clicking on the star icon next to it. This is similar to bookmarking a page in a catalog.
- You can also rename and tag these templates to make them easier to find and organize later, which is similar to adding labels or notes to items in your catalog to make them easier to find.

So, just like you would put books or other items in different sections of a library or catalog to make them easier to find and identify, Premiere Pro lets you organize and manage your video materials using libraries and panels. This makes it easier and faster to find what you need when editing your videos.

Browse and manage Motion Graphics templates

This is where you can find Motion Graphics templates: in the Essential Graphics panel. You can search for and look at your Motion Graphics designs as well as license-free and paid Stock templates in the Essential Graphics panel viewer.

In My Templates view, you can do the following:

- Type a word or phrase into the search bar to quickly find what you need. You can use the options as filters to see templates that are available in your Libraries or your local area.
- For themes with video clips, use hover touch to see previews of animations.
- Put the Motion Graphics file in order by Title or Most Recently Used.
- Click the star icon next to a Motion Graphics template to make it your favorite. Then, quickly see your picks by using the picks filter next to the search bar.
- Change the names of your Motion Graphics themes and add tags in the InfoView to make them easier to find and organize.
- You can change the size of the images in your MOGRT.

Note: You can also use the Libraries panel to bring Motion Graphics models into Premiere Pro from Adobe Stock or Creative Cloud Libraries.

Browse Multiple Libraries

You can also look through designs from more than one source at the same time.

- Clicking "All" shows all library results.
- When you select a single library, only designs from that library are shown.

- You can pick more than one library at once. Picking "All" undoes everything you've chosen.

Manage Extra Folders

Custom files that have been put as a path in Premiere Pro can be used, and you can also make your own. You can only see the Local Templates Folder check box if there is no special folder. These are the places in Premiere Pro where you can find a unique folder that you set up as a path.

Follow these steps to add new custom folders as paths:

1. If you want to add more paths, click the hamburger icon ▦ next to the Essential Graphics box.
2. Find Manage Additional Folders in the list that pops up. This will open the Manage Additional Folders dialog box.
3. Click "Add" to add a group. Click on a file and then click on Select Folder. The folder is added to the box that says "Manage Additional Folders."
4. To get rid of a folder, click on it and then click on Remove.

Drag and drop between locations

You can move or copy your MOGRTs from one place to another, just like you would with your operating system's file system. It's easy to move MOGRTs between local folders on the same disk. If the folders are on different drives, you can copy the MOGRTs instead. You can move MOGRTs from a folder on your computer to a collection as well. So, you can keep track of things, when you select a MOGRT in the Essential Graphics panel, a blue outline will show you where it is in the library.

Adding your local folders from the disk

To handle MOGRTs on disk, all you have to do is click the plus sign in the top right corner of the Essential Graphics panel. You can add a folder from a local drive, a cloud drive, or a shared network drive to the My Templates window. It's also easy to find your custom local files on disk; just right-click on the spot in the Essential Graphics panel and choose "Reveal in Finder/Explorer." **Note**: If you add a parent folder with MOGRTs in subfolders, the templates will not show up in the Essential Graphics panel. Make sure you add the folder with the MOGRTs inside. The Essential Graphics panel has a context menu that lets you manage your MOGRT files on disk. This menu includes the options to **Rename, Remove, and**

Reveal in Finder/Explorer. Changing the name of a place or deleting it from the Essential Graphics panel will not change the folder on your hard drive.

Removing default templates

We provide a set of basic templates in the Local Templates Folder to help users get started with MOGRTs in Premiere Pro. We know that some people would rather just focus on their material.

Just follow these steps to get rid of these templates:

1. Click the Local Templates folder in the browser tree and choose "Right-Click."
2. In Finder or Explorer, choose Reveal.
3. Get rid of all the MOGRT files in the Local Templates folder, but keep the.txt file (PrMogrtInstall13-0-0.txt).

If you ever want to get them back, all you have to do is delete the.txt file. The MOGRTs will be created again when you open Premiere Pro again.

Using the Essential Graphics panel, look for Motion Graphics templates in Adobe Stock

Select Adobe Stock from the Browse tab of the Essential Graphics panel.

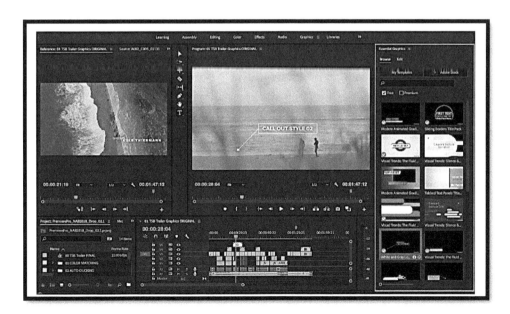

Once you've put in your search term, press **Enter**. Stock findings look like pages in a big book; they show you different Motion Graphics templates that you can use in your video projects. You can see a certain number of pages at a time in the browser panel, which is based on the number of themes and the size of the images you've chosen.

Here's how you can navigate and make the most out of these Stock results:

1. Browsing Methods:
- To move from one page to the next, use the "previous" and "next" arrows, like you would in a book.
- Similar to putting a page number into an index, you can enter a specific page number into the text edit box to go straight to that page.
- To license a Motion Graphics template, drag it into your video project or click on the "License and Download" button.
- Click the "I" icon below the image of a template to see more details or see how it will look animated.

2. Licensing and Downloading:
- From this view, click the "License or Download" icon to license the Motion Graphics template and save it in your Local Templates folder.

Here's how you can add a Motion Graphics template to your project once you've found one you like to use in your video sequence:

- In the Essential Graphics panel, go to the "Browse" tab. This will open the store area that has these themes.
- Drag and drop the template you want to use onto a video track in your sequence. This is similar to choosing an item from a store and putting it in your workspace.
- Keep in mind that Premiere Pro may show that the media is "offline" until the template is fully loaded after you add a template to your sequence. You can fix the missing fonts if the template needs fonts that aren't loaded.
- Once the template is added to your sequence, you can change how it looks even more by clicking on the "Edit" tab in the Essential Graphics panel. This is similar to changing the features of an item you've picked out from the store.

So, Premiere Pro lets you browse through a library of things, buy, and add Motion Graphics templates to your video projects. This gives you the freedom to change and use these templates in your editing workspace in the way that works best for you.

Add Motion Graphic templates to a Sequence

1. **Accessing Templates:**
   - Open the Essential Graphics panel and navigate to the 'Browse' tab. This tab acts as a window into a collection of available templates.

2. **Adding a Template to Your Sequence:**
   - Choose the desired template and drag it from the Essential Graphics panel onto a video track within your sequence. Think of this action as selecting an item from a shelf and placing it onto your workspace.

3. **Media Loading Status:**
   - Upon adding the template to your sequence, Premiere Pro might display that the media is 'offline'. This status indicates that the template is being loaded into your project. It's similar to having an item ready to use, but waiting for it to become fully available.

4. **Fixing Missing Fonts (if necessary):**
   - If the templates you've added require fonts that aren't currently installed in your system, Premiere Pro will notify you about missing fonts. You can address this issue by installing the required fonts, and ensuring the template looks as intended when used.

5. **Customizing Template Appearance:**
   - Once the template is in your sequence, you can modify its appearance and attributes. Head to the 'Edit' tab within the Essential Graphics panel, which is like having tools to adjust and fine-tune the selected item from your shelf. Here, you can alter various elements and make the template suit your project's needs.

Premiere Pro makes it easy to choose Motion Graphics themes, add them to your video project, and make changes to them. There are a lot of templates in the Essential Graphics panel, and you can also use it as a toolbox to change how these templates look in your working workspace.

Customize your Motion Graphics template

When you customize Motion Graphics designs in Premiere Pro, you can make changes that work for your project. **Here is a step-by-step guide on how to change these templates:**

1. Pick out the Motion Graphics template you want to change in your sequence.
2. Go to the Essential Graphics panel and click "**Edit**" to change the design settings to your liking.

3. If you go to Edit Template Properties, you'll see different options based on the type of template:

- Choose from a list of options given by the design owner to change colors, source text, and motion settings.
- Change things like fonts, text size, fake styles, and more.
- You can change the features inside groups of controls in themes by making them bigger or smaller.
- You can edit the values of the data using worksheet templates that support CSV (comma-separated value) or TSV (tab-separated value).
- Replaceable media designs let you use your pictures or videos instead of the ones that come with the template.

4. **Real-time updates**: Any changes you make to the features in the template settings are immediately seen in the template itself.

5. **Adjust Template Duration**: To change how long a Motion Graphics template plays, pick it in the timeline and use the red lines at its edges to make it play for longer or shorter amounts of time.

Regarding updating Motion Graphics templates

- Motion graphics templates made in After Effects that are used and modified in Premiere Pro sequences can be switched out for a more recent version of the template.
- To update, hold down Alt or Option and drag and drop the new template onto the sequence's current template.
- You can update the template for all instances in the project, or you can save the change for just one instance. Your changes are kept as much as possible during the update process.

Customizing Motion Graphics themes in Premiere Pro makes it easy to change visually appealing parts to fit the needs of a specific project. It also makes editing easier and gives you more freedom in the creative process.

Creating Animated Lower Thirds

Design your lower third, but don't worry about making it "move" yet.

Know what you want the bottom third of your screen to look like? Start by making it while the video is pausing. Use the square and circle tools (or the pen) to make shapes. Use the text tool to add your words. (To make sure everything fits, it's best to use the longest name, title, or place as an example when making a template that will be used more than once.) You can make images in Adobe Illustrator and bring them in **as.png files** if you have a more complicated plan. Watch your best videos or look for examples online to get ideas. It was easy for me to make this bottom third. It just had my name, the title, and a solid color background. The form is just two bars, and each one is the right length for the text.

Lock the elements in their final positions first.

In the beginning, everything should be off the screen or unseen in some way. In the end, everything should be in its right place. Start by setting the playhead to 2 seconds and making your entire layers stand out. Click the timers next to position, scale, and opacity on one of them. After the short 2-second animation is over, this will lock all the objects in the spot where you want them to be.

Animate the elements onto the screen.

There are a lot of different ways to add things to the screen. These are some options, but you can use keyframes and effects to make your own. In general, you should have the shapes move in the first second and the text move in the second.

You can change this to get the effect you want.

- Set a position keyframe and drag both rectangles off-screen with the playhead at 0. This will bring boxes in from the side. If you have more than one box, make sure the openings are not all at the same level.
- To make the boxes "unfold" down, unclick the "link" next to "scale" in the transform options for both rectangles. At second 1, the scale should be 100% and the position should be where you want them to be. Set both of their scale y-values to 0 at second 0. Place them so that the thin lines begin at the "top" of where they need to go.
- To add the word "type," look for "typewriter" in the effects panel and drag it onto your text layer. Press the "U" key on your keyboard to see the default animation keyframes. Change their positions so the animation lasts between one and two seconds.
- Two keyframes for opacity should be set: one for 0% at 1 second and one for 100% at 2 seconds. This will make the text fade in.

This is an example of the animation I made. It looks like a typewriter, and the text types itself as both boxes swing in from the left. The video is now 3 seconds long instead of 2.

Optional: animate the elements off-screen.

When the lower third leaves the screen, you can make it look like it did when it came in. You only need to copy the same keyframes backward at the end of the clip. Not interested in putting in that much more work? Do not worry. Most of the time, there's no need to animate off a lower third when the clip ends. A lot of the time, interview or b-roll clips in a video move so quickly that it would be annoying to pay too much attention to their coming and going.

Change the timing.

Once your keyframes are in the timeline, right-click on all of them to select them. To get to easy ease, go to keyframe assistant. Moving will be smoother after this. In the preview window, watch the animation a few times. Is it moving too slowly? Going too fast? Are the parts coming on at the right time? You can watch it more slowly by moving the playhead with your mouse. This is useful for checking out the animations you've made more closely.

Connect Premiere Pro and After Effects

When you open After Effects and Premiere for the first time, their interfaces will look a lot alike. They both have a player window, a sequence window, a browser window, and an effects tab. It would be easy to think that you can change in both, but you'll quickly see the main difference.

Premiere Pro: A Quick Overview

Premiere Pro is mostly used to cut, edit, and smooth out video clips, though it does have some moving text and transitions. The timeline is set up in a way that will allow for a free and creative video editing process, and the different edit areas allow the user a clean workflow from assembly to finish. You would use Premiere to cut together your video projects that use footage, like ads, music videos, and all sorts of creative video editing projects. Premiere is also great for audio because it lets you change, mix, and edit the sound in your project.

After Effects: A Quick Overview

For motion graphics, editing, and visual effects, After Effects is the best tool out there. It is much easier to make unique titles and animated parts in After Effects than in Premiere Pro because it has a lot of built-in animation types, and each one has its own set of options. It's hard to edit videos in After Effects because the timeline is so broken. Instead of moving back and forth between elements, the After Effects timeline focuses on the keyframing of a single element. When you add a keyframe to an element, it shows where the beginning and end of an animation begin. When you want to make a fake slow zoom on a clip in Premiere, for example, you will use keyframes. However, the key-framing sequence is secret and not very easy to find. Keyframes are right in the middle of things in After Effects, which makes working with motion graphics much easier. It's a beast for motion design and editing work because it has so many effects, tools, and third-party support.

Using Dynamic Links

In the past, you had to process and export one project before loading it into the other when you wanted to work between After Effects and Premiere. If you use it often, you know how annoying this was before it was made easier. When making changes to title sequences made in After Effects, you would have to export and load them into Premiere each time. To be honest, this was not only a big waste of time, but it also meant that you had multiple copies that took up valuable disc room. Luckily, those bad times are over thanks to the Dynamic Link function, which makes a link between the After Effects and Premiere projects and saves time and sanity. In simple terms, if you change a title in After Effects, the Premiere part will also be changed immediately. After you make a dynamic link between projects, the chosen After Effects comps will show up as clips in the Premiere browser. Here's a quick and easy way to get to all the shows you want to watch all at once.

How to Set Up a Dynamic Link

You can make an After Effects project to link to from within Premiere if you haven't already.

1. To make a new After Effects arrangement in Premiere, go to File > Adobe Dynamic Link > New...
2. Give the project a name and save it. It should become second nature for you to save the After Effects project in the same place as the Premiere project.
3. Just redo the steps if you want to add another match. Once you've done it once, it won't ask you to name the project again. Your comps will show up in the After Effects viewer.

Linking To an Existing After Effects Project

You can still link your motion graphics parts even if you have already made them. Don't worry—this will be easier if you get your After Effects files in order. Make sure the comps you want to link to are named and put in the right areas.

1. To import an After Effects creation into Premiere, go to File > Adobe Dynamic Link > Import When
2. In the file viewer, find the project.
3. Pick out the comps you want to bring in, and then click "OK."

ADDING & AMENDING YOUR GRAPHICS

After making your title in After Effects, you can find the Dynamic Link comps in the browser and add them to your timeline like you would any other clip. See, it's simple after linking; you can switch between programs to make any necessary changes to your motion graphics. The live link will change on its own, and the replay will be much faster.

Tips for Managing Dynamic Links

- Make sure your After Effects project is well managed. It's easy to get sidetracked and forget to name or file your works, but organization is key to having a clean linked project that's easy to find your way around.
- Keep the two projects together. You could lose both projects if you move them after they have been saved, but you can relink them like you would any other dropped clip.

- If you are using a title project that you got or that someone else gave you, open it and get used to how it is laid out. Before you use Premiere to make the dynamic link, write down the names of the comps you want to import.
- Keep all of your motion graphics in one place in After Effects so that you can use the same text and icon movements in different Premiere projects.

CHAPTER 12

USING MARKERS

Markers let you place and order clips by showing you where important moments in time are. You can use a label to point out an important sound or action in a clip or sequence. Markers are only there for reference; they don't change the video in any way.

You can use the following types of marks in Premiere Pro, as shown below:

Marker	Description
Comment	A comment or note about the selected part of the Timeline.
Chapter	Chapter markers in the project allow viewers seeing the finished video use the markers to quickly jump to those points in the video.
Segmentation Marker	Segmentation markers help you define ranges in the video to automate workflows. For example, you can identify certain areas as being leader or as segment where commercials go.
Web Link	Add a URL that provides more info about the selected part of the movie clip.

Markers are probably already a part of the way you work. Some editors use marks (like motion or a chosen sound bite) to make it easy to find parts of a clip. Others use marks to put and align parts in a Timeline. There is a strong marking system in Adobe Premiere Pro that can even connect to the Internet.

Markers panel

If you go to Window > Markers, you can see all the markers in a clip or sequence that is open. The information offered for clips includes color-coded tags, In-points, Out points, and notes. When you click on a clip thumbnail in the Markers panel, the playhead moves to where the marking is. The In and Out spots can be seen on a marker on a clip or in a sequence in the Marker box. You can move the marker from one frame in time to one that covers many frames by moving the In or Out point.

Add markers in the Timeline

The Source monitor, the Program monitor, or the Timeline can all have markers added to them. Any marks that are added to the Program monitor show up on the Timeline. When you add markers to the Timeline, they show up in the Program Monitor in the same way. In Premiere Pro, different marks can be added to a clip so that more than one note or comment can be made on the same clip on the Timeline.

1. **Position the Playhead:**
   - Navigate to the specific point in your timeline where you want to place a marker.
2. **Create a Marker:**
   - Press the "M" key for a quick shortcut or go to "Marker > Add Marker."
   - Note that the default color for markers is green.
3. **Modify the Marker:**
   - To make adjustments, enter the Marker dialog box by double-clicking on the marker icon.
4. **Choose Marker Options:**
- **In the Marker dialog box, you'll find various customization options:**
   - **Name:** Provide a name for the marker.
   - **Duration:** Adjust the duration value by dragging or clicking, then input a new value and press Enter/Return. This is particularly useful for sequence markers used in URL links and chapter markers.
   - **Comments:** Attach a note to the marker for additional context.
   - **Chapter Marker:** Check this option if you want the marker to function as a chapter marker.
   - **Web Link:** Opt for this option if you intend to link the marker to a website.
   - **URL:** If Web Link is selected, enter the URL of the website.
   - **Frame Target:** When Web Link is chosen, this field becomes active. If you're using an HTML frameset, input the target frame for the web page.
5. **Navigate Through Markers:**
   - Use the "Prev" or "Next" buttons to cycle through markers, add comments, or adjust settings as needed.
6. **Confirmation:**
   - Once you're satisfied with the modifications, click the "OK" button to save your changes.

Adding Markers to Clips

A lot of editors choose to use marks in their work. Clip marks can be used to add notes to clips or make it easier to line up two or more clips together. Notes can be added in the Source Monitor panel.

To add a label to a clip, do the following in the Source Monitor:

- Open the clip in the Source Monitor from the Timeline or the Project panel.
- Move the Playhead to where you want the marker to be.
- Press M or go to Marker > Add Marker. A mark has now been added to the clip.

Here are the steps you need to take to mark a file in the Timeline:

- To add a clip marker, go to Edit > Keyboard Shortcuts (Windows) or Premiere Pro > Keyboard Shortcuts (Mac) and make a shortcut.
- Pick out the clip you need. Move the Playhead to where you want the mark to go.
- Press the keyboard button you set up for "Add Clip Marker." A mark has now been added to the clip.
- You can see the marker text box in the Source Monitor if you double-click on the marker.

Create markers in the Effect Controls panel

You can see all the marks you made in the Timeline panel in the panel for effects. It is also possible to add markers to your sequence to show the Effect Controls panel where to put effects. You can also make and change marks directly in the Effect Controls panel.

- Move the playhead to the spot where you want to put the tag.
- For Windows, right-click on the timeline marker. For Mac OS X, control-click on it. After that, press M or pick Add Marker.

Change default marker colors

The first color of a pen is green. You can change this choice by setting computer shortcuts for each marking color.

The Keyboard Shortcuts box shows up.

- Select Edit > Keyboard Shortcuts on Windows.
- Select Premiere Pro > Keyboard Shortcuts on macOS.

Add keyboard shortcuts for each marker color in the Command section.

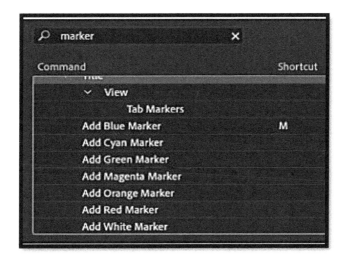

Navigate between the markers.

❖ To use the marker, just click it.
❖ **Choose one of the following options:**

- Go to **Next Marker** > Select **Marker**.
- Go to **Marker > Return** to the previous marker.

Move a marker

Choose one of the following options:

- To move a clip marker in a sequence, open a clip in the Source Monitor and drag the Marker icon in the time measure of the Source Monitor. It's not possible to change clip marks in the Timeline panel.
- To move a sequence marker, drag it in a Timeline panel or on the time measure in the Program Monitor.
- Moving a point in the Source or Program Monitor's Timeline panel's time measure changes the icon that goes with it.

Delete markers

Choose one of the following options:

- Move the playhead to the clip marker. 2. Open the clip in the Source Monitor to get rid of it.
- Move the playhead over a sequence sign to get rid of it.

You can get rid of all the marks by going to Marker > Clear All marks. When you use the Clear All Markers option in Premiere Pro, it gets rid of all sequence and clip markers from certain clips.

Display marker comments

When using Adobe Premiere Pro's time clock and markers, there is a handy tool that lets users quickly see marker information without having to open the Marker dialog box. If you move the mouse over a marker, a message will appear with important information about that marking. **The description for the sequence marker usually gives up to four pieces of information, such as**

1. **Marker Name (Optional):** The name of the marker will show up in the message if one has been given. If a specific name has been given for the marking, this information will only be shown.
2. **Start Timecode**: The start timecode for the marker is always shown in the message. The exact place in the sequence where the tag should go is shown by this timecode.
3. **Timeframe**: If the marker has a length, not just a place in time, but a set duration, the tooltip may include information about the marker's timeframe or duration in the sequence.
4. **Text or Comments (Optional):** If any notes, comments, or extra text were added when the sign was made, they will show up in the preview. This text is only shown in the window if comments or notes have been added to the marking.

Copy and paste sequence markers

You can add sequence markers to items you copy and paste from the timeline so that all of the markers and their data are copied and pasted at the same time. All marker information is saved during the copy/paste process. This includes color, notes, length, and marker type. To add sequence markers when you copy and paste, go to Markers > Copy Paste Includes Sequence Markers.

Using Sync Locks and Track Locks

There are two ways to put clips on tracks in the Timeline panel.

- Sync locks make sure that clips stay in sync, so when you enter or remove clips, they stay in sync on other tracks.
- Track locks let you keep a track in place so that it can't be changed in any way.

Using sync locks

In a normal editing job, there will be many levels of video clips. You will need all of the video tracks to stay in sync when you use ripple edits or inserts to change a sequence. In other words, if one track changes, so will the others. However, you can want one track to stay still while performing swirls or inserts. In Adobe Premiere Pro, you can stop one or more tracks from being moved in two ways: Lock Track and Sync Lock. When an actor's lips move in sync with the audio of someone speaking, this is known as bad lip sync. When this kind of syncing (sync) goes wrong, it's easy to see. Other kinds of sync faults might be harder to spot. When you think of synchronization, you can picture two things that should happen at the same time working together. It could be something as simple as a speaker's name in the lower third, or it could be music that plays at the same time as a moving end. If they happen at the same time, it's coordinated.

Using track locks

Track locks, which are different from sync locks, stop anyone from making changes to a track. They're a great way to keep your sequence straight and clips in place on certain tracks while you work. For instance, you could lock your song track while adding different video clips. The music track can't be changed when it's locked, so you don't have to worry about it while you type. Things that are on a locked track are still in the sequence; you just can't change them. You can lock and open a track by pressing the Track Lock button. You can use diagonal lines to draw attention to clips on a locked track. In this case, track locks are more important than sync locks, so moving the audio clips would throw off the timing of the video clips even if the sync locks are turned on.

Source Patch and Target Tracks

One popular way to work in Premiere Pro is to use source patching. If you don't want to mess around dragging and dropping clips by hand, you can tell the computer exactly where to put each clip. How do you do this, though? First-timers all over the world have this question. There needs to be a way for us to tell Premiere what to do right now. The ways we do that are through source patching and, by extension, track tracking.

What Is Source Patching

When most of us first start using Premiere Pro, we use it in a very basic way. We see it, want it, grab it, and throw it in with the rest. Most skilled editors will be able to do this without any issues when editing projects for fun or something small. When planning something more involved, though, you have to be able to work quickly and neatly. To put it simply, source patching tells Premiere which tracks should be filled in when you use any of the related controls on the Source Monitor, like when you overwrite or enter records. Without this method, we wouldn't be able to tell these tools what to do or where to put them. For projects that will be built from the bottom up, being able to work in stages can be helpful. In documentary work, this is useful because you lay down the sound bed and then add B-Roll on top of it, with each type of content staying on one or more specific tracks. The structure of video projects will be different, but the idea behind source patching can be used to make just about anything as an editor. In this group are projects with a lot of composited parts as well as pieces that are set to music and have no other sound.

How Does Source Patching Work?

Some of you may have noticed that you can turn songs on and off while you work. By choosing which clips to include in the sequence, you can show where you want them to go when you use the Insert or Overwrite command or when you copy and paste something. If you look closely at the picture below, though, you'll see that there are two rows of blue-highlighted track options.

Each track is named in the second column: **V1, V2, V3, A1, A2,** and **A3**. The first, on the other hand, only has two: **V1 and A1**. But you can see that the name doesn't change when we choose V2 and A2 in the first column. People are still calling them V1 and A1, even though the tracks that those names belong to are still below and above, respectively.

What Is the Difference?

When you work hands-free in the Source Monitor and enter or replace, this first column will be your go-to for hard source patching. One audio track and one video track can be chosen at a time. You can also turn off one or both of them completely. The second section does nothing more than turn tracks on and off. You can use these toggles to target tracks for any kind of automatic media movement that has nothing to do with the Source Monitor. For instance, anything you copy to the clipboard will be sent to the tracks you've chosen here. It doesn't matter which tracks you have chosen in the source patching column when you drag and drop. What counts is that you have both your audio and video source patches turned on if you want both to be included. People who hunt and peck will not care about track targeting at all; if all you do is drag and drop, without copying or pasting, they might not be there at all. We think you should take some time to understand how both of these tools work. It will help your job and your mental health in the long run.

How to Use Source Patching in Premiere Pro

It's possible that you already do source patching. If both your Source Monitor and your schedule show Ins and Outs, source patching will connect them. The Source Monitor has an In and an Out, and the schedule has an In point. Based on our source editing, we want our video to end up in tracks V1 and A1. But V3 is the only track that is being used. Press the button on the screen or the comma (,) key to add your option from the Source Monitor.

As you can see, the fact that we only chose V3 hasn't changed our final score in any way. When source patching; only the toggles in the first column are important. You don't need to target any tracks at all when you're only source patching.

But if we did the same thing but left V1 off in our source patching, only the part of the audio that was chosen in the Source Monitor would be added to the timeline. The video part was going to be left out.

The other way around is the same. This is a quick and easy way to get just the parts you need when you're changing speech or putting together a visual montage.

How to Target Tracks in Premiere Pro

In this case, there are already three clips in the frame, stacked on top of each other. There is an in and an out, and V1, V2, and V3 are being tracked. To go on, press the Lift button or the semicolon key (;), which is the usual option.

That part and both of our In and Out points will disappear without a trace.

Put down a new In or Out somewhere else. We're going to do something that's kind of like a standard three-point edit by sending this wedge of media to tracks V3, V4, and V5 instead of the three tracks it was in before. Turn off tracks V1 and V2 and turn on V4 and V5. Pressing Ctrl + V will put exactly what we lifted in front of or behind our new In or Out points on the tracks we chose. We can go back a few steps and only target V3. Premiere will then use this one targeted track as the base-level track that the whole stack will be added to again. First, let's try focusing on just the top and bottom tracks in the stack we chose.

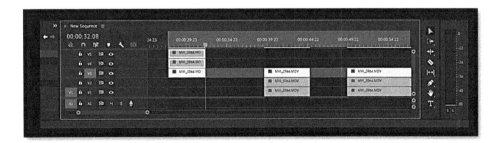

Even though the track in the middle hasn't been turned on, the whole block has been copied over anyway. This shows an important thing to keep in mind about track targeting: the pieces of content you Lift, Extract, or copy really can't be changed. Track aiming lets you move things around without changing what was picked up in the first place.

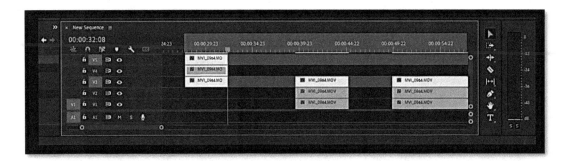

To Lift only the clips on tracks V1 and V3, for example, you must first turn off track V2 before you can Lift anything else. This way, only what you need has been Lifted, no matter what you had set as your goal. Because of this, only what you need will happen.

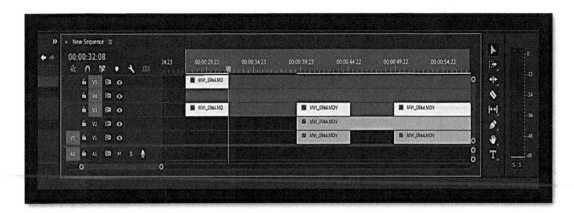

Again, Premiere doesn't make you choose just the two tracks that these two clips are on together, which includes the track in the middle. You only need to choose the track at the very bottom. The Lifted or Extracted part will be moved over exactly as it was, as long as there are enough tracks above the one you chose to fit them all.

CHAPTER 13
COLLABORATIVE EDITING AND MEDIA MANAGEMENT

Collaborative Workflows

A "*shared user workflow*" in post-production entailed working with either Media Composer or Resolve for a considerable amount of time. For many post-production processes, it is quite beneficial to have more than one person working on a shared set of materials or timelines. For example, an editor and assistant editor, a narrative producer and director, or any number of different combinations, are all examples of situations in which this is especially advantageous. On the other hand, Adobe Premiere and Final Cut Pro primarily concentrated on simplifying the lives of filmmakers who worked as part of a "one mule team." They built an increasing amount of capability for individuals who could work off of a single machine while neglecting features that enable many users to work together. Premiere took off after the collapse of Final Cut 7, with a rising user base in the social video and marketing area, but it was unable to fully penetrate into television and feature film usage without improved multi-user toolsets.

In circumstances in which it was necessary to have numerous users working on a project, some solutions were quite irritating. One of the older methods was straightforward but rather inconvenient: users would exchange .prproj files with one another while simultaneously maintaining identical media on some different workstations. Because of this, a significant amount of labor was needed as the complexity of the projects increased. This was because whenever new media was received, It was necessary to ensure that the editor, assistant, director, and other individuals received copies of the assets. If two persons worked on the same timelines at the same time, there was no way to reconcile their work together. Keeping track of the "current" version of the project was a major bother for the assistant or post-supervisor, and there was no means to reconcile their work together. On a shared network, multiple users can open a Premiere Pro project file at the same time. However, whoever clicks "save" last will overwrite all of the work that another editor has done while they are working. This is not an ideal solution, and it requires a lot of communication from room to room in the facility to ensure that nobody accidentally clicks save and destroys another editor's hours of hard work.

The past few years have seen Adobe take multi-user workflows more seriously as a method of moving in on Hollywood feature and television work. This has enabled workflows that will also appeal to those working in smaller facilities, where it is still sometimes a real timesaver to have even two users working on the same project at the same time at the same time. This needs all of the users to be pointing to the same pool of media to achieve the highest possible level of ease of use. Working on a shared network is currently the solution that offers the greatest functionality for circumstances involving several users. However, other options will be available shortly for cloud sharing, which we will cover below.

Shared Network

Premiere gives customers the ability to save their media in whatever location they want, in contrast to other platforms like Media Composer, which continue to function most effectively when all material is absorbed into a specific media folder. If the user so desired, they might conceivably edit straight from the camera capture card; however, this may not always be the most efficient approach, particularly if the card is going to be formatted shortly. In practice, this indicates that users will regularly store their material on a variety of external devices and infrequently on their desktops, which leads to a situation that is not conducive to scaling to accommodate additional users. Media Composer will actively migrate all of your content to a media file on a server if you specify it as your media drive. Premiere can do the same thing if you are savvy with your ingest settings. Both programs can successfully migrate your media. You will want to store all of your media in a central server of some kind, which is commonly referred to as a SAN, which stands for "storage area network." There are many options available to choose from, including hardware solutions from LumaForge, EditShare, Drobo, and even Avid, whose Nexis servers are compatible with Premiere. However, the most important thing is to have a server that is specifically designed for multiple users to pull from the same set of files at the same time so that they can work together.

Creating a separate folder on your server for each project that you are working on and including a "**media**" folder inside that folder is something that we suggest doing. Rather than going into the master media folder and attempting to figure out what belongs with what project, you can transfer the whole master folder, which contains all of the media, to your archiving solution all at once, and it will take all of the media with it. This will make it much simpler to archive a project once it has been delivered. You can set up Premiere to automatically ingest media, which means that it will move it to a new place. Premiere typically connects to media, which means that it does not move it from its current position. When setting up several editors on shared storage, it is generally worthwhile to do so to ensure that all of the media is transferred to the shared storage and that nothing is stored on the internal drive of a local editor. This is because file path routing can result in the loss of media. Having one of the editors save hundreds of assets to their desktop or an external drive, only to have those assets become inaccessible on a day when the editor is not there, is the single most annoying thing that can happen. To prevent such a problem, setting up for ingest rather than connecting is recommended. You can configure this intake route on the start window for new projects. If you are going to be using a significant number of processes that involve several users, you can wish to alter the default settings on all of the computers that are part of your system.

Multiple Projects at Once

One of the most important aspects of knowing how Premiere works for collaborative editing is the concept that it enables you to have many projects open at the same time. Premiere is a program that allows you to keep multiple projects open at the same time, in contrast to the majority of editing applications, which only allow you to open one project at a time (although **Resolve now** allows you to keep more projects "**active**" with fast project switching, it is memory intensive, and you are only keeping one project actively open at the same time). You can close each of the projects that you have opened at the same time by using the tabs that appear at the bottom of the project window. This occurs when you have more than one project open at the same time.

The significance of this cannot be overstated. On the other hand, in the past, if a user was working on a series consisting of six episodes, they would have been tempted to combine all six episodes into a single project. When all of the episodes are contained inside a single project, it is much simpler to flip back and forth between episodes, which helps to prevent duplication and ensures that transitions are seamless. It is now feasible to divide episodes into projects because numerous projects are now available. This allows users to quickly shift sequences and content across projects without having to wait for a lengthy process of closing one project and starting another. Additionally, this saves system memory since you may only need to access one to two episodes at a time rather than all six. Simply remove the text from one project, go to the other project, and then paste it into the other project.

Project Locking

You can activate **"project locking"** in Premiere by navigating to your settings panel for collaborative workflow. When you enable "project locking," only one person can make changes in a project at a time. This is only possible when there are no projects open in

Premiere. When other editors open the project, they will only have "locked" access, which means that they can see all of the project's components but will not be able to make any modifications to them. When they are working with a project that is locked, the little "lock" symbol that is located in the bottom left corner of the project panel will be locked and have a red color. This indicator will indicate that they are limited from working on the project. This is of significant assistance in situations in which a large number of individuals are collaborating to bring a project to a successful conclusion. Let's imagine you are working on episode 5 and you want to view the finish of the current edit of episode 4, even though an editor farther down the hall is working on it at the moment. You can quickly browse the project file (assuming that it is stored on shared storage and not on a local hard drive, of course) and open it in locked mode to evaluate what it looks like at the moment. This allows you to do so without disturbing the work of the other users or having to ask them to dismiss the project.

Not only can you lock projects, but you can also leave them locked even if you are the only person editing that project at that particular period in time. Take, for example, the situation in which you are aware that you will not be making any modifications to the project and you want to make it accessible to other people. Alternatively, if you are certain that you do not want to make any modifications and wish to prevent accidentally causing damage to an edit in a manner that you cannot be aware of. Simply click the clock symbol to lock it, and the next person who opens it will have it accessible and unlocked by default. There is no need to do anything more. The only time projects are updated is when they are opened; if a user is working at another workstation, the changes will not dynamically ripple to your workstation during that time. To see the modifications that they have saved, you will need to close and then reopen the application. It is important to ensure that you dismiss any more open projects by using the file menu or the hamburger menu that is located next to the tab at the bottom of the projects panel. This is because having many open projects will use more of your system's resources, particularly memory.

Project Sharing and Versioning

Keeping track of the many iterations or modifications that have been made to a project is made possible via the use of project sharing and versioning, which are essential components of collaborative work in video editing. These features enable numerous members of a team to work together efficiently. To further understand these ideas, here is an explanation:

Project Sharing

The concept of project sharing refers to the capacity to collaborate on the same video project with numerous members of the team at the same time or in separate periods from one another. When working with software like Premiere Pro, it is common practice to save project files, media assets, and editing choices in a centralized place or in a shared storage area that is available to all of the contributors. Because of this, members of the team can access, alter, and contribute to the project whenever it is required, which allows for increased cooperation and teamwork.

The following are some important characteristics of project sharing:

- **Centralized Storage**: All of the contents associated with the project, including video clips, audio files, graphics, and project files, are kept in a central place or on a shared server, where they are available to all of the individuals who are participating in the project activities.
- **Collaborative Editing:** This is the process by which members of a team can work on different sections of the project at the same time. This allows for concurrent editing, evaluating, and contributing to different areas of the video.
- **Real-time Updates**: Changes made by one member of the team are often reflected in real-time or upon synchronization. This enables other members of the team to see the most recent alterations, reduces the likelihood of encountering disputes, and guarantees that everyone is working with the most recent version of the project.
- **Version Control:** Mechanisms for version control are often included in project-sharing systems. These mechanisms make it possible to monitor the modifications that have been made to the project over time. This aids in retaining a history of revisions, which simplifies the process of reverting to earlier versions if it is required.

Versioning

The administration and organization of various iterations or versions of a video project is what is meant by the term "*versioning*." Maintaining a record of the modifications made at various stages of the editing process or by various contributors is a necessary step. Each iteration or version reflects a particular moment in the chronology of the project, exhibiting a variety of changes, adjustments, or variants that have been made.

Particularly important components of versioning in video editing projects are as follows:

- **Labeling or Numbering**: To differentiate between the many iterations of the project, it is common practice to label or number the various versions of the project in a sequential manner or with particular IDs, such as v1.0, v1.1, v2.0, and so on.
- **Documentation and Notes**: Editors may keep documentation or notes alongside versions, which record the changes that were done in each iteration. These notes and documentation provide context and insights into what was updated or added.
- **Retrieval and Archiving**: Older versions of the project can be preserved for reference or safekeeping. This provides editors with the ability to revert to an earlier version of the project if it is necessary. This is particularly useful in situations when the changes made in the current version do not meet expectations or need reviewing.

By enabling multiple members of a team to work on a project at the same time, project sharing makes it easier for them to collaborate on the project. Versioning, on the other hand, ensures the efficient management and organization of various iterations or versions of the project, which enables better tracking, collaboration, and revision control in video editing workflows.

Media Management Best Practices

To have a video editing process that is both efficient and well-organized, it is essential to have excellent media management in Adobe Premiere Pro.

Premiere Pro offers some best practices for managing media, including the following:

- **Folder Structure**: Before importing media into Premiere Pro, you should first create a folder structure on your computer or storage device that is well-organized. Files should be organized according to the project name, and then they should be subdivided into categories such as "Footage," "Audio," "Graphics," and so on. Using this structure, you will have an easier time locating and managing your files.
- **Media Browser**: Instead of importing your media files straight into your project, you can use the Media Browser in Premiere Pro to go to your media files. Since this tool enables you to preview and pick clips before importing, you can ensure that you only import the clips that you want.
- **Consistent File Naming:** Maintain a consistent naming convention for your files. It is helpful to include pertinent information such as scene numbers, takes, or

timestamps to distinguish clips more quickly. Maintaining this consistency is beneficial when looking for and locating assets inside Premiere Pro.

- **Metadata and Labels**: Make use of metadata and labels to include descriptive information in your clips. It is possible to improve the efficiency of finding and organizing inside Premiere Pro by tagging clips with keywords, descriptions, and other information.
- **The Proxy Workflow**: If you have huge or high-quality files that might potentially slow down your editing process, you might want to consider using proxies, which are duplicates of your media files that have a reduced resolution and are simpler to work with. Using the proxy processes that are available in Premiere Pro, users may edit using proxies and then relink to the high-resolution files for the final output.
- **Trimming Unused Footage:** This involves removing or trimming unnecessary sections of clips when editing to eliminate clutter and maintain a neat project. In addition, this activity contributes to the enhancement of performance.
- **Backup and Archive:** The files and media assets associated with your project should be backed up regularly to avoid any loss of data. In addition, archive finished projects and the media assets linked with them to free up space and maintain the organization of your storage resources.
- **Project Management:** Premiere Pro's sequences, bins, and markers can be used to arrange the various aspects of your project, which is an important aspect of project management. Bins can be used to organize clips or assets that are related to one another, sequences can be used to organize various edits or versions, and markers can be used to annotate your timeline or to indicate certain places.
- **Offline/Online Editing**: When working on complicated projects, you should think about using an offline/online editing approach. During the editing phase, you should work with files of lesser resolution or proxy files. After that, you should reconnect to files of higher resolution when you are working on the final output or completing stage.
- **Collaboration Tools**: If you are working in a group, you should take advantage of the collaboration tools that are available inside Premiere Pro. These tools include Shared Projects and Team Projects, which allow several editors to work on the same project at the same time while managing versions and modifications.

Your editing process can be streamlined, your productivity can be improved, and you can keep your library of media assets for your projects organized and easily available if you adopt these best practices for media management in Adobe Premiere Pro.

Replacing Clips and Media

Adobe Premiere Pro comes with a variety of tools that allow you to replace shots inside your project, as well as move keyframes and clip characteristics from one shot to the next across the project. Applying these tips can help you complete the process of video editing more quickly. At some point throughout the editing process, you will be required to modify a clip that is included in your project. It may be a total replacement, such as taking an earlier version of an animated logo and replacing it with a more recent one. It's also possible that you could want to alter a clip in your Timeline by replacing it with one from a bin. Depending on the mission at hand, there are some different methods in which you can switch pictures or media.

Techniques of Replacement

You can change clips in a Timeline in a few different ways. How careful you need to be when moving a clip will decide which method you use. No matter which method you use, any Timeline effects that were added to the original clip will stay on the new clip.

The following ways can be used:

- If you hold down the option key and drag (Alt-drag), you can change any file on the Timeline. Hold down the shift key and drag the new clip in its place. When the Option (Alt) key is pressed, the In point of the new clip will be used to find the start of the change.
- Hold down Shift+Option (Shift+Alt) while moving to use the original clip-in point instead of the new one. This method works best when video is recorded by multiple cameras at the same time and the timecodes match.
- The easiest and most exact way to do this is to use the Replace Clip command. You can change a clip in your bin or Program Monitor with this command. The playhead can be used to exactly sync the change, which makes this very useful.

Replacing a Clip in a Premiere Pro Sequence

Say you need to change a clip in a sequence but keep the filters, motion effects, and keyframes the same. Follow these steps to switch out one cutaway shot for another. It's an easy way to change shots while keeping the quality of the movie. Style and "***push-in motion***" (animated scale) that I've worked hard to create are things I want to keep in my example.

Set an "In" point for the clip in the Project window. If you don't, Premiere Pro will use the first frame of the clip. Hold down the Alt (for Windows) or Option (for Mac) key and drag the clip from the Source or Project panel onto the clip in the Sequence. After the clip has been selected, let go of the mouse. When the clip is changed, its features stay the same. Instead of moving the clip, you can choose the new clip in the Project box. If you choose the clip in Icon view, you can use hover scrub to find the best In point and hit I to set an In. To change the clip in the sequence, right-click on it and select Replace with Clip > From Bin. When you use Premiere Pro, the color grading settings from the clip above are moved to the clip below. What a great way to save time!

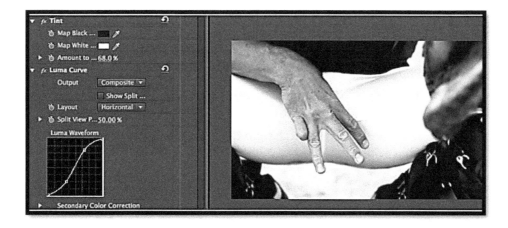

Using Replace Edit to Match Source Frame

You might find this method useful if you need to change a shot in Premiere Pro to a similar one. Replace Edit looks at where the playhead is in the Source Monitor and the sequence, but not at the In and Out places. If it were me, I'd want to switch out one dancer for another who is doing the same move. If the sync point was the same word in both takes, this would also work for a chat. Move the playhead to a word or action in the sequence, and then find the same spot in a different take. Right-click on the clip in the Sequence and choose **Replace With Clip > From Source Monitor, Match Frame.** When the clip is changed, its features stay the same.

Replacing a Clip in the Project

Let's say you want to use a clip in multiple sequences. This often happens when a user gives you a new file or when you need to change a brief fake clip. Press and hold on to the clip in the Premiere Pro project, then click and choose Replace Footage. The new clip takes the place of the old one in all sequences. When the clip is changed, its features stay the same.

Changing the Playback Speed of a Clip

When you compare how fast a clip plays back to how fast it was recorded, you get its speed. The length of time it takes for a clip to play from "In" to "Out" is known as its runtime. You can tell audio or video clips how long they need to be and have them speed up or slow down to fit. **Pick one of these options to change the speed or length of a clip:**

- Speed/Duration command
- Rate Stretch tool
- Time Remapping feature

Use the Speed/Duration command.

In the Timeline or Project boxes, choose one or more clips. In the Project box, press Ctrl (Windows) or Command (Mac OS) to select a group of clips that don't go together. To change the speed or duration of a clip, use the menu bar to select it and then right-click on it to bring up the context menu.

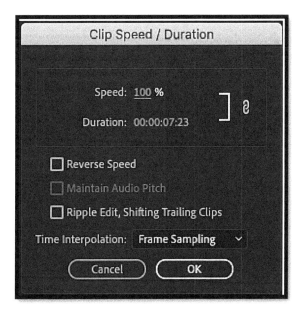

Do at least one of these things:

- If you want to change the length of the clips you've picked without changing their speed, press the "gang" button until it shows a broken link. By engaging, you can also change the speed without changing the time.
- To play the clips backward, choose "Reverse Speed."
- To maintain the audio pitch regardless of the speed or length, choose Maintain Audio Pitch.
- Choose Shifting Trailing Clips from the Ripple Edit menu to keep the clips moving when the clips next to them change.
- If you want to change the speed, pick one of the Time Interpolation options: Frame Blending, Optical Flow, or Frame Sampling.

Press the OK button. A fraction of the original speed is shown for clips whose speed has been changed.

Use the Rate Stretch tool

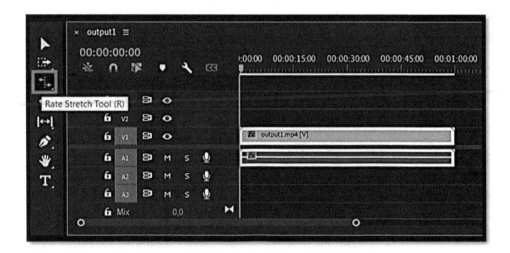

With the Rate Stretch tool, you can quickly change a clip's length in the Timeline while also changing its speed to fit the new length. Let's say you want to fill a certain length gap in your sequence with media that has been sped up. There is no need to worry about the speed of the video as long as it fills the gap. By using rate stretch, you can change the speed to any amount you want. You can change a clip's speed to fit a certain length with Premiere Pro's Rate Stretch tool. With the Rate Stretch tool, you can drag either side of a clip in the Timeline panel.

Make use of Time Remapping

You can change how fast the video part of a clip plays. Time Remapping lets you add effects of slow motion and fast motion to the same clip. When you right-click on the clip, the Context menu will appear. Select **Show Clip Keyframes > Time Remapping > Speed.** The clip has a blue tint to it. In the middle of the clip is a horizontal rubber band that lets you change how fast it moves. In the upper part of the clip, just below the title bar, there is a white speed-control track. If it's hard to see the clip, zoom in to make more room. You can change the speed of the clip by dragging the rubber band up or down. A tooltip shows the speed change as a fraction of the speed that it was at first. The video part of the clip plays at different speeds, and as the speed changes, the length of the video part grows or shrinks. The audio part of the clip stays the same during time remapping, but it is still connected to the video part.

Vary changes to speed or direction with Time Remapping

You can speed up, slow down, play backward, or stop parts of a video clip with the time-remapping effect. Let's look at a video of someone walking. You can show the person moving quickly forward, then suddenly slowing down, stopping in the middle of a step, or even walking backward before moving forward again. You can only change the time of cases of clips in a Timeline panel. You can't change the time of master clips. If you change the speed of a clip that has audio and video that are linked, the audio stays related to the video but plays at full speed. The audio doesn't match up with the video.

Vary change to clip speed

When you right-click on the clip, the Context menu will appear. Select Show Clip Keyframes > Time Remapping > Speed. The clip has a blue tint to it. In the middle of the clip is a horizontal rubber band that lets you change how fast it moves. In the upper part of the clip, below the title bar, there is a white speed-control track. Press and hold Ctrl (Windows) or Command (Mac OS) in at least one place on the rubber band to make a keyframe. At the top of the clip, speed keyframes appear above the rubber band in the white speed-control track. When you cut speed keyframes in half, you get two keyframes that can be used to mark the beginning and end of a speed-change transition. In the middle of the speed change, the rubber band's adjustment handles show up. **Choose one of the following options:**

- To change how fast that section plays, move the rubber bands on either side of the speed keyframe up or down. If you want to limit the speed changes to 5% steps, hold down Shift while moving.
- If you want to change the speed of the part to the left of the speed keyframe, hold down and drag it to the left or right.

Both the speed and length of the section change. Some parts of a clip get shorter when you speed them up and longer when you slow them down.

- To make a speed change, drag the speed keyframe's right half to the right or its left half to the left.
- If you drag either of the curve control's handles, you can change how fast the speed change speeds up or slows down.
- With the speed ramp's curve, the change in speed is slowed down or sped up.
- (Optional) To undo a change to the speed of a transition, pick the half of the speed keyframe that you don't want and delete it.

CHAPTER 14
MANAGING PROJECTS

It's possible that keeping organization won't seem like an urgent priority while you're just getting started using Premiere Pro. It is not too difficult to locate your original project on your storage disk, particularly if this is your first time working with video editing software. On the other hand, as you go farther into many projects, maintaining your organization becomes a more difficult task. Managing a wide variety of media assets from a variety of storage places is a need for working on many projects simultaneously. Some sequences are included in each project, each of which has its structure. Additionally, the production of various graphics and the possible use of some different effects presets and Motion Graphics templates are also included. To effectively handle this increasing complexity, a strong organizational framework is necessary. Establishing an organized way to manage your projects and having a clear plan for preserving projects that may need future revisiting are the two most important things you can do to ensure success. The difficulty, on the other hand, often occurs when these organizational mechanisms are more successful if they are established before they are required in an emergency. Imagine the following scenario: you are deeply involved in the creative process and all of a sudden you need to add a new video clip.

However, you can discover that you are too immersed in the creative process to pay attention to the titles of the files or the positions of the clips. Therefore, projects wind up having names that are similar to one another, being kept in places that are similar to one another, and containing a variety of data that does not logically belong together. Preparing and establishing your organizational structure in advance is the straightforward answer to this problem. The workflow route should be mapped out, beginning with the collection of source media files and continuing through the editing process until the final output, archiving, and future processes are reached respectively. Putting this strategy down on paper can be of great assistance in times like this. In this section, we will provide you with information on the capabilities of Premiere Pro that will enable you to preserve control over your creative pursuits while preserving the organizational parts of your work. Additionally, it will address collaborative methods that promote effective cooperation and seamless project management. These practices will be covered. Because you have a solid understanding of these components, you will be able to maintain control of your creative work without losing sight of what is important.

Asset management in Premiere Pro

When you are working on a project, you may want to change the way you look at your bins. Your whole project's structure can be seen in the standard layout, which is a useful feature to have. Nevertheless, there are circumstances in which you may want to open a bin in a new tab or a new panel from the beginning. To do this, you can focus on clips that are contained inside a certain bin, organize clips in the sequence of a storyboard while using icon mode, or use the search box to hunt for clips that are included within a bin. While some editors choose bin windows that are superimposed over the interface, others favor bins that open in new tabs.

If you want to open a bin in its floating panel, in situ, or a new tab, complete the following steps:

- To open a bin in a new tab, double-click on it. This panel, like any other panel, can be docked or grouped in the same way.
- Open a bin in situ by using the Ctrl-double-click (Windows) or Command-double-click (Mac OS) shortcut.
- You can open a bin in its floating panel by using the Alt-double-click option on Windows or the Option-double-click option on Mac OS.

Changing the default behavior of the bins in the Project panel can be accomplished by altering the Bins options.

- When using Windows, go to Edit > Preferences > General. Alternatively, in Premiere Pro (Mac OS), navigate to Premiere Pro > Preferences > General.
- To choose the options for double-clicking, you can use the menus in the Bins area of the Mac OS. Additionally, you can use the shortcuts + Ctrl (Windows) or + Command (Mac OS) and + Alt (Windows) or + Opt (Mac OS).
- Choose the OK option.

Using the Project Manager

Examine the Project Manager by going to the File menu and selecting Project Manager from the list of available options. There are some options available inside the Project Manager that makes the process of combining your project easier. The process of gathering (collecting) all of the media files that you have employed in one or more sequences is going to be included here. The use of this method of project management is advantageous if you want to archive your project or distribute it to other people. When you hand over the project to your coworkers or move it into storage for archiving, you can be guaranteed that nothing will be missing or offline if you use the Project Manager to gather all of your media assets. This brings you peace of mind. When you utilize the Project Manager, you will be provided with a new file that is unique to the project. Because the new project file is not connected to the project you are currently working on, you should do a thorough examination of the new project file before deleting the old media or project file. To ensure that you have all of the required files, it is a good idea to do a second check on the new project using a different editing system altogether. Check that the Project panel has all of the clips that are anticipated, and ensure that all of the information can be accessed online. First, go to the Sequence section of the new project and choose the sequences that you want to include in the new project.

Following that, choose one of the following options that are included in the section titled "*Resulting Project*":

❖ **Collect Files And Copy To New Location:** This option facilitates the creation of a duplicate set of media files used in your selected sequences, relocating them to a designated new location. This is particularly useful for archiving, sharing projects, or creating backups without affecting the original media files.

❖ **Consolidate and Transcode:** Generate new versions of media files based solely on the clips within the chosen sequences (trimmed clips). Various options become available with this selection.

Additional Options:

- **Exclude Unused Clips:**
  - Restricts the new project to only contain clips utilized in the chosen sequences, eliminating unused content.
- **Include Handles:**
  - Useful when creating a condensed project. This option includes additional frames, allowing flexibility in adjusting timing and trimming later on, at the expense of increased storage space.
- **Include Audio Conform Files:**
  - Incorporates existing audio conform files, saving time by eliminating the need for Premiere Pro to re-analyze audio. Particularly advantageous for lengthy projects.
- **Convert Image Sequences To Clips:**

- Transforms image sequences imported as clips into standard video files for streamlined file management and improved playback quality.
- **Include Preview Files:**
  - If effects have been previously rendered, this option includes them in the new project, saving time on subsequent renderings.
- **Rename Media Files To Match Clip Names:**
  - Renames duplicated media files to match clip names in the project. Useful for identification but be cautious about potential difficulty in identifying the original source content.
- **Convert After Effects Compositions To Clips:**
  - Replaces dynamically linked After Effects compositions with generated video files. Essential when the Project Manager cannot gather dynamically linked compositions or associated media assets.
- **Preserve Alpha:**
  - When transcoding, it preserves alpha channel information, ensuring transparency in sequences. Vital for sequences containing dynamically linked After Effects compositions with transparency.

Edit Videos to the Beat of the Music

An understanding of a few things is required before you can begin the process of synchronizing videos to the rhythm of the music. This is something that can be accomplished in two different ways: manually and automatically. It should be noted that the automatic method of doing this task is only applicable to Premiere Pro and does not function with other video editing tools such as Final Cut Pro, DaVinci Resolve, or more. To begin, let's begin with the automated way that Premiere Pro offers for synchronizing video to rhythms.

On the other hand, if you are working with a different video editing program or even Premiere Pro, you can scroll down and look at the manual technique to do the same thing. There is a possibility that it would be beneficial to examine your music track and play it a few times to determine the locations of the beats. As a result, you can alter the scene of the video in accordance with the sound that occurs whenever a string is struck to the beat. On account of this, you will be required to investigate the waveform of your music file and make use of the arrow keys to pinpoint the precise instant at which the rhythm shifts.

Automatically Sync Videos to the Beat of the Music in Premiere Pro

It is possible to synchronize your video to the rhythm of the music by using the Automate to Sequence option that is available in Premiere Pro. To synchronize the video recording with the rhythm, all you need are a few markers.

1. Import and Organize Your Media

At the beginning of every project including video editing, you should begin by organizing your media. Building a media library and organizing everything methodically will make it much simpler to maintain that collection. After the audio has been added to the media library, you can then drag it to the timeline. It can be positioned in the video in the manner that you like it to appear in. You can even adjust the In/Out range of the audio clip that you have picked, in addition to that if you want to. In this manner, you will not be required to cut away the unnecessary text.

2. Add Markers.

After you have finished adding media to your timeline, you can begin listening to the audio track to begin the process. During the time that you are listening to the music, you can begin adding Markers to your video to indicate the locations of the beats.

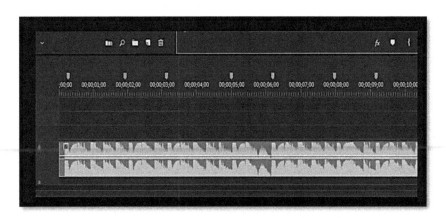

If you want to add markers to Premiere Pro as quickly as possible, you should utilize the shortcut key "M" on your keyboard. As soon as you recognize a beat, hit the M key on your keyboard to add a marker to your timeline. This will allow you to keep track of the beats while you listen to the audio. For the same reason, you should listen to the full track and continue to add beats to your timeline. At first, when you listen to the soundtrack for the first time, you could believe that adding markers would take a significant amount of time, but in reality, it is really simple. Nevertheless, it is essential to keep in mind that when you are adding markers, you are required to choose the full section of the audio clip, and not just the particular clip inside it.

3. Add Video to the Timeline

When you have finished adding markers to the audio, you can now drag the film into the timeline.

Click on the Clip tab in the top menu bar once you have selected all of the clips that are currently in your bin. From that point on, use the option that says "**Automate to Sequence**." When you are requested to specify settings, choose the options that are available to you, which are **Placement at Unnumbered Markers and Selection Order**.

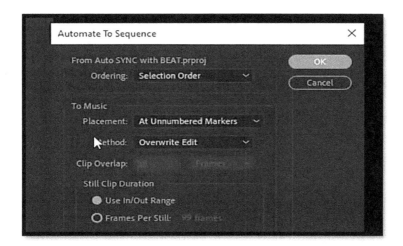

The footage will be automatically added to the timeline by Premier Pro, and the videos will be edited according to the markers that you put in the step before this one. When everything is finished, you can go back and look over the project to make sure that everything is in the correct place. On the other hand, it is essential to keep in mind that Premiere Pro does all of this via the use of algorithms; thus, it may not add the precise video points that you want to the timeline. There is also the option of using the manual technique, which can provide you with a more accurate outcome.

Manually Sync Videos to the Beat of the Music in Premiere Pro

Although Premiere Pro gives you the ability to automatically sync rhythms, the process can be difficult to understand, and the results are not always precise. Therefore, using the manual approach can present itself as a superior choice on its own. Additionally, it is not restricted to the usage of Premiere Pro alone; it can be used in any other video editing program.

1. Add Music to the Timeline and Analyze It

Your preferred video editor should be opened, and the audio clip should be imported into it. When you have finished doing that, you can drag the soundtrack into your timeline and make the waves more noticeable. You cannot be able to see the waveforms since their visibility changes depending on the music. When you have the waveforms in a prominent position and can readily see the peaks, you are ready to go further. You can tell where the music peaks and whether or not it is a beat by looking at those waveforms and analyzing them.

2. Add the Video to Timeline and Make Cuts

The video should be dragged to the timeline after you have determined the beats that are present in the audio. After that, make the edits in the video clips so that they are in sync with the rhythm. It is important to pay attention to the transients in waveforms, which describe the moment in the soundtrack when the beat begins to slow down. Cutting can now be done in accordance with the beat, and clips can be added if they are required.

Eliminating Mistakes

A dreadful sensation is experienced whenever a consumer or, even worse, a broadcaster contacts you to inform you that one of your projects is experiencing difficulty. However, certain flaws are quite embarrassing, such as black holes and flash frames. There are indeed times when there are issues with the media, problems with rights clearances, and other challenges.

Examining Flash Frames and Gaps

If you are using Adobe Premiere Pro, it is easy to locate a gap or flash frame by selecting Sequence > Go to Gap in your final sequence. The menu has a total of four different options. It is possible to detect gaps to the right or left of the sequence playhead using the first two, which are referred to as Next in Sequence and Previous in Sequence. This is accomplished while still covering all of the songs.

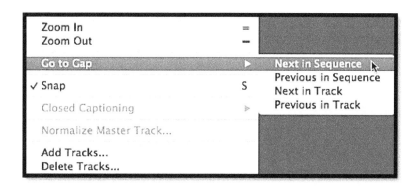

On a single track or a collection of tracks, gaps and flash frames can be located using the following two options: Following in Track and Previous in Track. These options make use of **tracks that are now focused, which can be audio or video. Immediately after recognizing a gap or flash frame, proceed with the following steps:**

❖ Select the gap by clicking the gap in the sequence
❖ To close the gap, conduct a ripple edit by pressing the Delete key on your keyboard. It is important to keep in mind that if you choose a gap in an audio or video track when Sync Lock is active with the related audio or video track, Adobe Premiere Pro will attempt to move the linked segment of the clip as well.
❖ Additionally, if another clip in your audio or video files is in the way, you will not be able to fix the gap. Changing the spacing between clips will result in clips that are not in sync with one another; however, this behavior can be stopped by turning off Sync Lock for those tracks.
❖ Select the gap, and then use the slash (/) key to mark In and Out points around the gap. Alternatively, you can select Markers > Mark Selection to mark In and Out points around the gap.
❖ After you have indicated a gap in the Program Monitor, you can employ the Extract keyboard shortcut by either clicking the Extract button or pressing the apostrophe (')

key using the keyboard shortcut. The removal of the gap and the subsequent sliding of everything from the right to the left will bring the gap to a close.

It is important to keep in mind that every time you designate a gap, it will be recorded for every song that you have selected. You can pick a track (and thus take part in the extraction process) or deselect (and hence not take part in the extraction operation) by clicking on the track header of the track in question. On the other hand, you should be mindful that removing songs from the selection may result in the audio and other tracks being out of sync with one another. Note that closing a gap by removing it may alter the overall duration of your sequence and may result in audio and other tracks, such as graphics, which are not in sync with one another. The clip on one side of the gap may also be clipped, which is another option for closing a gap.

Looking for Repeated Shots

There will be some photographs used during the project. When you begin, you will often begin with a large amount of raw media and then break it up into hundreds of smaller chunks. Some editors and producers are insistent about avoiding repeating the same footage in a sequence, even though this is very usual. For example, with Adobe Premiere Pro, you can easily determine the number of times a certain clip is used in a sequence. Act as displaying the Project panel in icon view inside the Project panel if you are not already doing so. It will display in the bottom-right corner of the screen that one or two orange icons are present if a clip is being used. A symbol that resembles a filmstrip is used to represent video, whereas an icon that resembles an audio waveform is used to represent audio respectively. It is only when a clip has simple video and no related audio that you will see the video sign, or vice versa, that you will appear. Note that if a clip is not currently being used, you will only see white symbols, and if a video clip contains integrated audio, you will only see a white sign for the audio that is linked with the clip.

Video Legalization

Even though the legalization of video may seem to be a challenging effort, it is rather straightforward. When it comes to the process of licensing your video, you will most likely feel at ease because you are an experienced editor. You can easily ensure that your movie is a legal video by using a few tactics and effects in Adobe Premiere Pro. This is true even if you are not aware of the controversy surrounding the topic.

Legalizing manually

To begin the process of legalizing video, the initial stages include color correction and grading. One of the key goals of color correction is to guarantee compliance with the law. As a consequence of this, the process of color correcting and grading film is equivalent to manually legalizing it. We will go over a few Adobe Premiere Pro effects that can assist you in legitimizing film; nevertheless, it is recommended that you do not depend on these effects. The first step is to manually legalize your film, and then you can utilize the legalization effects to repair any incorrect pixels that you may have mistakenly ignored.

Audio Legalization

The legalization of audio is very important, much like the legalization of video. According to an ancient proverb, audio is equivalent to half of the visual. While watching anything, you have most likely experienced frustration due to audio that is either excessively modulated or excessively quiet at some time. The "*laws*" that govern the legalization of audio vary from broadcaster to broadcaster; nonetheless, if you can comprehend a few simple techniques, you will be able to produce legal audio.

Getting to the right levels

When it comes to producing legal audio, getting the levels just right is perhaps the single most crucial piece of advice. Levels are monitored by utilizing the audio meters that are included in the Audio Mixer of Adobe Premiere Pro for each track in a sequence. Additionally, the Master audio track can be seen in the mixer or by choosing Window > Audio Meters at any time. In any particular sequence, how you mix your music is entirely up to you; nonetheless, the overall master (levels) is the most important thing to consider. Depending on the application you submit, different degrees can be considered legal qualifications.

PART IV
SPECIALIZED WORKFLOWS

CHAPTER 15
360-DEGREE VIDEO EDITING

Understanding 360-Degree Video

If you want to see what's going on from every angle, a 360-degree experience video is exactly what it sounds like. For this to work, the cameraman has to be in the middle of the action, which puts the watcher in the right place. Find out more about this new type of video that is getting more and more popular.

Undoubtedly, you've heard surround-sound audio. This time, you can do the same thing with video.

- ❖ *How do I watch a video in 360 degrees*? Most 360-degree videos are made for virtual reality headsets, which put the person wearing the gear in the middle of the video so they can see everything around them. If you're on a phone or a computer browser, you can also pan through a 360-degree video by moving the phone or mouse around the screen.
- ❖ **How do you make a 360-degree video?** A special rig with several cameras or one camera with multiple lenses that record from different angles at the same time is usually used to make this kind of video. When you fix it, it all comes together so well. By "stitching," the videos are put together to make a circular video. The colors, brightness, light, and shadow are adjusted so that the video looks like it's all one long piece.

Introduction to VR Editing

Virtual reality (VR) has changed how we see and interact with digital media in general, and editing videos is no different. Adobe Premiere Pro, a popular video editing program, has recently added powerful tools and features to better meet the needs of making VR content. Because of this merging of technologies, there is now a specialty field called VR editing. In this field, editors use immersive technologies to make virtual experiences that are interesting and appealing.

Understanding Virtual Reality Editing

1. **Immersive Storytelling**: VR editing goes beyond the standard straight story, giving artists a three-dimensional surface to work with. In a 360-degree area, editors can

direct the viewer's attention, making the story more engaging and livelier. This means that traditional editing methods need to be replaced with ones that are more physical and experienced.

2. **Adobe Premiere Pro Integration**: Adobe Premiere Pro has become a leader in VR editing, with tools that make the process easier. The software works with many VR files, so editors can easily bring in, change, and send VR content. Integration with other Adobe Creative Cloud apps makes it easier to work on VR projects as a whole.

Key Features in Adobe Premiere Pro for VR Editing

❖ **VR Preview**: Editors can see previews of VR media right in Adobe Premiere Pro's editing interface. This feature lets you see how the audience will interact with the realistic world in real time, so you can make exact changes to improve the story and visual effect.

❖ **Spatial Markers and information**: Editing in VR means moving around in a 3D space. Adobe Premiere Pro makes this easier by giving you tools for adding spatial markers and information. Editors can carefully put marks in the VR area to direct viewers' attention and improve the flow of the story as a whole.

❖ **VR Effects and Transitions**: Adobe Premiere Pro has built-in effects and transitions that are specifically made for VR video. These tools can help editors make the media more engaging by making sure there are smooth changes between scenes and keeping viewers interested.

❖ **Editing ambisonic audio**: Adobe Premiere Pro lets you edit ambisonic audio, which is an important part of immersive audio experiences in VR. With this feature, editors can make a sound setting that fills the whole room, making VR media feel more real and improving the sense of presence.

Workflow in Adobe Premiere Pro

❖ **Adding VR footage**: Adobe Premiere Pro can handle some VR files, such as binoculars and monoscopic. Editors can easily add VR videos without changing the quality of the experience.

❖ **Editing in 360-Degree Space**: Editors can move around in Adobe Premiere Pro's VR world, changing the layout of elements and changing the way space is used to make the best view for the user. Putting clips in the right order, adding effects, and adding spatial audio features are all part of this.

❖ **Preview and fine-tuning**: Adobe Premiere Pro's VR preview tool lets editors see their work as it's being made in real-time. This iterative process is necessary to fine-tune spatial features and make sure the VR experience flows well and is fun.

❖ **Exporting VR Content**: Adobe Premiere Pro has export options that are designed to work with VR devices. You can easily share your projects in files that keep the realistic qualities of the content, whether you want to use them on VR headsets, online platforms, or other devices.

Editing 360-Degree Footage

Step 1

Enable VR in Sequence Settings

You can bring your 360 videos into Premiere just like any other video. While Premiere automatically finds VR properties when you load media, here are the steps you need to take to directly turn on VR in sequence settings.

1. Select **Sequence > Sequence Settings** from the menu.
2. There will be a VR Properties area at the bottom of the button

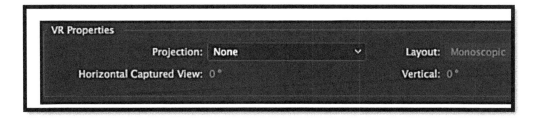

Pick an image to turn on VR for your sequence. Equirectangular is the only projector type that Premiere Pro offers right now.

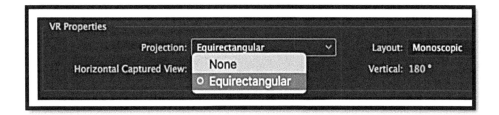

Next, pick the style based on the camera you used and the video you recorded. You can do a monocular view, an over/under view, or a side-by-side view in full stereo. One type of video can only be played at a time in this sequence. Keep reading to learn more about these changes.

3. You can choose how many degrees of view are in a full picture by using the Horizontal and Vertical Captured View fields. All the time, the usual setting of 180 degrees up and 360 degrees down is fine. This makes a full sphere.

4. Your changes should now be saved when you click OK. You can now use the VR Video show with your sequence.

What is an Equirectangular Projection?

Picture a map of the world: It shows a circular globe on a flat surface. With equirectangular projection, the sphere is just unwrapped, and the longitude is mapped to the X coordinate and the latitude to the Y coordinate.

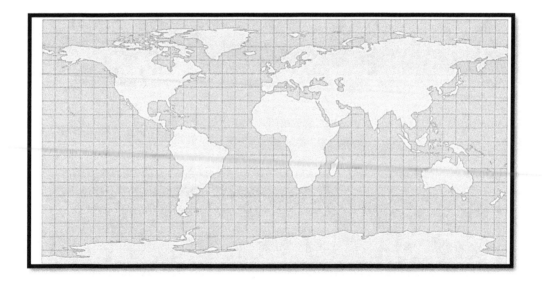

In the same way, equirectangular film is a popular file for 360 video that lets it turn into a sphere for a more realistic experience. It may look flat, but it can also look like a skewed landscape. The raw video that you put together will be in an equirectangular shape, but you can switch between this shape and the VR view while editing in Premiere.

Step 2

Preview the VR Video Display

The next step is to play the clips on the monitor now that VR editing is turned on for your sequence. You can watch your video in 360 degrees in two ways:

1. To turn on VR video, either right-click the monitor or click the gear icon (wrench) on the right side of the screen.

2. Click the button maker (+) and drag the Toggle VR Video Display button to the menu to make it easy to find!

Once the VR Video Display mode is turned on, go to VR Video > Settings. In the VR Video Display mode, the Monitor View areas let you choose what part of the sphere you see and create different watching experiences. For instance, 160 degrees by 90 degrees is like watching YouTube. Keep in mind that these choices affect how the view window is sized. In this case, 160 degrees by 90 degrees shows a 16:9 view window.

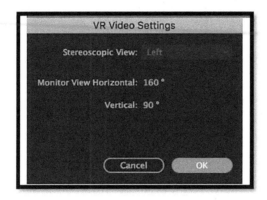

Step 3

Edit Video and Set Center Point

After that, you can edit your 360 video like you would any other video. This includes things like trimming, adding pictures, audio, text, and more, as well as color correcting and adding slices. Just keep in mind that the text will be fixed on a certain spot on the video; it won't move with the viewer's head or eyes. When the text is stretched to a circular view, it will look a little off. Take note that effects that change things, like warp adjuster, will not work for 360 videos.

Example of text distortion in 360 video

The camera's center point is another important thing to think about. You can't change where the viewer is looking like you can with a regular camera. The middle point, or starting point, of the shot, can be set to draw attention to the subject, though. Users shouldn't have to turn their heads to see the subject again when you start cutting together shots.

That being said, the Offset effect is the best way to set the center point in Premiere Pro:

1. Go to **Video Effects > Distort > Offset** in the Effects window.
2. In the timeline, give your clip the Offset effect.
3. Pick out the clip in the timeline and open the dialog box for the effects.

4. In the middle of the shift If you want to pan the clip horizontally, drag the first number left or right. Moving the second number would go against its upright position, so don't do it.

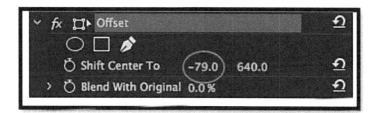

When you switch between shots in Premiere, keep in mind that the viewer's direction does not return to the middle. This means that if the watcher is looking at the back of the scene in the first shot, they will still be looking at the back in the second shot and might miss what you aimed at in the middle.

Step 4: Export

To export your video, pick out the timeline and press Ctrl/Cmd+M, or go to File > Export > Media. This will open the window where you can share. After picking the codec you want, go to the very bottom of the Video tab and make sure the Video Is VR box is checked and the Frame Layout is right.

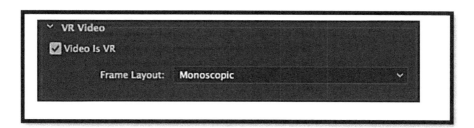

Working with the Bins

Bins work the same way as folders on your hard drive and have the same icon. With them, you can sort your clips into different groups and store them more efficiently. Like on your hard drive, you can put many bins inside of other bins to make a folder system that is as detailed as your project needs. One important difference between bins and groups on your hard drive is that bins only appear in your Adobe Premiere Pro project file. You will not be able to see individual project containers on your hard drive.

Creating bins

Find the "**New Bin**" button at the bottom of the Project panel and click it. When you start Adobe Premiere Pro, it makes a new file and gives it a name that you can change later. For better order, you should quickly change the names of your bins. If you need to manage film clips, give them their bin. The name for it is "Theft Unexpected." You can also use different ways to make bins, like going to the File menu and selecting "New > Bin." Make a new folder called "PSD Files" to store those kinds of files. Premiere Pro gives you a lot of options for making bins. You can right-click in the Project box, choose "**New Bin** ," and give it a name that fits. To try this, make a folder called "Illustrator Files." To quickly make a new bin for clips that are already in your project, drag and drop them onto the "**New Bin** " button at the bottom of the Project panel.

For quick creation of a new file, press the keyboard shortcut Control+/ (Windows) or Command+/ (Mac OS). Use this method to make a bin called "Sequences." If your Project panel is set to List view, the clips will be grouped by the name of the bins. This setting helps you arrange your bins in a way that makes it easier to find things and handle your project files. If there are a lot of clips in your Project panel and it's hard to find a blank spot to click, try clicking just to the left of the icons in the panel to make a bin there.

Opening the bins

1. **Opening a Bin in a New Window:** To open a bin in a new, separate window, simply double-click on the bin. This action launches a stand-alone window that can be independently docked or moved to any desired location on your screen. This method provides a dedicated space for focusing on the contents of that specific bin.

2. **Opening a Bin in a New Tab:** Double-click on it and hold down the Option (Alt) key at the same time. When you click this button, the file will open in a new tab in the Project panel. The bin is shown as a different tab in the Project panel, next to other tabs. This makes it easy to get to its contents without opening a new window.

3. **Opening a Bin In Place**: Hold down the Command (Ctrl) key and double-click on the bin to open it in the same view as before. This method lets you move around in the view inside the bin while hiding the rest of the project's parts. This way, you can only see what's inside the bin. To go back to the main project view from the bin view, just click on the project name or the folder at the top of the window.

Customizing Bin and Clip Views

You'll need to be able to see your media moving once you've put all of your stuff in bins. It's easy and helpful to look at your picture when each shot is indicated by a sign. Sometimes it's helpful to be able to see a photo's information, like when you need to figure out what camera took the picture. You can occasionally add to the information by adding a brief description. To see what you can do, let's start by changing the view you're seeing.

Changing Views

You can see a bin as either a list or an icon. The list view is what most editors like to use because it lets them see more clips at once. If you look at things in the icon view instead, you can see a plan, scrub while hovering, and quickly sort things graphically. Press the buttons in the bottom left area of the Project panel to change between the list view and the icon view. To switch between list and icon views, press Command + Page Up (Ctrl + Page Up) and Command + Page Down (Ctrl + Page Down).

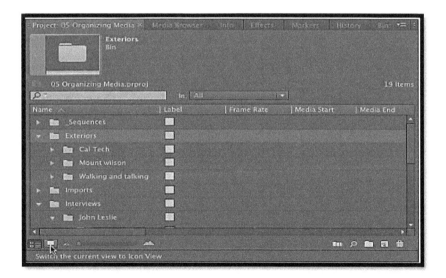

List view

Most writers spend a lot of time in the list view while working on a project. As you can see, it's a simple list, with the name of the movie at the top. These views are the most useful because they let you show a lot of information and let you choose how to arrange it.

When looking at a list, you can look at the images of the photos. Go to the Project panel menu to change the size and color of the icons. In the Project box, go to the menu and choose Thumbnails. The same keys (Shift+ and Shift+) can be used to make the pictures bigger or smaller in icon view.

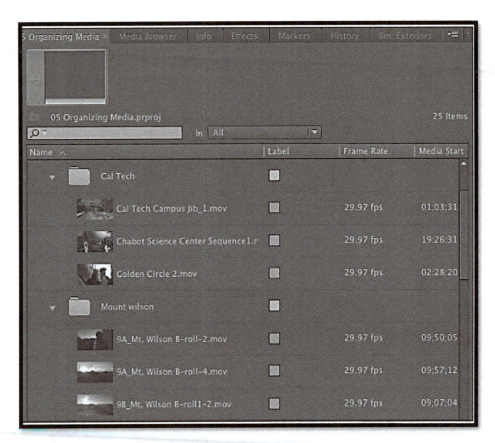

Icon view

"**Hoverscrub**" lets you move your mouse over a clip and "scrub" over it to watch the video more interactively. This quick way to clean up your video has become one of our favorites, especially when the clips are really big. It's not the same as the Source Monitor, but it's a lot faster to get to know the video, especially if you make the bin full-screen.

Here are some of the good things about icon view:

- You can see a clip by its title without having to load it into the Source Monitor.

- Hoverscrub lets you quickly skim through the content of a clip by running the mouse over it.
- It's a fantastic way to get acquainted with the footage you haven't seen before.
- The clip titles on many file-based cameras (still or video) are a sequence of digits. Icon view is a great method to see what the clips are without having to change the labels they were given by the camera.

Reviewing Footage

If your movie is interlaced, Premiere Pro needs to know the frame rate, the pixel aspect ratio (pixel shape), and the sequence in which to show the fields so that it can play the video correctly. Premiere Pro can usually get this information from the file's metadata, but you can change that if you want to.

To begin, do what's written below:

1. **Getting a Video In:**
   - To bring in a video, head to the Media Browser panel. Think of it like opening a drawer where you store your video files.
2. **Checking Out the Clip:**
   - If you want to check out a specific part of the video, just double-click it. You'll notice it's in widescreen format, wider than the usual screen you're used to.
3. **Adjusting the Clip's Properties:**
   - Now, if you want to tweak how the video looks, right-click on the clip in the Project window and choose Modify > Interpret Footage.
4. **Dealing with Audio:**
   - If your video has no sound, you won't be able to mess with the audio settings.
5. **Playing with Pixel Shapes:**
   - The clip is set up to use a particular pixel shape called Anamorphic 2:1. This just means the pixels are twice as long as they are wide.
6. **Changing Pixel Aspect Ratio:**
   - You can play around with the pixel aspect ratio. Go for Conform To, Square Pixels (1.0), and click OK. Your video might start looking more like a square.
7. **Aspect Ratio Experiments:**
   - If you're feeling exploratory, try different aspect ratios. Right-click the clip in the Project window, choose Modify > Interpret Footage, and this time go for

DVCPRO HD (1.5). Click OK, and see how the video looks in the Source Monitor again.

Premiere Pro will now think that the clip's frames are 1.5 times wider than they are tall. This changes the image's size to a standard 16:9 widescreen ratio. Changes to the pixel aspect ratio rarely lead to creative decisions because they make the image's horizontal space bigger or smaller. For example, all circles will turn into ovals when the aspect ratio is changed. There can be a technical reason why the pixel aspect ratio reading needs to be changed if, on the other hand, all circles look like ovals and all squares look like rectangles.

Freeform View

The Freeform View option in Premiere Pro lets you arrange things in creative ways. In Freeform View, you can do the same things you can in Icon View: explore images, set in and out points, and change the order of your clips. You can order clips in Freeform View in any way you like since they don't have to fit into a grid. You can edit individual clips or put clips on top of each other to make any layout you want. Last but not least, this will give you more options in how you think about your project. In the spring of 2019, Premiere Pro version 13.1 added Freeform View. To use this new feature, make sure you always have the most up-to-date version of Adobe Creative Cloud.

How to Use Freeform View in Premiere Pro

Here are the steps you need to take to start using Freeform View. Once you know all the options, you can start making the screen work for you.

Getting Started with Freeform View

To get to the Freeform View button, go to the Assembly workspace in the Project screen. You can use the scale or a mouse to change the zoom level in your workspace. To start putting clips in order, drag and drop them into the box. Nothing stops you; you can even stack clips on top of each other! You can change the size of a single clip or a group of clips by picking them, right-clicking, and choosing Clip Size.

Freeform View Customization

Custom Metadata Display

You can change what information shows under each picture by going to the panel menu and clicking on Freeform View Options. You can show up to two information descriptions for each clip.

Placing Poster Frames

The small picture that shows up next to your clip in the Project panel is a Poster Frame. If you use a Poster Frame that shows the clip correctly, you can tell right away which one is which. Move your mouse over the clip to pick out a frame, and then press Command + P (or Shift + P on a PC) to select it.

Assign Labels

Use the drop-down menu to give clips color names when you right-click on them. These color names will also show up on the calendar.

Save Layouts in Freeform View

If you've already made one layout in Freeform View, trying out different storyboards might help your process.

- Right-click in the Project box and pick "**Save as New Layout**."
- Give the layout a name.
- In the future, try out different flows and combinations.
- When you want to bring back a saved plan, right-click and select "**Restore Layout.**"
- Right-click on the project box and pick "Reset to Grid" to start over with a grid. From here, you can sort by any information.

Freeform View Editing

In Freeform View, you can not only manage video but also start making a rough cut.

- Move your mouse over each clip and drag it across the screen to set it in and out points. Press I to make an in point and o to make an out point.
- To play and pause clips while working in Freeform View, press the spacebar or the J, K, and L keys.
- Put your clips in a sequence in the Project panel to begin.
- To add the changed clips to your Timeline, pick them and drag them there.

Creative Ways to Use the Freeform View

You can be very creative when you use Freeform View, but there are two main ways to think about your footage:

- Sort the items by type
- Arrange in a logical order

1. Sorting Clips in Freeform View by Type

One great way to start editing is to put clips into groups. In List View, you could use Bins to organize things in this way, but in Freeform View, you can see what you're doing much better.

Here are some types of footage that could be put together:

- **Shot**: Does the same shot come in different forms? First, stack them. Then, go back through and pull out the ones you want.
- **Angle**: Don't put close-ups and wide shots in different shots.
- **Character**: When editing a talk, it might be helpful to keep all the shots of the same character together.

- **B-Roll**: Have your cutaway shots ready to add in while the video is being put together.
- **Action-Items**: Are there any clips that need extra work, like color fixing, effects, or titles? Make groups of action items out of them.

There are several ways to arrange clips in Freeform View so that they look good. Your approach will depend on how you work, how much video you have, and what kind of footage you have. It's possible to arrange the clips in a row or put them on top of each other.

2. Storyboarding in Freeform View

Since editing videos is a visual process, it makes sense to plan a sequence visually. When you're storyboarding, think about how stacked or overlapping clips in Freeform View could show cuts in the final edit. You can save plans, which is another great tool for storyboarding. Try out different cuts and save the ones that work as Layouts. When you make different versions of the same movie for different systems, you should also think about the design. You might save one plan for an IGTV video and another for a YouTube video. This is an easy but effective way to review and put your footage in context: organize your clips. Getting ready ahead of time could help you see your project in new ways and save you time while you're editing. The Freeform View in Adobe Premiere Pro lets you see what new footage will look like. Check out the Freeform View and let us know how you've used it in other ways!

CHAPTER 16

ADVANCED EXPORTING AND DELIVERY

Export Settings for Different Platforms

Exporting your videos from Adobe Premiere Pro involves choosing the right export settings, which can vary depending on the platform or destination you intend to use.

Below are guidelines for exporting to different platforms:

1. YouTube:
- Format: H.264
- Preset: YouTube 1080p HD or YouTube 4K, depending on your project resolution.
- Bitrate: Use the target bitrate for the chosen preset, or adjust based on your preferences.
- Frame Rate: Match your project frame rate.
- Audio: AAC, 320 kbps, 48 kHz.

2. Vimeo:
- Format: H.264
- Preset: Vimeo 1080p HD or Vimeo 4K, depending on your project resolution.
- Bitrate: Use the target bitrate for the chosen preset or adjust based on your preferences.
- Frame Rate: Match your project frame rate.
- Audio: AAC, 320 kbps, 48 kHz.

3. Facebook:
- Format: H.264
- Preset: Facebook 1080p HD or Facebook 4K, depending on your project resolution.
- Bitrate: Use the target bitrate for the chosen preset or adjust based on your preferences.
- Frame Rate: Match your project frame rate.
- Audio: AAC, 320 kbps, 48 kHz.

4. Instagram:
- Format: H.264
- Preset: Instagram 1080p HD or Instagram 4K, depending on your project resolution.
- Bitrate: Use the target bitrate for the chosen preset or adjust based on your preferences.
- Frame Rate: Match your project frame rate.

- Audio: AAC, 320 kbps, 48 kHz.

5. Twitter:
- Format: H.264
- Preset: Match Source – High Bitrate.
- Bitrate: Adjust based on your preferences.
- Frame Rate: Match your project frame rate.
- Audio: AAC, 320 kbps, 48 kHz.

6. Adobe Stock or Other Stock Footage Sites:
- Format: H.264
- Preset: Match Source – High Bitrate.
- Bitrate: Adjust based on your preferences but ensure it meets the stock footage site's requirements.
- Frame Rate: Match your project frame rate.
- Audio: AAC, 320 kbps, 48 kHz.

7. Television Broadcast (NTSC):
- Format: H.264 or MPEG-2 (Check with the broadcaster for their preferred format).
- Preset: Choose the broadcast standard and resolution.
- Bitrate: Follow broadcaster specifications.
- Frame Rate: Match the broadcast standard (usually 29.97 fps for NTSC).
- Audio: AC3 or AAC, 48 kHz.

8. Film Festival Submission:
- Format: ProRes or DNxHD/DNxHR (Check the festival's submission requirements).
- Resolution: Follow the festival's guidelines.
- Frame Rate: Match your project frame rate.
- Audio: PCM or AAC, 48 kHz.

9. Archiving/High-Quality Master:
- Format: ProRes (for Mac) or DNxHD/DNxHR (for Windows).
- Resolution: Choose the highest resolution of your project.
- Frame Rate: Match your project frame rate.
- Audio: PCM, 48 kHz.

Remember to always check the specific requirements of the platform or destination you are exporting for, as these guidelines may change based on their preferences and specifications. Additionally, keep in mind the importance of maintaining a balance between file size and video quality based on the intended use.

Presets and Custom Export Configurations

Adobe Premiere Pro provides users with both preset and custom export configurations, offering flexibility and convenience when exporting projects. Presets are predefined export settings tailored for specific platforms or use cases, while custom configurations allow users to fine-tune export settings according to their preferences.

Let's explore both options:

1. Presets:
- **Accessing Presets:**
    1. After completing your project, go to the "File" menu.
    2. Select "Export" > "Media."
- **Choosing Presets:**
    1. In the Export Settings panel, you'll find a variety of presets on the left side.
    2. Presets are categorized by platforms or use cases (e.g., YouTube, Vimeo, H.264 High Quality).
    3. Click on the preset that matches your intended destination.
- **Adjusting Preset Settings:**
    1. Once you've selected a preset, you can further customize the settings within that preset.
    2. Modify parameters such as bitrate, resolution, and codec to meet your specific requirements.
- **Saving Custom Presets:**
    1. After making adjustments, you can save your modified preset for future use.
    2. Click on the floppy disk icon next to the preset list to save your custom settings as a new preset.

2. Custom Export Configurations:
- **Starting with a Preset:**
    1. Begin by selecting a preset that closely matches your requirements.
    2. Make sure you've chosen a preset similar to your desired output format.
- **Fine-Tuning Settings:**
    1. Scroll down to the "Basic Video Settings" and "Audio Settings" sections.
    2. Adjust parameters like resolution, frame rate, bitrate, and audio settings to your liking.
- **Choosing the Format and Codec:**
    1. Navigate to the "Format" dropdown menu to select the desired file format (e.g., H.264, ProRes, MPEG-2).

2. Choose a compatible codec within the selected format.
- **Saving Custom Configurations:**
  1. Once you've fine-tuned your settings, you can save them as a custom export preset.
  2. Click on the "Save Preset" button at the bottom of the Export Settings panel.
  3. Name your preset and choose a location to save it.
- **Accessing Custom Presets:**
  1. In future projects, your custom preset will be available in the "Preset" dropdown menu.

Additional Tips

- **Experimentation:**
  1. It's beneficial to experiment with different presets and custom settings to find the optimal balance between file size and quality for your specific needs.
- **Checking Specifications:**
  1. Always check the specifications and requirements of the platform or destination where you plan to share or distribute your video.

Using Adobe Media Encoder

As a flexible tool for transcoding and compressing, Adobe Media Encoder is an important part of Adobe Premiere Pro that makes the output and release processes possible. Changing files into different editing types can make them work better on the Web, DVDs, Blu-ray Discs, and mobile devices, among other platforms. The program's 64-bit design and ability to use multiple processors and cores make processes quick and efficient.

To use Adobe Media Encoder, you can do one of two things:

1. **Directly from Adobe Premiere Pro:** Users can get to the Export Settings box in Premiere Pro by going to **File > Export > Media**. The user interface here looks a lot like the version of Adobe Media Encoder that you can run on its own. This connection makes it possible to switch between Premiere Pro and Media Encoder without any problems, which makes the process easier.

2. **As a stand-alone application**: Adobe Media Encoder is a separate program that can work without any other programs. You can drop self-contained files, source clips, or project files from Adobe Premiere Pro or Adobe After Effects right into Media Encoder to encode them. The Watch Folder tool also lets you start

encoding automatically when files are put into a certain folder. This feature speeds up the encoding process, making it easier to use and more effective.

Adobe Media Encoder is a powerful tool that can be used directly from Adobe Premiere Pro or as a separate program. It gives users a lot of options for encoding and transcoding, and it works well both ways. It works well with other Adobe programs and can handle many types and output files, which makes it an important part of the video creation process.

Using Adobe Premiere Pro to access Adobe Media Encoder

Adobe has spent a lot of time and money-making processes easier in its Creative Suite. This includes making it easier for Adobe Media Encoder to work with Adobe Premiere Pro.

You can use its power right from within an Adobe Premiere Pro project by following these steps:

1. **Exporting Individual Clips:**
   - Select an individual clip within the Project window.
   - To export that specific clip into your desired format and preset, choose File > Export > Media or use the shortcut Command + M (Ctrl + M) on your keyboard.
   - You have the option to define specific In and Out points to export either the entire clip or a particular range within it.
2. **Exporting Sequences:**
   - During review or delivery phases, there's often a need to export parts or entire sequences.
   - With either the Timeline panel selected or the sequence chosen within the Project panel, go to File > Export > Media.
   - Additionally, you can drag multiple sequences directly from the Adobe Premiere Pro Project panel into the Adobe Media Encoder program window for exporting.

Because Adobe Premiere Pro and Adobe Media Encoder work together so well, it's easy to share both single clips and whole sequences. Whether you're fine-tuning individual clips or getting whole sequences ready for review or delivery, Adobe has made these easy-to-use tools available to ensure a smooth and flexible process. These tools let users share their projects in a variety of forms and settings, depending on their needs.

What Are the Benefits of Using Adobe Media Encoder?

As a key tool, Adobe Media Encoder is mainly made for reducing audio and video data. This feature is very important because the files that are made when finished projects are rendered tend to be very big. Compression is needed so that projects can play easily on a variety of devices that are connected to mobile networks, Wi-Fi, or that don't have a lot of processing power or memory, like devices with slower CPUs or limited RAM.

Compression makes sure that the media can be streamed or played back quickly without losing quality, even on devices that can't do that. To put it simply, almost all audio and video media on all devices is compressed at some point during the production or delivery process. This process reduces the size of files while keeping the quality. This makes the content easier to access and play on a wider range of platforms and network situations.

Download or Update Media Encoder

1. **Open the Creative Cloud Desktop App**: On your computer, open the Creative Cloud app. Take care of your Adobe software changes and payments from this one place.
2. **Look for updates or new installations for the media encoder**: You can find the list of "All Apps" in the Creative Cloud app. In the list, look for Adobe Media Encoder. You'll see an "**Update**" option if it's already there but needs to be updated. An "Install" option will appear if it hasn't been installed.
3. **Add or update Adobe Media Encoder**: From the drop-down menu next to Adobe Media Encoder, choose either "Update" or "Install" based on your needs. The app will begin to install or update itself. How long this process takes may depend on how big the update is or how fast it is installed.
4. **Finishing and Accessing**: After the update or download is done, Adobe Media Encoder will show up in the Creative Cloud app's "All Apps" list. To use the latest or brand-new Media Encoder, all you have to do is click "Open."

Adding Your Source to the Queue

There are different ways to add things to the Adobe Media Encoder list because it works with the whole Adobe Creative Suite. Here are some of the easiest ways to start using Media Encoder.

Adding Files to Media Encoder

The Add Source option lets you quickly add files that are already finished and saved on your computer so they can be compressed. As an option, you can add any AE composition or Premiere Pro sequence that you have already made and saved.

- Open Adobe Media Encoder by going to that name.
- Pick out a file.
- You can select Add Source, Add After Effects Composition, or Add Premiere Pro Sequence based on the project you're working on.

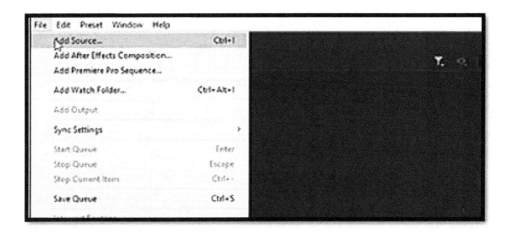

Browsing for Media Encoder Files

Is the fastest way to add files that you already have before you format them to use the file search option? This lets you choose more than one file to add to the queue at the same time.

- Open files Encoder are a free program that lets you encode files.
- Click the plus sign (+) in the Queue panel.

- Pick out the file you wish to send.
- Press the OK button.

Importing from After Effects

It's easy to add things to the Media Encoder list in After Effects. How to do it:

- Open up your After Effects project.
- From the File menu, choose File > Export.
- From the drop-down menu, choose "Add to Media Encoder Queue."

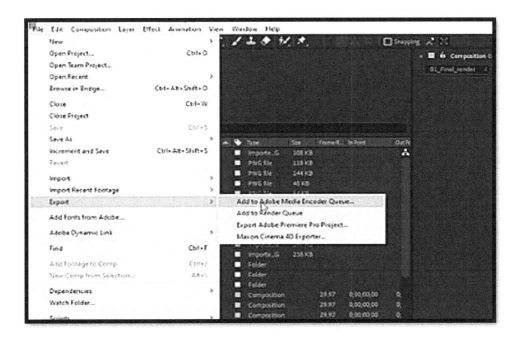

Importing from Premiere Pro

From Premiere Pro, you can send your files directly to the Media Encoder queue with the click of a button. This lets you keep working in Premiere Pro while your project encodes.

- Open your project in Premiere Pro.
- Click on File > Export in the File menu. Then pick the format you want to use.
- Pick Queue when the Export Settings box comes up.

Changing the Media Encoder's Options

Media Encoder comes with built-in settings for the most common types of videos. By default, Media Encoder will use the setting you picked for your last project.

But here's what you need to do if you need to change your last project:

- Choose the pre-set text in the Media Encoder Queue's Preset box. In the pop-up box, you can change the style. Most people use H.264, which has built-in settings for YouTube, Vimeo, Facebook, Twitter, and many other popular sites. If you want to post to a certain site, you should usually check its needs twice before making any changes to these settings.
- From the Preset dropdown list, choose an option.

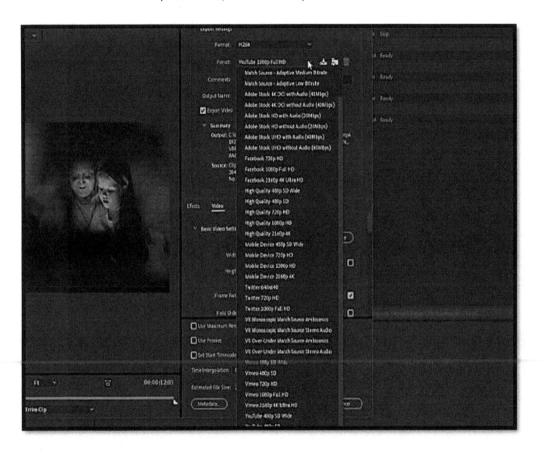

- Pick an output name and tell it where to save the files after they've been made.
- Get to the place where you want to save the file. You can now also pick a new name for the file.
- Click "Save" when you're done.

This window also has some other options for customizing how things work. If you choose the setting for the site you want to post to, you shouldn't have to make any other changes.

How to Stop Encoding

If you think of a way to change your project or if you forgot to change your settings, you may need to stop the decoding process. Stopping the decoding process is easy and quick.

Should you decide to end the encoding process, you can do any of the following:

- To stop encoding the current item, go to File > Stop Current Item. Media Encoder will convert the rest of the things in the Queue.
- To stop encoding everything in the Queue, go to File > Stop Queue.

Clearing Your Queue

1. Open Adobe Media Encoder on your computer. This will let you see your list and handle your jobs.

2. **Choose Files to Delete:** In the Media Encoder screen, find the jobs or files that you want to remove from the Queue. You can choose to delete a single file or a group of files.

- Hold down the Shift key and click the first and last things in the list to pick a set of files.
- To pick several files that are not next to each other, hold down the Ctrl key (or the Command key on a Mac) and click on each one separately.

3. **Right-click and remove:** Once you've picked out the files you want to delete, right-click on any part of the files you choose. When you do this, a secondary option will appear.

- Select the "Remove" option from the menu that shows. If you click this button, the files or jobs you picked will be deleted from your Media Encoder Queue.

Uploading to Social Media

Once you've compressed your video, the next step is usually to share or post it. In the Export Settings dialog box of Adobe Media Encoder, you can set up publishing settings. This way, your video will be posted automatically once the encoding process is done. With the Publish options in the Export Settings dialog box, you can set up how your video will be sent to places like your shared Creative Cloud Files folder, Adobe Stock, Adobe Behance, Facebook, FTP sites (File Transfer Protocol), Twitter, Vimeo, and YouTube. When you can save the settings you've chosen as an export standard, this feature becomes very useful. When you use presets, you can speed up your social media posts by setting the parameters only once. Then, when you share media in the future, you can just select the preset to use those parameters.

Here's how to get to these settings in Premiere Pro, step by step:

1. Now go back to Premiere Pro.
2. From the Timeline panel, go to **File > Export > Media**. To open the Export Settings dialog box, you can also press **Command + M (macOS) or Ctrl + M (Windows).**
3. In the Export choices dialog box, click on the "Publish" tab to get to the choices for sharing or releasing your video.
4. After making the necessary changes to the settings to get to where you want to go, click "**Cancel**" to close the Export Settings dialog box and finish the setup.

It's important to keep in mind that every site or location has its own transportation rules. Most of the time, you can pick a high-quality master file and let the tool make smaller versions of it for you. For example, when sending to Adobe Stock, making a high-quality UHD (3840x2160) file lets the server handle the compression and editing needs of the different video types and codecs that the platform supports. This method makes the sharing process easier while keeping the quality at the best level for all devices.

Exchanging Projects with Other Editing Applications

For loading and publishing, Premiere Pro works with some common file types, such as EDLs (Edit Decision Lists), OMF (Open Media Framework), AAF (Advanced Authoring Format), ALE (Avid Log Exchange), and XML (Extended Markup Language). When working with writers who use different programs, these forms are necessary to make sure that project data can be shared easily. As an example, using AAF as a bridge file can make working together with Avid Media Composer editors easier by letting them share clip information, changed sequences, and certain effects. In the same way, XML acts as a bridge for working together with Apple Final Cut Pro producers.

Here's what you need to do to save an AAF or XML file from Premiere Pro:

1. Pick out the sequence you want to send.
2. Choose the type you need from the File menu and then choose **File > Export > AAF or File > Export > Final Cut Pro XML.**
3. This step makes the AAF or XML file that has all the project information you need to share it with other people or edit suitable systems.

Premiere Pro also lets you save a project's data into a file that describes the project and lets you make it again using the same media or a different editing system. One example is that a project can be exported as an edit decision list (EDL) in the CMX3600 format. Of all the different EDL types, CMX3600 is one of the most popular and effective ones for moving files between editing systems. Premiere Pro supports a wide range of import and export files, which makes sure that different editing platforms can work together easily. This means that editors can use their chosen software and tools while still working together.

Using the EDL files

EDLs (Edit Decision Lists) work best with simple projects that have no more than one video track, two stereo audio tracks, and no stacked sequences. They can be used with most common transitions, frame holds, and clip speed changes. All source contents must be recorded and logged with the correct timecode for EDL to work. Whether it's a capture card or a FireWire port, the capture device should be able to be controlled by timecode. Also, before filming a video, each record should have its unique reel number and be set up with a timecode so that cutting and syncing is done correctly.

To save a project as an EDL file in Premiere Pro, follow these steps:

1. Open or save the project that you want to turn into an EDL file.
2. Make sure that the project has a Timeline panel open.
3. From the File menu, go to **File > Export > EDL**.
4. In the **EDL Export Settings (CMX 3600)** box, pick out the video and audio tracks you want to send. Keep in mind that you can send out one video track along with two soundtracks or up to four audio channels.
5. Say where the EDL file is saved and what it's called.
6. Hit "**Save**" to confirm where the file will go and what it will be called.

7. Click "**OK**" to start the download process.

If you follow these steps, you can send a project from Premiere Pro in the CMX 3600-compliant EDL format. This method works best for simple projects with few tracks and simple changes. It also makes it easier to use with editing systems and processes that support EDL import.

Exporting to OMF

By making an Open Media Framework (OMF) file in Premiere Pro, audio data can be sent between computers, which is often used for mixing audio. Most of the time, OMF files combine all the audio files in a sequence into a single file. The clips on the audio tracks stay organized the same way they are in the Premiere Pro sequence.

Here's a step-by-step guide to creating an OMF file in Premiere Pro:

1. **Select Sequence and Open Export Settings:**
   - Choose the sequence you want to export.
   - Navigate to File > Export > OMF.
2. **Configure OMF Export Settings:**
   - In the OMF Export Settings dialog box, specify a name for the OMF file in the "OMF Title" field.
   - Ensure that the "Sample Rate" and "Bits Per Sample" parameters align with your video settings. The default settings are commonly 48000 Hz and 16 bits.
3. **Choose Export Options:**
   - **Under the "Files" menu, select one of the following options:**
     - **Embed Audio:** This option creates an OMF file containing project information and all audio files within the sequence.
     - **Separate Audio:** Splits all audio files (including stereo audio) into individual mono audio files saved in the omfiMediaFiles folder, which is standard for complex audio mixing procedures.
4. **Select Audio File Format:**
   - If using the "Separate Audio" option, choose between the AIFF and Broadcast Wave formats. Both are high-quality formats, so ensure compatibility with your system. AIFF files are often suitable for various systems.
5. **Configure Audio File Handling:**

- Under the "Render" menu, choose between "Copy Complete Audio Files" or "Trim Audio Files" to reduce the file size. Adding handles (additional seconds) to the clips offers flexibility when editing and combining them.

6. **Initiate OMF File Creation:**
   - After configuring all settings, click "OK" to start creating the OMF file.

Following these steps allows you to generate an OMF file from Premiere Pro, providing a comprehensive and organized representation of audio clips from your sequence. This file format is beneficial for transferring audio projects across compatible programs or systems involved in audio mixing and editing.

Exporting Premiere Pro Videos to MP4

It might seem hard at first to convert Premiere Pro movies to MP4 format since Adobe Premiere Pro doesn't have a straight "MP4" option for saving files. But MP4 movies are usually converted with codecs like H.264 or the high-quality H.265/HEVC. You can find these codecs in the sending options. When you export Premiere Pro movies to MP4, even if you choose the right options, the files you get might be saved in a different format for reasons that aren't immediately clear. When this happens, Premiere Pro movies need to be converted to the MP4 format because MP4 is a flexible file that works with a lot of different devices and systems. **These steps will help you change movies from Premiere Pro to MP4:**

- Open **Adobe Premiere Pro** and open the project that has the video you want to send.
- On the project schedule, choose the video clips you want to use. Usually, certain parts show up with a light blue tint.
- Select the "Export" option from the File menu in the top left area. You can also use the keyboard shortcut (Ctrl/Command + M) or click on the Media icon to get to the export options.
- It will pop up a box with options. Click on "Format" and scroll down to choose the H.264 or HEVC codec that works best for you.
- Change the video quality, give the file a name, and pick a place to save the copied file.
- Finally, choose the "Export" option to save your Premiere Pro project as an MP4 file.

By following these steps, you can send your Premiere Pro project as an MP4 file using either the H.264 or HEVC codec. This makes sure that it works on a wide range of devices and systems.

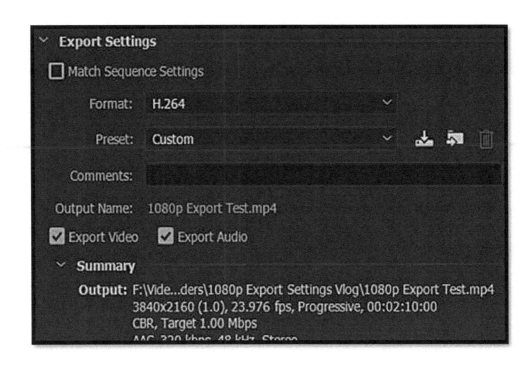

CHAPTER 17
WORKING WITH KEYFRAME INTERPOLATION

In digital video and film, interpolation is the process of guessing or figuring out numbers in the middle of two known places or keyframes. This is the most important thing you need to know to make smooth animation changes and moves. Let's say you need a visual element, like a title, to move fifty pixels across the screen throughout 15 frames. To do this, you would use keyframes to set the starting and ending points and let the software interpolate the frames in between to make the action look smooth. "Tweening," which is another name for interpolation, makes frames that fill in the gaps between two keyframes. In this method, movement, effects, audio levels, visual changes, color changes, and other things are easily transitioned between these set key times, giving images life.

Interpolation can be broken down into two main types:

1. **Temporal Interpolation**: This method looks at how changes in motion happen over time. It tells whether something is moving slowly or quickly along its way. On the other hand, only a few effects in programs like Premiere Pro fully allow keyframe blending over time.
2. **Spatial Interpolation**: This type of interpolation changes shapes. It tells you things like whether corners should be smooth or sharp, for example. To control these changes in Premiere Pro, spatial interpolation can be used on the keyframes of some effects.

These are two popular ways to interpolate:

1. **Linear Interpolation**: This method makes the change from one clip to the next smooth. Because each intermediate frame gets an equal amount of the change, there are sharp starts and stops and a smooth transition between keyframes.
2. **Bezier Interpolation**: With Bezier interpolation, the rate of change can be sped up or slowed down. It has the shape of a Bezier curve, which lets the speed slowly go up from the first keyframe to the next and then slowly go back down again.

Depending on the result you want, you can use either linear or Bezier approximation. Linear interpolation makes changes that are smooth and steady; while Bezier interpolation lets you change the rate of change in more subtle ways that you can control. This gives the animation a more natural and smoother feel.

Change the keyframe interpolation method

If you change and tweak keyframe interpolation, you can fine-tune how fast things change in your movies. You can change the keyframe type directly by changing the keyframe or handles, or you can choose an interpolation type from a context menu.

Choose one of the following options:

➤ Right-click a keyframe marker in the Effect Controls panel.
➤ Right-click a keyframe in a Timeline window.

From the context menu, choose an interpolation method:

❖ **Linear**: This setting keeps the speed of change the same between keyframes.
❖ **Bezier**: You can change the shape and rate of change of the graph by hand on each side of a keyframe. With this approach, changes go very smoothly.
❖ **Auto Bezier**: Auto Bezier makes a smooth rate of change with a keyframe. When the value of a keyframe changes, the Auto Bezier direction handles the change. This makes sure that the shift between keyframes is smooth.
❖ **Continuous Bezier**: This method uses a keyframe to make a smooth rate of change. In contrast to Auto Bezier interpolation, Continuous Bezier lets you change the direction handles by hand. If you change the shape of a graph on one side of a keyframe, it also changes on the other side of the keyframe to make the shift smooth.
❖ **Hold**: This changes a property's value quickly and without a smooth shift. After a keyframe, the graph looks like a horizontal straight line with the Hold interpolation turned on.
❖ **Ease In**: This slows down how quickly the value of a keyframe changes.
❖ **"Ease Out"**: This speeds up the changes in value slowly until a keyframe is reached.

Using the Auto Reframe Effects

Auto Reframe figures out what's going on in your video and reframes it automatically to fit different aspect ratios. For example, if you want to share your video on Instagram, YouTube, or Facebook, this option will come in handy. You can change the aspect ratio of sequences to square, vertical, or widescreen 16:9, and you can also crop high-resolution videos up to and including 4K. You can instantly resize single clips or a whole sequence.

Add the Auto Reframe effect to a clip

- Move the mouse over Transform in the Video Effects menu.
- Drag the Auto Reframe effect to a clip to change its frame.
- To fine-tune the Auto Reframe effect, go to the Effect Controls panel and pick the right Motion Tracking option. Premiere Pro makes motion keyframes that follow the action in your video while the effect is being applied.
- **You can choose from the following options: The three options are Slower, Default, or Faster Motion.**
  - ➤ **Slower Motion**: It's helpful when the camera doesn't move at all or moves very slowly, like when a talking head is being interviewed. When this control is used, the clip doesn't have many keyframes, and the effects are pretty much fixed.
  - ➤ **"Default"** means it works for most things. The Auto Reframe effect moves with the action. If the action is fast, though, the results may not be good.
  - ➤ **Faster Motion**: This option should be used when the clip is moving quickly and you want the Auto-Reframe effect to keep up. This could be in action sports or skateboarding videos. It makes sure that the moving object stays in the frame and that your clip has a lot of keyframes.
- You can change the Generated Path if you want to.
- Adjust Position; Reframe Offset, Reframe Scale, and Reframe Rotation are some other fine-tuned options that you can choose from.
- If you want to, you can play the video after the effect has been made. You can make the effects even better if you need to by copying and changing the keyframes in the Effect Controls window.

Resize a Picture

It's quick and easy to change the size of a landscape picture that is still in Premiere Pro. You'll need to add the pictures you want to use in your video project first. That can be done by going to File > Import, but it's easier to just drag and drop the files. Before you add the picture, you need to drag it to the spot on the schedule where you want it to go. Then, right-click (or press control + mouse on a Mac) and choose Scale to Frame Size from the list of options that comes up.

From the two dropdown options below the picture, you can choose Fit or Full if the picture doesn't fit the frame.

How to Fit a Portrait Image in Your Video

It's a little trickier to change the size of a portrait picture than a landscape picture, but it's

still easy to do. To make a color finish first, go to the project tab and click on New Item in the bottom right corner. Expand your screen or press the three lines on your video and choose Panel Group Settings > Maximize Panel Group if you still can't see the icon.

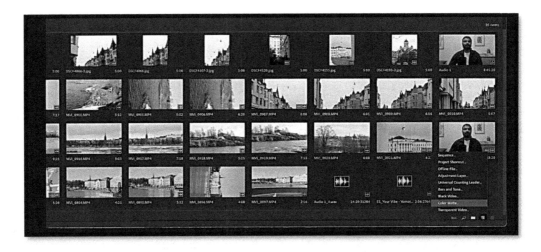

Before you pick the best color and click OK, you can choose how big you want the color matte to be.

Add your color finish to the project by dragging and dropping it. Put it in a video number above your main project so that it covers the footage, then drag and drop your picture into the video number above that. Remember that dragging and dropping can cause Premiere Pro to crash, so it might be better to import it by hand. Once you've chosen the picture you want to change, click on Scale to Frame Size. After you do these things, your picture should fit on the screen within the color background.

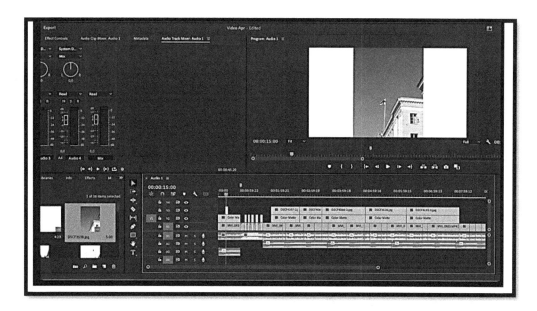

CHAPTER 18
WORKFLOW OPTIMIZATION

Keyboard Shortcuts and Customization

10 Useful Default Keyboard Shortcuts

These work with the default layout. Go to the File menu (or Premiere Pro CC menu on Mac) and choose Keyboard Shortcuts > Keyboard Layout Preset > Adobe Premiere Pro Default if it isn't already selected.

❖ In video editing software, changing your timeline means making the visual picture of your project bigger or smaller. When you press Shift and the plus (+) or minus (-) keys, you can make these changes. For example, Ctrl and or minus keys change the height of the video track, while Alt and or minus keys change the height of the audio track. It's the same as expanding or contracting the editing workspace area set aside for your video and audio clips.

❖ The backslash key (/) can be used as a tool to quickly zoom out your whole project timeline. You can see everything in the timeline at once with this key instead of using the scroll bar to move between pieces of work. This is a much faster way to get a sense of your whole project.

❖ In and Out points are popular editing tools used to mark the beginning and end of a section you want to work with. There are different key combinations you can use to clear these points: To clear the In point, press Ctrl+Shift+I (or Opt+I on a Mac). To clear the Out point, press Ctrl+Shift+O (or Opt+O), and to clear both the In and Out points at once, press Ctrl+Shift+X (or Opt+X).

❖ The 'X' key helps mark the clip right under the Playhead, and the '/' (forward slash) key sets the In and Out places for all the clips that are currently chosen. It lets you quickly mark certain parts of several clips in your timeline.

❖ The letter "D" on the computer can be used to pick the clip that is where the Playhead is in the timeline. You can use this tool to quickly work with certain clips in your project.

❖ Press Shift+Ctrl+A (or Shift+Cmd+A on a Mac) to remove everything that is currently chosen, including clips, effects, and other things. In other words, it removes or "un-highlights" everything you've clicked on or chosen before.

- ❖ Pressing Ctrl+K (or Cmd+K) quickly cuts a clip in half, like using a knife tool but faster. When you use this command with the Shift key pressed, all clips under the Playhead are cut.
- ❖ The Q and W ripple trim instructions are very important for making quick cuts in your video. If you put the playhead where you want it and press Q or W, the part between the playhead and the previous or next edit point will be erased. The fastest way to get rid of parts of a clip that you don't want is to use Top & Tail Editing.
- ❖ To get to Match Frame, press "F" on the computer. It helps you find the first or master clip in your sequence and open it in the Source Monitor at the exact frame where the Playhead is.
- ❖ Pressing Shift+R brings up the Reverse Match Frame, which works backward. To go back to the first time that frame appeared in your sequence, press Shift+R while you're on a certain frame in the Source Monitor. By hitting Shift+R over and over, you can see all of the cases of that frame in your project. It lets you quickly find the spot in your video where a certain frame shows.

Best practices when editing keyboard shortcuts

It's important to follow best practices when working with and changing keyboard shortcuts in Adobe Premiere Pro to make sure the editing process goes smoothly.

Here are some tips on how to use computer tools to get more done:

- **Avoid conflicts**: It is important to avoid giving a key combination that is already in use when creating shortcuts, as this can cause misunderstandings or actions that were not meant to happen. If you get a warning when you try to set up a new link, you might want to try a different key combination to avoid problems.
- **Learn existing shortcuts**: Before you make big changes, you should learn and use the computer tools that come with Premiere Pro. There are a lot of these tools that work in all Adobe programs and can help you get things done faster.
- **Create mnemonic associations:** Use the first letter of a function to make mnemonic associations. For example, "C" for Cut or "V" for Paste are mnemonic associations that can help you remember the methods. For some people, this can help them remember their methods.
- **Build up your list of shortcuts slowly**: Start by changing a few shortcuts to fit your needs. As you learn more about Premiere Pro, add to your unique settings. This will help you keep from getting too many new options.

- **Put your custom shortcuts in order and write them down**: Make a list of your unique tools and what they do so you can find them quickly. This can be very useful if you work on different computers or share your passwords with other people.
- **Make a copy of your shortcuts**: Make a copy of your custom button set and save it so you don't lose your changes if there are problems with the software or if you need to restart Premiere Pro.

Ten Essential Right-Click Commands for Adobe Premiere Pro

You can do a lot of useful things in Adobe Premiere Pro by right-clicking on a clip in the Project or Sequence! For Adobe Premiere Pro editors who want to work faster, these must-know settings can speed up the post-process. You can change the speed, audio, and effects of a clip by right-clicking it.

1. Editing>interpretation of the footage

As many DSLRs now record at 60 frames per second, slow-motion clips need to be set to play in slow motion instead of fast motion. You can change the frame rate of video clips right away in Adobe Premiere Pro. Click and hold on to the clip in the Project. Then, go to the menu and choose "Modify" > "Interpret Footage." If you are modifying with a different frame rate, choose either 23.94 or 29.97 as the overall rate in the "assume this rate" box. The length of the clip will change, and it will now play more slowly.

2. Alter the Audio Channels

You can quickly convert the audio in your clips from mono to stereo. Press and hold on to the clip in the Project for a moment, then select "Modify" from the drop-down menu. You can go from mono to stereo or back again.

3. Reveal in…

If you right-click on any file, it will be easy to find on your hard drive. You can also right-click on a Premiere clip and select Adobe Bridge to see it. From there, you can name, play, and rate the clip.

4. Speed and time

If you change the speed of a clip in the Project, it will change everywhere that clip appears. It happens more often to change the speed of a clip in a sequence, which only changes that clip.

5. Blending the frames

This should be turned on when you change the frame rate of an output or clip. Select a clip in the Sequence by right-clicking it and selecting Frame Blend.

6. Remove Effects

Pick out the clips whose effects that you want to be removed. There will be a dialogue box showing up. To get rid of Effects that you don't want, uncheck them.

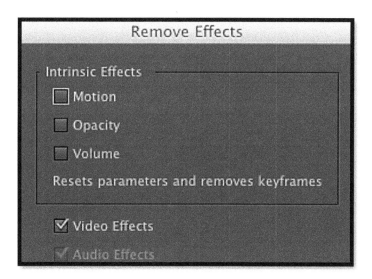

7. Reveal in Project

Right-click on a clip in a Sequence to see where it is in the Project.

8. Examine the content

Pick a clip from the Project to analyze speech (planned results are better) and/or identify faces. Visit Adobe's website to learn more about information in general.

9. Edit the Clip in the Audition

This starts Adobe Audition and sends the clip from the Sequence that was picked. Editors can get rid of background noise in audio files using Adobe Audition's "Noise Reduction" tool. Then, when you go back to Premiere Pro, it will remember the changes you made in Audition.

10. Replace with After Effects Composition

To change the clip from the Sequence, an After Effects Composition will be used. You can use this method when you need to do Motion Tracking in After Effects or use an AE effect that isn't available in Premiere Pro. If you change your mind later, I suggest making a copy of the Sequence with the clip you want to change.

Instead of going through the menu bar, you can instantly access these actions by right-clicking a clip in Adobe Premiere Pro. Boost your productivity!

PART VI
ADVANCED TECHNIQUES IN EFFECTS AND ANIMATION

CHAPTER 19
ADVANCED VIDEO EFFECTS
Exploring the Effects Panel

Adobe Premiere Pro is a powerful video editing tool. It contains countless features that let you make cinematic edits with ease. Many of these are called effects. These effects are controlled with the **Effect Controls** panel in Premiere Pro. The Effect Controls panel in Premiere Pro is very flexible and has many options. It's simple to use. When you use Effect Controls with the Effects panel in Premiere, they work together. It's also a strong tool that you can use on its own with any video, without any extra effects. So, where is Premiere Pro's Effects panel? We'll do everything one step at a time.

1. Open the Effect Controls Panel

As we work in Premiere Pro, let's get used to how the screen is laid out. I've used some stock videos for this case. We're going to use this beautiful stock video of the Blue Ridge Parkway to show you how to use Effect Controls. The clip can be seen ahead of time in the upper middle of the screen. The Program Monitor is the name of this part of Premiere Pro. It shows you the video you're changing in real-time, as you can see. Any changes you make with the Effect Controls will show up right away here. It shows you exactly what the video will look like when you download it.

The Timeline is to the right of the Program Monitor. With this tool, you can order, combine, and sequence video clips. With this, you can change how and when clips play and how they connect. First, let's look at how to get to the Effect Controls. This could make you wonder, "Where are the controls for the effects in Premiere Pro?" You can see your clip next to Effect Controls in the Program Monitor. By default, Premiere Pro won't show it to you. You have to launch it first. Find the "**Window**" dropdown menu at the top of your screen to open the Effect Controls. Drop-down menu: Click Window, then click Effect Controls from the list of options that comes up. The Effect Controls app will start right away! It'll be to the left of the clip you already saw in the Program Monitor.

2. Use Effect Controls to Transform Clips

Let's use Effect Controls now that it's open. There are three drop-down options there. Some of these are **Time Remapping, Motion, and Opacity**. You can see more options when you click on the lines next to each one.

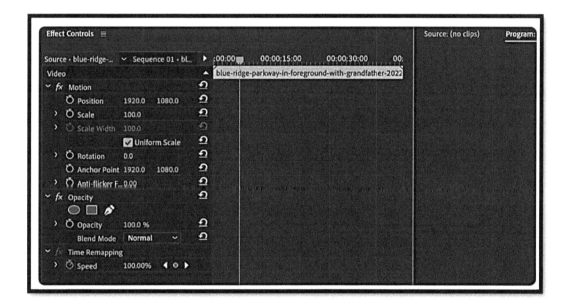

You can change where a video clip is in the frame by going to the **Motion** group. One example is that you can move things around. The editing canvas's middle is where videos by default show. The position numbers can be changed to move a video up, down, or side to side. The **Scale** menu can be thought of as a zoom tool. Let's say you set the size of this clip to 125.0. It will zoom in by 25%. You can also change the direction, the center point, and other things.

❖ **Opacity** lets you change how see-through a video clip is. This is very helpful if you want clips or effects on other clips to show through. Another clip, for instance, could be overlaid so that it will show through. The Opacity tool makes this easy to change.

❖ **Time Remapping** helps you use keyframes to change the speed of a video clip. This is one way to make things more exciting and cooler. For instance, you could add dramatic effects like slow motion. You could also speed up a clip to make it fit better into the schedule for your project.

You can see that Premiere Pro's Effect Controls are a good place to start making changes. To make even stronger changes, which we'll look at next, this step is helpful.

3. Add Effects and Adjust with Effect Controls

The above-mentioned Effect Controls are built-in tools that come with every movie. However, these are only the very beginning of what Premiere Pro can do. You can use Effect Controls to add and change a huge number of other effects. To do this, open the Effects panel. Go to Window > Effects to get to it. Then, go to the top right part of your screen and select Effects from the toolbar menu. There will be an Effects sidebar to the right of the Program Monitor and Timeline when the window opens.

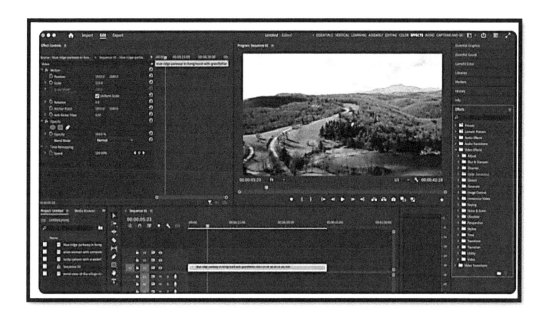

You can find dozens more unique effects here. They are very different in style and form. They do the same thing, though. For instance, go to the dropdown menu and click on Video Effects. Let's open Blur & Sharpen to see a simple example. Inside, look for the Sharpen effect. Click and drag an effect from the Effects panel onto your clip to add it. In the Timeline, move it on top of your clip and drop it where you want it. A black bar shows the clip. The sample in the Program Monitor won't change right away. But take a look at what's in the Effect Controls panel. Here, you'll see a new dropdown: **Sharpen**. The Effect Controls let you change any effect you add to Premiere Pro. You can quickly and easily change how strong the result is.

Let's change the **Sharpen Amount to 30** as an example. Keep an eye on the Program Monitor after you do that. The clip gets clearer. This shows you how to add controls for effects in Premiere Pro! You can use the Effect Controls menu to change how an effect works after dropping it into place. Remember that you can give a clip more than one effect. It's always the same process. You can add an effect to the Timeline. As soon as you do that, settings for it will show up in the Effect settings. There are many things you can do. Think outside the box and try out different results. They're an easy and quick way to make big changes to any video you work on in Adobe Premiere Pro. You can see that Effect Controls in Premiere Pro are easy to use. In just a few easy steps, you learn how to add Effect Controls to Premiere Pro. Your most important answer is "**Where are the effect controls in Premiere Pro**?" These tools will come in handy over and over again as you start editing in Premiere.

Using Masks for Creative Effects

Masking is a great skill to have in Adobe Premiere Pro because it can help you make movies and fix many problems with your shots. A mask is most often used to add a vignette or crop the footage into a certain shape, but once you know how to use the tools, you will find many more uses for the effect.

Create a Mask with Shape Tools

A circle and a square are the two set shape masks in Premiere. These are both simple things that you can add to your clip with just one click. Find the Crop effect in the Effects panel and add it to the clip you want to hide. This will make the other clips in the sequence invisible. The cropping effect will be put in the Effects Control panel. The settings will show up when you click on the Crop drop-down. Next, we'll look at the pen tool. First, we'll look at the square and circle tools.

If you click on either shape, the mask will be added to your clip in the media player. Now you can change the size and style of your mask until you're happy with it.

To make the cutting effect, go back to the Effects Control panel and cut out the parts of the shot using the Crop percentages. You can choose whether the effect is applied to the inside or outside of the mask by checking the "Inverted" box.

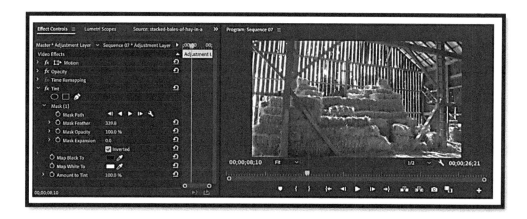

It's not as hard as you thought! Let's move on to something a little harder.

Create a Custom Shape Using the Pen Tool

You can use the pen tool to make your video into a shape other than a circle or square. You can draw right onto your video in the media player once you choose the Pen tool. When you click on the video, a point will be added to the shape. Keep adding points until you're happy with the shape, then click on the first point to finish the loop. With just one click, you can make a corner point that will give your shape a sharp edge. When you click and drag on a point, it will get handles that let you make bent lines. It takes time to get good at using the pen tool, especially when you need to make balanced shapes. Don't stress, you'll get it.

How to Modify and Move Masks

Once your mask has a full shape, you can change the points on it until it looks just right.

- By clicking on any part of the mask line, you can add another point to your shape.
- If you hold down ALT and click on a point on a mask, you can add or remove handles.

Move Your Mask

If you click in the middle of the shape and pull it, you can move the mask around the screen over your video.

Feather and Adjust Mask Edges

You will find three more settings in the Mask Effect options. These are **Feather, Opacity, and Expansion. Each one of these can help to define your mask and give your pieces amazing style looks.**

- With the Expansion control, you can change how close the footage is to your shape line. When making complicated shapes, changing the description of your mask can help smooth out some of the rougher edges. This way, you don't have to spend hours perfecting every angle.
- Feathering lets the impact fade in or out from the edge of the mask slowly. Both in the Effects Control panel and the media player, you can change how much feathering there is.
- The opacity feature works pretty much the same way in all Adobe programs. If you put it on a mask, it will change how opaque the footage you cut out is.

How to Copy and Paste Masks

It's very easy to copy a face to another clip. In the Effects Control box, click on the clip with the mask you want to copy. Then, press Cmd+C or Ctrl+C to go to Edit > Copy. Press Cmd+V or Ctrl+V and choose the clip in the sequence where you want to paste the text. You can copy and paste masks to specific clips by copying and pasting them, but adding an adjustment layer is much easier if you want to change the whole sequence.

- To add an adjustment layer, open the Project window and select **New Item**. It will add a new layer to the Project window by itself.

- Drag this to the sequence and put it on top of the clips you want to change.
- Follow the steps above to add a mask to the change layer. This time, the effect will be added to all clips in the sequence that are below the layer.
- Masks can be copied and pasted between adjustment layers or between clips and adjustment layers.

When you use an adjustment layer, it can save you a lot of time when you need to change your mask later. You're already editing better than before!

Premiere Pro Masking Tips

You already know how to use masks to crop, but you can also add them to almost any effect that changes the way your clips look.

Here are a few of our favorites:

Color Effects

You can add masks to any color effect, which lets you make more beautiful images in your movies than just the usual fade-to-black vignette. In this case, we used the Tint effect to get rid of all the colors around the mask's edge. You can also fix shots with a lot of contrast by using masks with color effects. This lets you choose which parts of a scene to lighten or darken.

Blur Effect

Blurs are a great way to make a main point in your video. You can blur certain parts of your shot with the same blocking settings that show up in the Effects Control panel after you add a blur effect. This will help you if you want to give a clip a title.

Color Mattes

Because Premiere has so many built-in text boxes, there are times when only a custom effect will do. Masking color mattes is a great way to add color to your videos without having to use Illustrator, Photoshop, or After Effects.

Troubleshooting Premiere Pro Masks

Masks can be hard to get right every time. Let's look at some of the most common mistakes and how to fix them.

Twisted Handles

You can have made a perfect shape and can see all the handles, but it doesn't look the way you want it to because one point is now a small, sharp loop. Most of the time, this is because the handles were turned the wrong way. Pick out the point and turn the handles until the edge is smooth.

Point Clusters

If moving a point doesn't seem to change the shape all the way, it might be because there are other points close to it. The video player will be quite small unless you are working on a very large screen, and you won't always be able to see every single point on the mask. Check the Zoom to see if there are any extra points. If there are, delete the ones you don't need by holding down Command or Control and clicking on the point you want to get rid of.

Playback

When you use masks, you might sometimes have trouble with replay. Do not worry, this is most likely due to the effect you are using and not the mask. However, you should always check that your sequence has been created. It's helpful to know how to use masks when editing because they can help you make beautiful images and fix mistakes made while shooting. You have the tools you need to address specific issues, such as white spots in your footage, thanks to the ability to place your color changes carefully. While you can rely on apps and effects like the standard Premiere Vignette, learning how to use Adobe Premiere masks without using any additional tools will give you more freedom to try new things and figure out how to fix problems.

CHAPTER 20
PUTTING CLIPS IN MOTION

In video projects that focus on motion graphics, many shots are combined into complicated compositions with many layers. These levels are used a lot of the time. A video clip could be shrunk down and put next to a presenter on camera, or a bunch of video clips could be shown moving by in boxes that float in the air. With the Motion effect, you can move, scale, or spin a clip inside the video frame. You can add the Motion effect to any clip in the Timeline panel, and it will always be there. You can see and change the properties of the Motion effect by clicking the triangle next to its name in the Effect Controls panel. By setting keyframes for Motion features, you can also make clips move.

Adjusting the Motion Effects

Click the triangle next to the Motion word in the Effect Controls panel to see and change the features of the Motion effect. There is a reference point on the clip that tells you its position, size, and spin. Anchor points for clips are always in the middle of the clip. You can change the center point on the Effects Control page.

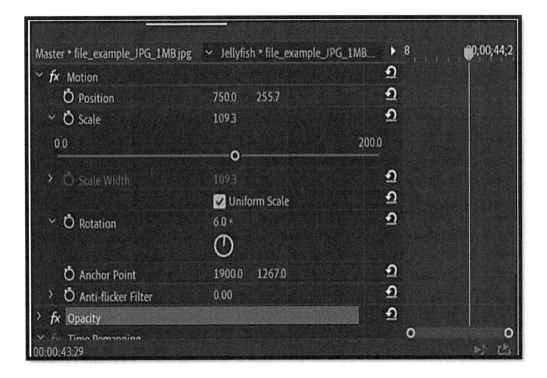

Changing a Clip Position, Size, and Rotation

Scale Clip

Scaling a Clip:

1. **Select the Clip in the Timeline:**
   - Open your project in Adobe Premiere Pro.
   - Navigate to the Timeline and choose the clip that you want to scale.

2. **Access the Effects Control Panel:**
   - Go to the menu bar and select the Effects Control panel. This panel displays various parameters and effects for the selected clip.

3. **Adjust the Scale Parameters:**
   - Within the Effects Control panel, locate the "Scale" parameter under the "Motion" effect.
   - Click on the triangle or the disclosure triangle to the left of "Scale." This expands the Scale options.

4. **Modify Scale Settings:**
   - To uniformly adjust both height and width together:
     - Drag the slider to the right to increase the clip's size.
     - Drag the slider to the left to reduce the clip's size.

5. **Adjust Height and Width Independently (Optional):**
   - If you wish to change the height and width separately:
     - Deselect the "**Uniform Scale**" option.
     - Now, you can adjust the height and width values individually to scale the clip in different proportions.

6. **Fine-Tune the Scaling:**
   - Keep adjusting the Scale parameters until you achieve the desired size or proportions for your clip.

Clip Rotation

1. **Select a Clip in the Timeline:**
   - Open your project in Adobe Premiere Pro.
   - From the Timeline, click on the clip that you want to rotate.

2. **Access the Effects Control Panel:**
   - Go to the menu bar and choose the "**Effects Control**" panel.
   - This panel displays various properties and effects for the selected clip.

3. **Adjust Rotation Properties:**

- Within the Effects Control panel, locate the "**Rotation**" property under the "Motion" effect.
- Click on the triangle or disclosure arrow to the left of "Rotation" to reveal its properties.

4. **Apply Rotation Effect:**
   - Input a specific value in the "Rotation" coordinate to set the desired rotation angle.
   - Alternatively, you can drag the line within the circular control to visually adjust the rotation.

Adjust Anchor Point

Follow these procedures to alter the anchor point:

- ➢ In the Timeline, choose a clip.
- ➢ Select the Effects Control panel from the menu bar.
- ➢ Click on the Anchor coordinate and enter a value to update the Anchor Point.

Manipulating Using Clip Handles

Making adjustments to a video clip within the Program Monitor involves using handles, which are intuitive tools to modify its position, size, and orientation.

Here's a step-by-step guide to effectively use handles for creating motion effects:

1. **Selecting the Clip:**
   - Within the Timeline panel, choose the specific clip you want to work on by moving the playhead to a frame within that clip.

2. **Accessing the Clip in the Program Monitor:**
   - Click on the chosen clip in the Program Monitor to ensure it's actively selected for editing.

3. **Navigating to the Effect Controls:**
   - Head over to the Effect Controls panel and click on the "Motion" label or the full line related to the clip you're modifying.

4. **Utilizing Handles:**
   - As you hover your mouse over the clip in the Program Monitor, handles will become visible, indicating areas where adjustments can be made.

5. **Relocating the Clip:**
   - Click and drag the clip to move it to the desired position on the screen.

6. **Scaling the Clip:**
   - To resize the clip, hover the mouse near a corner until a resizing handle appears. Drag the handle to adjust the clip's size. For maintaining proportions while resizing, hold down the Shift key while dragging.
7. **Rotating the Clip:**
   - Position the mouse slightly outside the clip until the cursor transforms into a rotation icon. Drag to rotate the clip to the desired angle.

This method provides a user-friendly way to manipulate video clips within the Program Monitor, allowing you to precisely adjust their placement, size, and orientation to achieve the desired visual effects.

Adjusting Size

Get a movie that needs to be cropped in Adobe Premiere Pro. Click on the Import button on the File tab. Another way to add a clip to the timeline is to drag and drop it.

Open the Effects panel.

The Crop tool can be found in the Effects tab, under the Transform file. As you click and drag it, it will move to the movie.

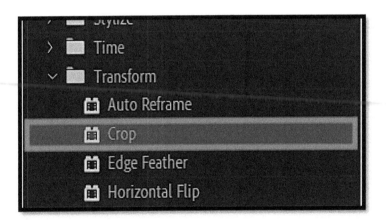

If you need to, you can change the settings on the Effect Controls screen. You can choose from Left, Right, Top, and Bottom. You can change other numbers to crop your movie as well. To change the frame size, go to the timeline, pick out the movie you want to change, and then choose **Set to Frame Size** from the dropdown menu.

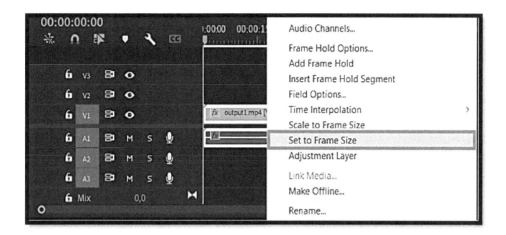

When you right-click on the movie, a drop-down menu will appear. Select "**Scale to Frame Size**." You can change the size of the source clip here instead of using settings that have already been set.

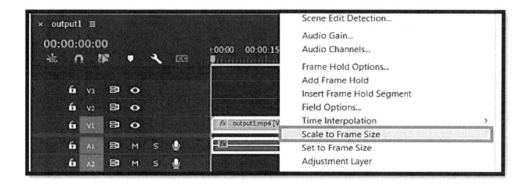

Back to the Effect tab to use the Motion effect. It is in the Effect Control Panel where you can find the Motion drop-down list.

To get the best scale, use a slider.

A few key factors to consider

- By default, a clip shows up in the middle of the Program Monitor at full size.
- The clip reference point, which is in the middle of the clip by default, is used to figure out the position, scale, and rotation values.
- The Position, Scale, and Rotation parameters are easier to change in the Program Monitor because they are spatial.

CHAPTER 21
EXPRESSIVE COLOR GRADING
Advanced Color Grading Techniques

When you use advanced color grading in Adobe Premiere Pro, you use complex methods to improve and change the way a video project looks. This complicated process goes beyond simple color fixing and includes changing colors, tones, and differences in small ways to get the look or feeling you want. Let's look at some advanced Adobe Premiere Pro color grading tips that will make visual stories better.

1. **Look-Up Tables or LUTs**: One basic but strong method used in advanced color grading is the use of Look-Up Tables. LUTs let producers give their footage certain looks by using pre-set color profiles or custom maps. Third-party LUTs can be imported into Premiere Pro, which opens up a lot of creative options. LUTs are a quick and easy way to make sure that the color grading is the same across multiple clips, whether you want a dramatic feel, an old-fashioned look, or a styled mood.

2. **Color Wheels and Curves**: Premiere Pro's Color Wheels and Curves give you fine-grained control over how colors are changed. With the Color Wheels, you can fine-tune the shadows, midtones, and highlights separately. By changing these factors, editors can carefully boost or lower certain color ranges, making the mix look better and more balanced. Curves are a feature that lets you precisely control the brightness and color strength by showing you a picture of the tonal distribution.

3. **HSL Secondary Color Correction**: Premiere Pro's HSL (Hue, Saturation, and Lightness) Secondary tool lets you use specific color correction. Editors can pick out certain colors, change their intensity and brightness, and then fine-tune particular parts of the picture. This is especially helpful for making skin tones look better, drawing attention to a certain color in a scene, or adding dramatic effects.

4. **Vignettes and Graduated Filters:** Vignettes and graduated filters are often used in advanced color grading to direct the viewer's attention and give a scene more depth. These tools are in Premiere Pro's effects panel, and they let editors slightly darken or lighten certain parts of the frame. You can use this method to draw attention to a certain part of the design, make the subject stand out, or control the contrast.

5. **Adjustment layers and blend modes**: The use of blend modes and adjustment layers in creative ways is a big part of advanced color grading. Editors can try out different combos to create their unique style by adding adjustment layers with different effects

and blend modes. This method makes it possible to work without destroying the source footage, so changes can be made easily.

6. **Keyframing and Dynamic Color Changes**: Keyframing is an important part of advanced color grading for making color changes that happen over time. Editors can change color factors like hue, intensity, and brightness to make stories more interesting or to make people feel certain feelings. This method works especially well in commercials, music videos, and other projects that need to tell a story visually interesting.

7. **Use of Filmic Effects and Grain:** Filmic effects and grain can be used to give projects a movie-like look. Premiere Pro has built-in film grain effects and lets you add third-party tools for even more customization. By adding minor movielike elements, editors can make the video look more like traditional video by giving it the same structure and feeling.

Creating LUTs for Consistent Looks

- **Step 1: Importing Your Footage**

You need to import your video into Premiere Pro before you can use LUTs. You can drag and drop your files right into your project panel or click "File" > "Import" to automatically add them.

- **Step 2: Accessing the Color Workspace**

Once your video is in the timeline, go to the "Color" workspace. It's at the top of the screen, or you can get there by going to "Window" > "Workspaces" > "Color." This action will open the Lumetri Color panel located on the right side of the screen.

- **Step 3: Different Tabs for LUT Application**

There are different tabs to look through on the Lumetri Color screen. The "Input LUT" dropdown menu is under the "Basic Correction" tab. This is where you can add LUTs. Usually, this is where you'd use a LUT to change log footage to the standard Rec. 709 color space.

On the other hand, the "Creative" tab lets you play around with how your movie looks. You can use different artistic LUTs here to give your video a certain mood or style.

- **Step 4: Import and Apply the LUT**

Click on "**Browse**" in the LUT area of either the "Basic Correction" or "Creative" tab to find the LUT file you want to use. Don't forget that the LUT file type must be .cube. After you've found and chosen the LUT file, click "Open" to add it to your video.

- **Step 5: Adjust LUT Intensity**

That's not all. You can change the LUT's strength or sharpness to make it work better with your footage. You can change this by moving the "Intensity" tool under the "Creative" tab on the Lumetri Color screen.

- **Step 6: Fine-tuning and Additional Adjustments**

Putting on a LUT is only the first step in the color grading process. You'll likely need to tweak other settings, such as contrast, brightness, whites, blacks, color, and more, to get the look you want. The Lumetri Color area is where you can make all of these changes. Utilizing LUTs can greatly improve your color grading process in Adobe Premiere Pro, giving all of your scenes a uniform visual tone. Color grading for your video projects will look much better and flow better if you learn how to use and change LUTs properly.

How to Use the Color Wheels

You can change your footage's shadows, midtones, and highlights with the Color Wheels, which are powerful and flexible tools. Let's go over in more depth how to use and learn the Color Wheels so that you can get the best color grading results. Learn the basics of how to use the Color Wheels in Premiere Pro before moving on to more advanced methods. Shadows are shown by the blacks, midtones are shown by the grays, and highlights are shown by the whites. Each wheel can be changed on its own to change the color balance of its tonal range. You can change how warm or cool your footage is generally by moving the Temperature tool in the Color Wheels panel. A natural look can be achieved by making sure that the color temperature matches the scene's lights.

The Color Wheels are great for fixing footage that has strange color casts. If there is an unwanted tint, find the main color that is causing it and change the opposite color wheel to get rid of it. For example, if you can see a blue cast, move the scales that go with them to make the midtones and highlights warmer. If you change the shadows, midtones, and highlights separately, you will get more contrast and depth. Try making small changes to each wheel until you find the right balance. In particular, this works great for making your footage look better. You can do specific color grading once you know how to use the Color Wheels. You can, for example, make certain colors stand out more or less in certain tonal areas. This helps to focus on a subject or give a picture a styled look. Getting skin tones that look real is very important when working with footage of people. To get skin tones that look natural and good on you, use the Color Wheels to change the mix of reds and yellows in the midtones. The RGB Parade in the Lumetri Scopes screen works great with the Color Wheels. It shows you how the red, green, and blue bands of your video images are balanced in terms of color. Use this tool to find gaps and use the Color Wheels to make exact changes. Keyframing can be used with the Color Wheels to make color changes happen automatically over time. This is especially useful for telling stories or making sequences that look interesting. Try keyframing to change the color balance gradually for certain scenes or effects on the viewer's emotions. The Color Wheels are only one part of the Lumetri Color panel in Premiere Pro. You can get more complex and complete color grading by mixing their use with other Lumetri effects, like the Curves and Color Correction tools.

HDR Editing and Display Considerations

The **Rec. 709** color space is no longer the only one used for image processing. Premiere can correctly understand and work with different color space types. Users can select from **Rec. 601, Rec. 709, Rec. 2020, Rec. 2100 HLG, and Rec. 2100 PQ** in the color management part of the Interpret Footage dialog box. There is also an option to give input LUTs to source footage. There is now **Rec. 709 and Rec. 2100** options in the Working Color Space drop-down menu of the Sequence Settings dialog box. In the same way, the export options now have HDR options for some file types. With the right information, H.264 and HEVC files can be exported to be sent in HDR10.

Monitoring

At the moment, monitoring is the big catch. Yes, you do want to see how your HDR video looks. Image has to go from software to Windows to the graphics driver and then over a digital wire to an HDR display. It then has to be properly read on that end so it can be seen correctly. The last three steps should work with HDMI-2.0b, but the step where you go through the operating system and graphics driver adds a lot of factors that Microsoft, Apple, Nvidia, AMD, or Intel could change. A specialized hardware output that supports Adobe's Mercury Transmit is the only way to be sure you can see your HDR video in Premiere. This makes a strong connection between the software and the HDMI 2.0 (or SDI) output, which can then be watched in the usual ways. AJA's Kona cards, Thunderbolt devices, and Blackmagic's DeckLink cards are some of the hardware output options that are currently enabled. Then, these are hooked up to your HDR display, which could be a regular HDR TV or a mastering-quality Canon DP-V3120, which is what I tested with (a Kona 5 card powered it).

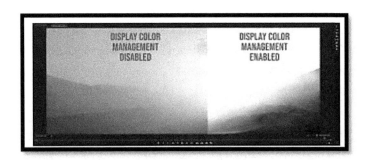

I tried using an HDMI 2.0 adapter to connect my HDR display to my Quadro GPU, but Premiere's output was limited to the brightness I set for the SDR program in Windows. This was true for both the Program Monitor Panel and the full-screen Transmit output. If you turned on Display Color Management in Premiere's settings, all the numbers above 100 were clipped instead of setting the peak brightness to 100%.

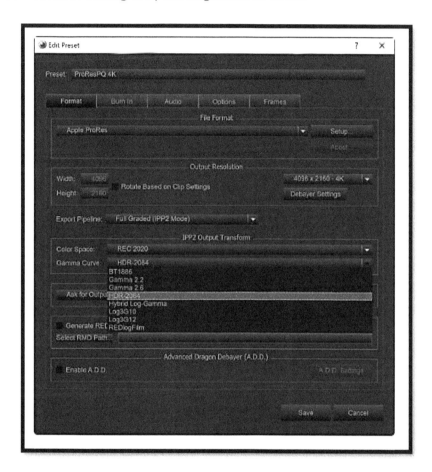

I'm not sure if running it in OS X produces the same results, but neither is officially supported by Adobe at the moment because changes to either the OS or the graphics drivers could have a big impact on how accurate the output is. This will be a lot easier in the future when operating systems and apps make their user interfaces work better with HDR screens. But until that happens, checking will be the hardest part of working in HDR or even just watching HDR media on a computer. Getting your footage into an HDR file that can be edited is the first thing you need to do. Some cameras, like the Panasonic GH5 that records to HLG HEVC files or the Sony cameras that record to X-AVC in HLG, can get HDR right away. Some cameras record raw images that can be read or changed into HDR color spaces.

At the moment, Premiere can't turn R3D files straight into HDR. However, RedCineX can convert R3D files to ProRes in either HLG or PQ, and you can then drop those files into Premiere HLG sequences. I hope that one day we will be able to edit R3Ds and other raw files straight in Premiere sequences in HDR without any problems.

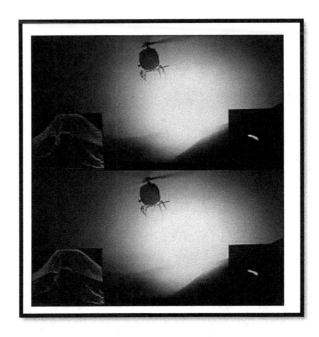

If your video is in the right file, it should be easy to import into Premiere, and any new sequences made from it should be in HLG by default. You will need to set your display to match if necessary and change the settings on your output device to send either HLG or PQ output. This is usually done in the Playback Preferences menu. For HDR media, color with a high bit depth makes a big difference. By default, Premiere plays back at 8 bits.

When you pause playing, the frames are reprocessed at 32 bits. If you turn on "**High-Quality Playback**" in the Program Monitor Wrench menu, you can change this behavior so that it always stays 32-bit. This needs more computer power, but banding will show up at 8-bit with HDR media for sure. There is also a new Project setting that lets you choose the HDR Graphics White point. The three options are 100 (old SDR), 203 (new de facto standard), and 300 (very bright). Setting it to 203 will make your SDR content match your HDR media better. Until you play around with color fixing, editing is pretty much the same. The Lumetri Scopes screen should instantly be set to Rec.2100, but you might need to change the scale in the bottom right corner to HDR.

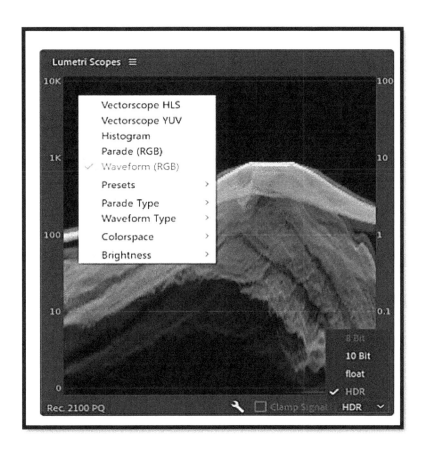

The scale on the right changes to a logarithmic scale. The normal range for SDR video is 0–100, the maximum range for most market HDR screens is 1000, and the possible maximum range for the format is 10,000. A lot of the Lumetri Color tools work the same way they do on SDR footage. However, some numbers may need to be set differently to get the same result as they would in SDR. You have to export your work in HDR format if you want to show it to other people when it's done.

You can share high-quality content with ProResHQ, ProRes444, JPEG2000, and X-AVC Intra, but most people will watch your HDR content from H.264 or HEVC files. Although H.264 is good for backward compatibility, most HDR-enabled devices can play HEVC files, which is a better codec. In either case, you need to turn on "Render at Maximum Bit Depth" and choose the "High10" setting so that the "Rec. 2020 Primaries," "High Dynamic Range," and "Include HDR10 Metadata" checkboxes can be used. We hope that one day there will also be an HLG export option.

PART VII
SPECIALIZED EDITING WORKFLOWS

CHAPTER 22
DOCUMENTARY EDITING TECHNIQUES
Storytelling through Documentaries

Documentaries are an interesting form of art that tells real-life stories in a way that is both engaging and powerful. They use a combination of visual elements, plot structure, and emotional connection. Strong video editing software called Adobe Premiere Pro is an important tool for filmmakers and documentarians who want to tell complex stories that touch people deeply. The Adobe Premiere Pro canvas gives writers a huge range of artistic options. The timeline tool makes it easy to arrange clips in a way that makes sense, which helps you tell a story that flows smoothly. Interviews, historical videos, and extra images are common parts of documentaries. Premiere Pro's easy-to-use design makes it easy to combine all of these different elements. Establishing a strong emotional link with the audience is one of the most important components of successful documentary storytelling. Premiere Pro gives producers the tools they need to change sound and images to evoke specific feelings. With color editing tools, you can set a specific mood, whether you want to use warm tones to remind you of good times or cold tones to show how harsh reality can be. The audio editing tools also give you fine control over background noise, music, and conversation, making sure that the story's emotional beats stand out.

An engaging documentary often gets its point across by putting together things that are very different from each other. The split-screen and multicam editing tools in Adobe Premiere Pro let you show different points of view at the same time, which helps the viewer's connect different parts of the story. By giving a more complete picture of the subject, this lively method improves storytelling. The pace of a documentary is very important for keeping people interested. The powerful editing tools in Adobe Premiere Pro, like the ability to precisely trim and rearrange clips, help you tell a story that flows well. The software can work with many file types and sizes, which makes it easier to combine different video sources and make sure the result looks clean and professional. When making a documentary, the story usually builds up slowly, showing different levels of complexity in the subject. To organize information, provide context, and lead the audience through the story as it develops, Adobe Premiere Pro's titles and graphics features are crucial. The motion graphics features of the program let you make beautiful opening sequences that make the whole watching experience better.

Working together is also an important part of making a documentary film, and Adobe Premiere Pro's ability to work seamlessly with other Adobe Creative Cloud apps makes the process easier for directors. For example, the interoperability of Premiere Pro and Adobe After Effects makes it possible to add complex visual effects that can give the storytelling a movie feel. Also, Adobe Premiere Pro's export options meet the wants of documentary producers in a variety of ways. The software lets you choose from some choices to make sure the result meets the standards of the industry, whether it's for online streaming services, television, or film events. In conclusion, Adobe Premiere Pro is a flexible and powerful tool for making documentaries that people will want to watch. Its powerful features let writers create stories that are visually stunning, emotionally powerful, and mentally stimulating. Real stories can come to life in Adobe Premiere Pro by careful cutting, skilled layering of elements, and attention to the little details of storytelling. This helps the audience feel more connected to the subject and the story.

Edit Documentaries in Premiere Pro

Create Vivid Still Photos

1. **Put your picture on the timeline and make changes to it.** First, bring your photo into the editing software and put it on the timeline. Change its size and position until it's where you want it to be.
2. **Set the first keyframe for Position**: Move the playhead (or player line) about 8 frames before the beginning of the clip. This is where you should set the first keyframe for the photo's Position property.
3. **Set the second keyframe and change the position**: Go back to the start of your clip and set the position of the second keyframe. Move things around so that the picture comes up from the top of the screen.
4. **Apply Ease In effect:** Right-click on the last Keyframe created (the one where the photo stops moving) and navigate to Temporal Interpolation > Ease In. This will give the movement a smoother transition.
5. **Access the Graph Editor:** Click on the downward arrow next to the Position settings to reveal the Graph Editor, which shows the trajectory of the movement.
6. **Create a curve in the Graph:** Adjust the handles of the second Keyframe in the Graph Editor. Drag the handle toward the first keyframe to create a curved trajectory, influencing the motion path of the photo.
7. **Gaussian Blur effect**: Look for the Gaussian Blur effect and add it to the picture. This effect will help make things look blurry.

8. **Keyframe the Blur effect**: Make keyframes for the Blur effect at the same points where you made keyframes for the Position animation.

9. **Adjust the first Blur Keyframe**: To set the initial blur level, change the setting of the first Blur keyframe to around 50 (or a number you like).

10. **Add sound effects**: To go with the video, add a sound effect of an old camera or projector. This audio effect can be timed to the motion to make the video more powerful as a whole.

Match Cut on Text

For interesting names in your project, the Match Cut on Text effect is a great option. The process can take a while, depending on how many pictures you want to use, but the result is worth it.

1. **Gather Text Examples**: Write or look for text that has the word or phrase you want to use. Take pictures or screenshots of at least 12 different examples of this text from different places, like books, websites, or written materials.

2. **Make Sure Text Positions Are Different**: Make sure the line or phrase you want to draw attention to shows up at different places on the page or paragraph, including in the pictures. When shown in the video sequence, this change will make it more interesting to look at.

3. If you want to use the pictures you've collected, you need to bring them into Adobe Premiere Pro and arrange them in the Timeline the way you want to use them.

4. To use rulers for alignment, go to the "**Show**" menu and pick "**Rulers**." To get a better sense of accuracy, line up the blue lines on the markers in the middle of your editing screen.

5. **Move Pictures to Get the Best Focus:** Move each picture so that the word or phrase you want to draw attention to is in the middle of the screen. This makes sure that the important text gets people's attention.

6. **Adjust Image Duration**: Change how long each picture in the timeline is. As the sequence goes on, slowly shorten the length of each picture, making the pace change from longer show times to faster shifts.

7. **Add Sound Effects**: At the start of each clip, add sound effects of a camera clicking in time with the picture cuts. This sound cue improves the visual change and makes the sequence more interesting.

8. **Nesting the Sequence:** To "nest" the sequence of pictures, right-click on all of them and choose "nest." This action puts the chosen pictures into a single nested sequence. This makes it easier to handle and change the sequence as a whole.

9. **Simplify Adjustments with Nested Sequence:** If you need to change the size or placement of text or pictures, you can do so within the nested sequence. By using this method, you can change the whole sequence at once instead of each picture separately.

Organizing and Structuring Documentary Projects

Using Adobe Premiere Pro's powerful features to ensure a smooth workflow and interesting storytelling is a dynamic process that includes organizing and planning documentary projects.

Here are the steps you need to take to organize and structure a documentary project in Adobe Premiere Pro:

1. Project Setup:
- **Create a New Project:** Launch Adobe Premiere Pro and initiate a new project. Set project settings such as frame rate, resolution, and scratch disk locations.

2. Media Organization:
- **Import Footage:** Use the Media Browser to import your footage into the project. Adobe Premiere Pro supports various file formats, ensuring flexibility.
- **Organize Bins:** Create bins to categorize your media assets. Organize footage into folders based on interviews, B-roll, and additional content.

3. Editing Workflow:
- **Timeline Structure:** Use the timeline to arrange your footage. Create a rough assembly by dragging and dropping clips onto the timeline in chronological order.
- **Labeling and Marking:** Utilize labels and markers to highlight significant moments or themes within the footage. This aids in quick navigation during the editing process.

4. Storyboarding and Sequencing:
- **Storyboard Panels:** Utilize the storyboard panels in the Adobe Premiere Pro interface to plan the visual sequence of your documentary.
- **Sequencing Clips:** Arrange clips in a logical order to tell a coherent and engaging story. Experiment with different sequences to find the most impactful narrative flow.

5. Transitions and Effects:
- **Transitions:** Apply transitions between clips to create a smooth visual flow. Adobe Premiere Pro offers a variety of transition effects.
- **Effects Panel:** Explore the Effects panel to enhance storytelling through visual effects, color grading, and adjustments.

6. Audio Management:
- **Import Audio:** Import and organize audio files, including interviews, ambient sounds, and music.
- **Audio Mixing:** Use the Audio Track Mixer to balance and enhance the audio elements. Ensure that the dialogue is clear and the music complements the mood.

7. Text and Graphics:
- **Text Layers:** Integrate text layers for titles, captions, and informational graphics. Use the Essential Graphics panel for easy text customization.
- **Lower Thirds:** Incorporate lower thirds to introduce interviewees or provide context.

8. Multi-camera Editing:
- **Multi-camera Sequence:** If applicable, use the multi-camera editing feature to sync and switch between multiple camera angles seamlessly.
- **Angle Selection:** Easily switch between different camera angles during the editing process.

9. Collaboration with Other Adobe Apps:
- **Dynamic Link:** Leverage the dynamic link feature to collaborate with other Adobe Creative Cloud applications like After Effects and Photoshop for specialized effects and graphics.

10. Export and Distribution:
- **Export Settings:** Choose export settings based on your distribution platform. Adobe Premiere Pro offers presets for various output formats.
- **Online Platforms:** Directly export and upload your documentary to online platforms or create a high-quality export for film festivals and broadcasting.

11. Project Backup:
- **Regular Backups:** Ensure regular project backups to prevent data loss. Adobe Premiere Pro provides auto-save features, but manual backups are also recommended.

12. Final Review and Feedback:
- **Test Screenings:** Conduct test screenings with a diverse audience to gather feedback.
- **Iterative Refinement:** Make adjustments based on feedback, fine-tuning your documentary for maximum impact.

By leveraging Adobe Premiere Pro's features throughout the entire documentary production process, you can efficiently organize and structure your project, resulting in a visually compelling and impactful story. The software's intuitive interface and extensive toolset empower filmmakers to bring their vision to life with precision and creativity.

Balancing Information and Entertainment

Balancing information and entertainment in video content is a delicate art, and Adobe Premiere Pro is a powerful tool that can significantly aid in achieving this balance. Whether you're creating educational content, documentaries, or any form of video where information dissemination is crucial, it's essential to keep your audience engaged.

Here are several tips and techniques to strike the right balance in Adobe Premiere Pro:

1. Storyboarding and Planning:
- Begin with a clear plan. Outline the key information you want to convey and identify the moments where entertainment elements can be integrated.
- Create a storyboard to visualize the flow of your video. This will help you allocate time for both informative and entertaining segments.

2. Dynamic Editing:
- Use dynamic and varied editing techniques to keep the visual experience engaging. Experiment with different cuts, transitions, and pacing to maintain viewer interest.
- Utilize Premiere Pro's built-in transitions and effects to add flair to your video without overshadowing the informational content.

3. Effective Use of Graphics:
- Incorporate graphics, text overlays, and animations to highlight key information. Adobe Premiere Pro offers robust tools for creating visually appealing titles and graphics.
- Ensure that graphics are clear, concise, and aligned with your overall style.

4. Audio Enhancements:
- Pay attention to audio quality and clarity. A well-mixed soundtrack can enhance the overall viewing experience.
- Experiment with background music or sound effects to create a mood without distracting from the information being presented.

5. Engaging Visuals:
- Incorporate engaging visuals such as charts, graphs, and relevant B-roll footage. Visual aids can make complex information more digestible and interesting.
- Leverage Premiere Pro's color correction and grading tools to enhance the visual appeal of your footage.

6. Narration and Scripting:

- Craft a compelling script that seamlessly integrates information and entertainment. A well-written script sets the tone for an engaging video.
- Use a confident and engaging narrator. The tone and delivery can greatly impact how information is received.

7. Interactive Elements:
- Implement interactive elements within your video, such as quizzes or clickable links for further information. This can enhance viewer engagement.
- Adobe Premiere Pro allows for the integration of interactive elements through plugins and external tools.

8. Consistent Branding:
- Maintain a consistent visual and tonal style throughout your video. This helps in establishing a brand identity and keeps the viewer connected.
- Utilize Premiere Pro's project management features to organize and streamline your workflow.

9. Test and Gather Feedback:
- After creating a draft, test your video on a sample audience to gather feedback. Adjustments can be necessary to ensure the right balance.
- Premiere Pro's collaboration features enable seamless sharing and feedback integration.

10. Accessibility Considerations:
- Ensure your video is accessible to a diverse audience. Use closed captions and subtitles to make the content available to those with hearing impairments.
- Adobe Premiere Pro provides tools for easy captioning and subtitling.

Post-Production Strategies for Documentaries

In the process of making a movie, post-production is very important. When it comes to documentaries, cutting methods must be used carefully to make the story interesting. Adobe Premiere Pro is a giant in the world of post-production.

It has a huge number of tools and features that are specifically designed to meet the needs of documentary filmmakers.

- **Logging and organizing**: The trip starts with carefully organizing the footage, which is one of the most important parts of post-production. The easy-to-use bin system in Adobe Premiere Pro makes this process easier. Editors can name and put clips into groups, which makes it easier to find clips in the large amounts of video that are usually gathered during documentary shoots. Adding information, tags, and marks makes it easier to find important parts of the video, which saves time during the editing process.

- **Story Structure and Scripting**: The most important part of making a documentary film is coming up with an interesting story. Using the writing and plot tools in Adobe Premiere Pro, editors can make a plan for their documentaries. The software lets you write a script right inside the project, which makes the change from planning to doing much easier. Editors can try out different ways of putting together stories to make sure that the final result gets the point across clearly.

- **Advanced Editing Techniques**: Adobe Premiere Pro has a lot of advanced editing tools that documentary filmmakers can use to turn raw video into a finished and interesting visual story. The timeline is a blank medium for precise editing. It lets producers cut, trim, and rearrange clips without any problems. Adding tools like the ripple edit tool makes changes easier, making sure that scenes run smoothly into each other. Also, the software allows multicam editing, which is very useful for documentaries where different cams record the same event from different points of view.

- **Color Grading and Correction**: To evoke feelings and improve storytelling, a documentary's visual tone is very important. The powerful color grading and correction tools in Adobe Premiere Pro let editors precisely change the way their footage looks. You can make small changes to color, contrast, and brightness on the Lumetri Color panel. The color wheels and curves give you even more control over how the documentary looks overall.

- **Audio Enhancement**: Effective storytelling goes beyond images, and Adobe Premiere Pro understands the importance of audio in documentaries. The software has a complete set of tools for changing audio, such as tools for getting rid of noise, adjusting the volume, and moving sounds around in space. Editors can easily add background noise, music, and voiceovers, creating a smooth sound experience that goes well with the visual story.

- **Adding Graphics and Animation**: Documentaries often use graphics and videos to show facts, figures, or historical background. Adobe Premiere Pro makes it easy to combine these parts without any problems. Within the program, editors can add graphics, text, and movements that are fun to watch. This feature gives the documentary a higher level of visual complexity, which makes it more powerful overall.

- **Collaboration and Versioning**: Working together is an important part of post-production, especially when making a documentary and a lot of different people are involved. The working together tools in Adobe Premiere Pro, like locking and versioning projects, make sure that everything runs smoothly and efficiently. Editors can work on different parts of the project at the same time, and the version history makes it easy to see what changes have been made. This makes it easier for team members to work together.

- **Output and Distribution**: After the video has been carefully edited, Adobe Premiere Pro gives you some file options that can be used on different platforms for release. By exporting their projects in different forms, sizes, and aspect ratios, editors can make sure that the documentary is best suited for airing on TV, online, or in theaters. Having Adobe Media Encoder included speeds up the export process and makes sure the result is of the best quality.

In conclusion, Adobe Premiere Pro becomes an important tool for documentary producers to have after the film is finished. Its flexibility, advanced features, and easy-to-use layout make it possible for editors to turn raw video into a powerful visual story. Documentarians can use Adobe Premiere Pro to its fullest extent and take their documentaries to new heights of storytelling greatness by adopting the techniques mentioned above.

CHAPTER 23
MULTI-CAMERA EDITING

You can edit video of the same scene or subject that was shot from different cameras and views. This is called multicam editing. You can make the video more interesting to watch by showing the same scene or subject from different points of view. This method can also be used to show the same picture from various points of view. Music videos, soap shows, reality TV, live performance records, business videos, and weddings all use more than one camera.

Simple Steps to Multi-Camera Editing

Step 1: Create a Multi-Camera Source Sequence

Make a bin (Premiere Pro's word for a box) called "Multi-Cam" in your Project Panel and put all of your video clips from different angles inside it.

I have three camera views, and I've given each one a name:

- Cam 1 (this one contains the high-quality audio track)
- Cam 2
- Cam 3

Audio Tip: If you're editing with more than one camera, I suggest that you take sound from all of them and put the high-quality audio track on one of them. To edit a multi-camera source sequence, you need at least one camera angle with high-quality audio. The other views can have bad quality, like on-camera sound.

Select "Create Multi-Camera Source Sequence" from the Context menu by right-clicking on the bin (or ctrl+click on a Mac). When you do this, the Multi-Camera Source Sequence dialogue box will appear.

Here is where you can pick how to mix the video clips from different cameras. You can put clips together by in-and-out places, timecodes that match, or audio waves. I'm going to use Premiere Pro's advanced audio-sync waveform tool to put the clips together now. After you click "Audio," you need to pick the Audio Sequence Settings.

You can choose from these three options:

- **Camera 1:** When this setting is used, all video clips will be synced with the audio track from camera 1. The audio tracks from the other cameras will be muffled. As a result, throughout your multi-camera source sequence, the audio from camera 1 will be dominating and steady.
- **All cameras**: All of the audio tracks from the video clips will be mixed in this setting.

- **Switch Audio**: If you want each camera angle to use its source audio, this setting is great. While revising (see Step 4), if you choose Camera Angle 2, you will hear audio from that angle. If you then choose Camera Angle 3, you will hear audio from that angle, and so on.

I don't want to choose the "Switch Audio" option in this case because the high-quality audio track I want in my end video is only in Camera Angle 1. I also don't want to choose "All Cameras" because I don't want to hear the audio tracks from other rooms. So that all camera angles will sync with the audio from Camera Angle 1, I'm choosing the "Camera 1" option.

Step 2: Create a Multi-Camera Target Sequence

You can change and switch between different camera views in the target sequence. Right-click on the new multi-camera source sequence in the Project Panel and select "New Sequence from Clip" from the Context menu to make a target sequence from the multi-camera source sequence. Just double-click on this sequence to open it and start making changes.

3. Enable Multi-Camera Editing in the Program Monitor

To start editing, click on the "+" button in the Program Monitor and drag the "Toggle Multi-Camera View" icon to your toolbar. This will turn on multi-cam editing mode. To turn it on, click on it.

- **Quick Tip:** You can also enable the multi-camera editing mode using the keyboard shortcut Shift+0.

There will be two windows in the Program Monitor once you are in multi-camera editing mode. You can see all of the camera views in the multi-camera source sequence in the left window. There should be three camera angles there right now. By choosing "Edit Cameras" from the Source Monitor's pop-up menu, you can also reorder the camera views to change the sequence order or turn them off. The finished video will look like what you see in the right window, which is the combined goal sequence.

You will only see Camera Angle 1 if you skip through the sequence right now since we haven't told it to switch to a different angle yet.

Step 4: Editing and Switching Camera Angles

To start, press the spacebar to play the sequence. Then, click on the camera point you want to see in real-time based on the time code you chose.

- **Editing Tip:** To change directions, press the number keys on your computer. 1. For Camera Angle 1. 2. for Camera Angle 2. 3. For Camera Angle 3. Finally, for Camera Angle 4.
- Change between the views over and over until you get the sequence you want. To stop, press the spacebar when you're done. If you zoom in on the sequence, you'll see that Premiere Pro has cut and pasted the new angle for each timecode you chose. Multiple camera magic!

5. Adjusting and Refining Your Multi-Camera Target Sequence

Use the Rolling Edit tool to change and improve cuts. Choose the rolling edit tool from the menu or press "N" to start it. Then, select the cut and roll it to the timecode you want in the sequence.

Or, let's say you want to switch from Camera Angle 2 to Camera Angle 3. You can change the angle by clicking on the clip in the sequence and pressing the number of the angle you want to use. It's really that simple! Finally, go ahead and add any effects that you want to the sequence, like color correction, music, or transitions, just like you would with any other Premiere Pro sequence.

Synchronizing and Switching Between Camera Angles

Use the number keys on your computer to change the video in real-time while you're playing. It's really simple: pressing number 1 will bring in view camera 1, pressing number 2 will bring in view camera 2, and so on. Simple, right?

Change between the camera views as many times as you need to until you get the effect you want. Press the spacebar to end. You will notice that Premiere Pro has cut and pasted the new camera views for each timecode you chose if you look closely inside the timeline. This is the magic of multiple cameras!

PART VIII
CAREER AND INDUSTRY INSIGHTS

CHAPTER 24

BUILDING A PROFESSIONAL EDITING PORTFOLIO

Selecting and Showcasing Your Best Work

One important part of making a name for yourself as a video maker is putting together an impressive portfolio of your best work. There are many tools and features in Adobe Premiere Pro that can help you make a beautiful reel that shows off your skills, imagination, and flexibility.

Here is a step-by-step guide on how to use Adobe Premiere Pro to choose and show off your best work.

1. Organizing Your Portfolio:
Before diving into Adobe Premiere Pro, carefully curate your portfolio. Select a diverse range of projects that showcase your proficiency in different styles, genres, and technical aspects of video editing. Ensure that your portfolio reflects both your creative flair and technical expertise.

2. Gathering High-Quality Footage:
The success of your showcase relies heavily on the quality of your footage. Gather high-resolution clips that exemplify your best work. Use Adobe Premiere Pro's robust import features to bring your footage into the editing environment.

3. Creating a Project in Adobe Premiere Pro:
Open Adobe Premiere Pro and create a new project. Organize your workspace by creating bins for different types of footage or projects. This step ensures a systematic and efficient editing process.

4. Setting the Tone with an Intro:
Start your showcase with a captivating intro that reflects your style. Use Adobe Premiere Pro's motion graphics templates or create custom animations to introduce yourself and set the tone for what viewers can expect.

5. Sequence Organization:
Create a master sequence where you'll assemble your showcase. Use nested sequences for individual projects to maintain a well-organized timeline. This allows for easy navigation and fine-tuning.

6. Trimming and Cutting:

Begin the editing process by trimming and cutting your footage. Remove any unnecessary or less impactful segments to keep your showcase concise and engaging. Adobe Premiere Pro's razor tool and trimming features simplify this task.

7. Highlighting Your Skills:

Showcase a variety of editing skills such as pacing, storytelling, and creativity. Use Adobe Premiere Pro's effects and transitions judiciously to enhance the visual appeal. Highlight specific techniques or unique approaches that distinguish your work.

8. Incorporating Audio:

Pay attention to the audio quality in your showcase. Adobe Premiere Pro allows for precise audio editing. Ensure that your music or voiceovers complement the visuals and contribute to the overall storytelling.

9. Color Grading:

Consistent color grading enhances the visual cohesiveness of your showcase. Utilize Adobe Premiere Pro's Lumetri Color panel to achieve a polished and professional look. Ensure that the color grading serves the narrative and style of each project.

10. Adding Text and Graphics:

Integrate text and graphics to provide context or additional information about each project. Adobe Premiere Pro's text tools and essential graphics panel enable you to create visually appealing titles and annotations.

11. Review and Refinement:

Regularly review your showcase to ensure a seamless flow and maintain viewer engagement. Seek feedback from peers or mentors and make refinements as needed. Adobe Premiere Pro's playback features facilitate this iterative process.

12. Exporting the Showcase:

Once satisfied with your showcase, use Adobe Premiere Pro's export settings to create a high-quality video file. Consider multiple export formats to accommodate different platforms or delivery requirements.

13. Creating a Demo Reel:

For a more condensed version, consider crafting a demo reel that encapsulates the essence of your work in a shorter duration. Adobe Premiere Pro's timeline tools make it easy to create a dynamic and impactful reel.

What is a demo reel?

A demo reel is a short video that actors and filmmakers put together of their best on-screen clips. A typical demo clip is about two minutes long or less because its only purpose is to show the range of the maker through a collection of short videos. For their demo reel, actors may use scenes from a range of types of work, such as drama, comedy, historical drama, or parody. Editors or animators may use clips from a variety of projects they've worked on. They show this video to casting directors, agents, and producers to show how talented they are and how long they've been working in the business.

Why are demo reels important?

Demo reels are an important part of an actor or director resume because they show off their skills and range. As part of the screening and application process for many projects in the film business, people are asked to send in demo reels. You will almost certainly need a demo reel if you are trying to find an agent, which is a person who specializes in finding projects for entertainment workers to work on. Before moving you forward in the casting or hiring process, agents and directors want to know what you specialize in, how much experience you have, and how talented you are.

Demo reel examples

Here are some examples of what different entertainment professionals might include in their demo reels:

On-screen actor

A normal demo reel for an actor on television can include a variety of clips from various acting projects. You could use clips from projects where you had to act in different types of roles, like drama or comedy. When you pick clips, try to pick the ones that you think best show how good an actor you are. This is a chance to show how versatile you are as a talent and how well you can handle different styles and themes.

Filmmaker

If you're a director or editor, clips from your different projects might be on your demo reel. If you're good at a certain kind of movie, like science fiction or horror, you might want to include clips that show off your cutting and art skills for those types of movies. You can also add clips from other projects you edited or directed, like commercials, ads, or videos of special events, like a wedding.

Animator

If you're an artist, your demo reel should show off your drawing skills. You can do this by adding clips of what you think are your best works of art. When picking clips for your demo reel, you might want to pick ones that show how versatile you are as an artist. For instance, you might have worked on a very realistic video game that you can use on a different animation project that has a more fun, kid-friendly style.

Voice actor

Whether you're a voice actor or not, your demo reel should show off your singing ability. You can include voice-overs for ads, TV shows, documentaries, or movies, among other types of work. When putting together a demo, it can help to include the real clips where your voice was used, even if you're not in the shot. Putting this in context can help the casting director or agent who is watching your demo understand what you are doing in each clip.

Crafting a Demo Reel

In the highly competitive world of video editing, one of the most important things you can do to demonstrate your talents and leave a lasting impression is to create a demo reel that is going to attract people's attention. You can create a demo reel that successfully showcases your knowledge, originality, and variety with the help of Adobe Premiere Pro, which offers a powerful platform for these purposes.

This is an in-depth tutorial that will walk you through the process of creating an engaging demo reel using Adobe Premiere Pro:

Crafting an attention-grabbing demo reel is a crucial aspect of showcasing your skills and making a lasting impression in the competitive world of video editing. Adobe Premiere Pro provides a robust platform for creating a demo reel that effectively highlights your expertise, creativity, and versatility.

Here's a comprehensive guide on crafting a compelling demo reel using Adobe Premiere Pro:

1. Define Your Purpose: Before diving into Adobe Premiere Pro, clarify the purpose of your demo reel. Are you targeting a specific niche or industry? Understanding your audience helps tailor your reel to their expectations.

2. Curate Your Best Work:

Select a diverse range of your absolute best work. Choose clips that demonstrate a variety of editing skills, from storytelling and pacing to visual effects. Ensure the selected clips align with the goals of your demo reel.

3. Storyboarding and Structure:

Plan the structure of your demo reel. Create a storyboard or outline that outlines the flow of the reel. Adobe Premiere Pro allows you to organize your clips systematically on the timeline.

4. Create a Dynamic Intro:

Grab your viewer's attention with a dynamic and engaging intro. Use Adobe Premiere Pro's motion graphics templates or create a custom animation that reflects your style. Keep it short and impactful to set the tone for the rest of the reel.

5. Pacing and Variety:

Pay attention to the pacing of your demo reel. Keep it dynamic and engaging by avoiding long, monotonous segments. Ensure a good balance of different styles and genres to showcase your versatility.

6. Transitions and Effects:

Use Adobe Premiere Pro's transition effects judiciously to smooth transitions between clips. Experiment with creative effects, but avoid overusing them. The goal is to enhance the overall viewing experience without overshadowing your work.

7. Music and Audio:

Select a fitting background music track that complements the overall mood of your reel. Ensure that the audio levels are balanced, and consider using Adobe Premiere Pro's audio editing tools to enhance the sound quality.

8. Showcase Editing Techniques:

Highlight specific editing techniques that set you apart. This could include innovative cuts, seamless transitions, or any unique approaches you've employed in your projects. Adobe Premiere Pro's editing tools provide ample opportunities for creative expression.

9. Color Grading:

Maintain a consistent and polished look by applying color grading to your clips. Adobe Premiere Pro's Lumetri Color panel allows for precise control over color correction and grading. Ensure a cohesive visual style throughout the reel.

10. Text and Graphics:

Integrate text and graphics strategically to provide context or additional information about each project. Use Adobe Premiere Pro's text tools and essential graphics panel to create visually appealing titles and annotations.

11. Create a Seamless Flow:

Ensure a seamless flow between clips. Use Adobe Premiere Pro's timeline tools to finesse the pacing, timing, and overall coherence of your reel. Smooth transitions contribute to a professional and polished presentation.

12. Review and Refinement:

Regularly review your demo reel and seek feedback from peers or mentors. Make refinements as needed to ensure that every second of your reel contributes to showcasing your skills effectively.

13. Exporting and Delivery:

Once satisfied with your demo reel, use Adobe Premiere Pro's export settings to create a high-quality video file. Consider exporting in different formats to accommodate various platforms or delivery requirements.

Building an Online Presence

1. Understanding Your Audience: Before diving into video editing, it's crucial to define your target audience. Understand their preferences, interests, and the platforms they frequent. This information will guide your content creation and help you tailor your videos to resonate with your audience.

2. Developing a Content Strategy: Outline a content strategy that aligns with your goals and resonates with your audience. Consider the type of content you want to create—whether it's educational, entertaining, or promotional. Develop a consistent theme or style that sets your content apart.

3. Video Planning and Scripting: Effective videos often begin with careful planning and scripting. Outline your video's structure, including an engaging introduction, informative or entertaining content, and a compelling call to action. This planning phase is essential for a smooth editing process.

4. Adobe Premiere Pro Basics: Familiarize yourself with the basic features of Adobe Premiere Pro. Learn to import media, arrange clips on the timeline, apply transitions, and use effects. Mastering the software's fundamentals will enable you to edit videos seamlessly.

5. Enhancing Visual Appeal: Adobe Premiere Pro offers a range of tools to enhance the visual appeal of your videos. Experiment with color grading, adjust exposure and fine-tune your footage to create a polished look. Consistency in visual style can contribute to a recognizable brand image.

6. Incorporating Graphics and Text: Integrate graphics and text elements to enhance the storytelling aspect of your videos. Adobe Premiere Pro provides tools for adding titles, captions, and other graphical elements. Well-designed graphics can reinforce your brand and convey information effectively.

7. Audio Enhancement: Pay attention to audio quality, as it significantly impacts the viewer's experience. Use Adobe Premiere Pro to clean up audio, add background music, and synchronize sound with visuals. Clear and well-balanced audio is crucial for maintaining audience engagement.

8. Branding Elements: Consistent branding is key to building a recognizable online presence. Incorporate your logo, color scheme, and other brand elements into your videos. This not only reinforces brand identity but also establishes a cohesive visual language across your content.

9. Optimizing for Online Platforms: Understand the specifications and requirements of different online platforms. Adobe Premiere Pro allows you to export videos in various formats and resolutions. Tailor your content to each platform to maximize visibility and engagement.

10. Engaging with Your Audience: Building an online presence goes beyond content creation. Actively engage with your audience through comments, messages, and social media. Foster a sense of community around your content to encourage ongoing interaction.

Frequently Asked Questions (FAQs)

What is Premiere Pro?

Premiere Pro is a video editing program that was created by Adobe and is known for its unique and powerful features. It functions as a full toolset that gives users the ability to produce, edit, and improve videos by using a broad variety of advanced features and tools. Premiere Pro gives developers, filmmakers, and video fans the ability to create contents that are both visually appealing and compelling. It does this by providing a user-friendly interface in addition to editing features that are compatible with professional editing software.

What are the minimum system requirements to run Premiere Pro?

When using Premiere Pro, it is essential to fulfill the minimum system requirements to guarantee a smooth and optimum performance when using the program. A 64-bit multi-core CPU is required for effective processing; compatibility with Windows 10 (64-bit) version 1809 or later, a minimum of 8 gigabytes of random-access memory (RAM) to meet the processing needs of the program, and a minimum of 8 gigabytes of accessible hard-disk space for installation are also required. During the installation process, it is essential to pay attention to the fact that more free space is required, and the program cannot be loaded on flash storage devices that are detachable. It is also essential to have a display resolution of 1920 by 1080 (at a scale factor of 100%), a sound card that is compatible with the ASIO protocol or the Microsoft Windows Driver Model, and an Internet connection to activate the product and download content to have the best possible experience.

Where can I get a trial version of Premiere Pro?

Accessing a trial edition of Premiere Pro is a simple and straightforward process when using the official website for Adobe Premiere Pro. Users have the opportunity to have a personal experience with the program via the trial version, which gives them the chance to investigate the product's broad capabilities and features before committing to using it.

How can I purchase Premiere Pro?

Through the official Adobe Premiere Pro website, the process of purchasing Premiere Pro is a simple and easy one. The website guarantees a smooth and safe transaction, enabling customers to purchase the software license and get unrestricted access to the program's collection of tools and features for use in their video editing projects.

What is the difference between Premiere Pro and Premiere Elements?

Both Premiere Pro and Premiere Elements are designed to meet quite different editing requirements and user groups. Filmmakers, television broadcasters, and other professionals in the video industry are the primary users of Premiere Pro, which is a complex and professional-grade video editing program. It provides powerful tools and functionality for editing very difficult jobs. Premiere Elements, on the other hand, is designed for home users and amateurs, and it offers a more user-friendly interface as well as simpler tools that are ideal for basic video editing tasks.

What is the cost of Premiere Pro?

As a result of Premiere Pro's subscription-based business strategy, consumers have the option of selecting either a monthly plan that costs $20.99 per month or an annual plan that costs $239.88 per year. With these subscription levels, you will have access to the whole set of tools and capabilities that Premiere Pro has to offer.

What are some alternatives to Premiere Pro?

Alternatives to Premiere Pro include some other powerful video editing software options, such as Final Cut Pro, DaVinci Resolve, and Avid Media Composer, amongst others. Every one of these options comes with its collection of features and functions, making it possible to meet a variety of editing needs and preferences according to the user.

What is the best computer for running Premiere Pro?

Adobe advises utilizing a machine that satisfies the minimum system requirements to get the best possible performance while running Premiere Pro with the software. This entails having a CPU with a minimum of 16 gigabytes of random-access memory (RAM), a strong graphics card (NVIDIA or AMD) with a minimum of 4 gigabytes of video memory (VRAM), and a minimum of 16 gigabytes of RAM. Having a computer that satisfies these requirements will guarantee that your editing experiences are more fluid and that your performance will be enhanced.

What is the difference between Premiere Pro and After Effects?

The primary purpose of Premiere Pro is to serve as a video editing program that focuses on organizing, cutting, and improving video contents. To put together video clips and use a variety of editing methods, it is used. After Effects, on the other hand, is a program that is specifically designed for motion graphics, the production of visual effects, animation, and compositing. When used in combination with Premiere Pro, it is a great tool for more sophisticated post-production activities since it is used to build elaborate special effects, construct animations, and develop visually attractive features to improve videos. In addition, it is used to enhance videos.

Recommended Plugins and Extensions

The video editing program known as Adobe Premiere Pro is an excellent piece of software. There are a variety of good tools for both video and audio that can help you get started and guarantee that you can generate material of the highest possible quality, regardless of whether you are a novice or an experienced expert. Adobe Premiere Pro continues to be one of the most well-liked and widely used pieces of video editing software, even though there are competing programs such as Final Cut Pro and Avid Media Composer. It is important to note that not every video package includes every tool that you could need. Although Adobe Premiere Pro is loaded with excellent editing tools, there are instances when you will want an additional tool that is not included. The plug-ins are what come into play here. Plugins provide you the ability to increase the number of tools that are accessible inside Adobe Premiere Pro. It doesn't matter whether you're looking for a straightforward one-shot effect or something that's considerably more complicated; there is a vast selection of third-party plug-ins accessible, and you can get them for free or for a fee. Some of these are added to a video clip or project to improve its quality and ensure that your audio clips continue to sound as magnificent as they possibly can. When it comes to plug-ins, the choices are almost limitless but also quite diverse. On the other hand, since there are so many plug-ins accessible, it can be challenging to explore and locate what you need. To add even more confusion to the situation, there are both free and commercial plugins available for usage with Premiere in Pro.

Best Plug-ins for Adobe Premiere Pro (Free and Paid)

1. Knoll Light Factory

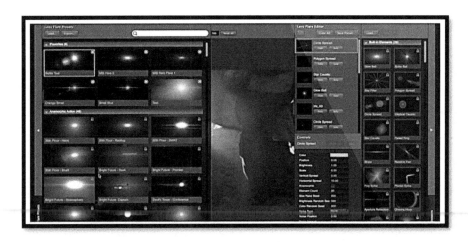

Your videos can go from being merely alright to being extremely breathtaking if you pay attention to the lighting and make it perfect. You might think of Knoll Light Factory as a magical tool that assists you in accomplishing this goal. On the other hand, it is similar to having a collection of really interesting lighting effects at your disposal, which you can utilize to make your videos appear incredible. You can build a wide variety of lighting effects and flares that look awesome using Knoll Light Factory. These effects will help your videos stand out from the crowd. Regardless of the kind of video you are creating, you can apply these effects since they have a very natural and strong appearance. What is the most enjoyable aspect? These effects can be modified to meet your specific requirements in a variety of ways. You don't need to get a large quantity of them if you just desire one or two of them. By allowing you to pick and select the effects that you want, you can save money while still achieving the precise appearance that you are looking for. This tool is comparable to a professional when it comes to the process of producing stunning lighting effects for videos. Simply said, the outcomes that it produces are extraordinary. **The positive aspects of it are as follows:**

Pros:

- **Super High-Quality Results:** The effects that you get from this tool look like they were made in a professional studio. They're that good.
- **It's Quick:** Even though the effects look awesome, it doesn't take forever to make them. It's pretty fast.
- **Lots of Different Lights:** You've got a whole range of cool lighting options to choose from. You can pick what suits your video best.
- **You Can Buy Only What You Need:** Instead of buying a bunch of stuff you don't need, you can just get the specific effects you want. Saves money!

But, there's a little downside:

Cons:

- **It's Not Cheap:** Unfortunately, this cool tool comes at a price. It might be a bit expensive for some people.

If you pay $99.00 a month (paid annually), you will get access to all of the cool effects. Don't worry, however, since there are a variety of price plans available, and you can choose the one that is most suitable for your requirements and financial constraints.

2. Motion Array

Motion Array stands as an alternative catering to those on a different financial scale. Rather than being only a tool, it is a full hub for collaborative work that is accessible to anybody interested in the fields of video creation and post-production initiatives. Even if it provides a wide variety of resources, such as stock footage, stock audio, and other things, the Adobe Premiere Pro plugins that they provide are the primary focus of our attention since they are especially exciting. The plugins in question are known as video presets, and they are libraries of pre-saved visual effects that are developed specifically for use in video editors. They enable users to quickly apply particular appearances or styles to their videos without having to go into complicated settings, which is a huge time saving for the users.

To avoid the effort of manually adjusting the settings, all you need to do is choose the preset, apply it, and you are good to go. These presets support a broad range of activities, ranging from simple lettering and graphic design for titles to more difficult jobs such as mimicking camera shaking or including unique transitions between clips. These presets cover a wide spectrum of functionalities. Users can replicate the nostalgic colors of early cinematic color processes or the retro appeal of VHS tapes by using the options that are available in Motion Array's library, which gives options to imitate a variety of film stocks. There are a plethora of options to investigate thanks to the amazing size of Motion Array's collection, which is a stunning expanse. Users can experiment with a variety of presets to get the visual styles that they choose, thus the only thing that can restrict them is their creativity.

Pros:
- **Extensive Array of Presets:** The availability of a vast number of presets grants users a wide array of options to choose from for their video editing needs.
- **User-Friendly Interface:** Motion Array's interface is designed for easy navigation and hassle-free usage, ensuring a straightforward experience for users.
- **Comprehensive Resource Pool:** Besides plugins, Motion Array offers an incredible resource repository, including stock footage and music, catering to various creative demands.
- **Regular Updates:** The library is not stagnant; Motion Array frequently adds new assets, ensuring users have access to fresh content beyond a static collection.
- **Valuable Investment:** Users find the subscription to be worthwhile, given the wealth of resources and benefits it offers.

Cons:
- **Overwhelming Options:** The sheer abundance of options might overwhelm users, making it challenging to determine where to start amidst the extensive selection.

For those interested in the cost, a membership to Motion Array can be purchased for $29.99 per month or $19.99 per month if paid yearly. The plugins and all of the other resources that are included within Motion Array are available to members at no extra cost, which makes it a solution that is both comprehensive and cost-effective for those who create videos.

3. FilmConvert

FilmConvert stands out among plug-in sets that are specialized for recreating certain film stocks. It provides users with the ability to imbue their video with not just genuine grain but also precise color profiles that are similar to the film stocks that they wish. This tool makes the procedure easier to understand by giving an interface that is easy to use while still holding a wide variety of parameters for users who are interested in fine-tuning additional configurations beyond the default settings. FilmConvert gives customers the ability to precisely modify their film to their tastes by providing a variety of editing options, including the ability to alter lighting levels, manipulate gradients, and manipulate median tones. The support that FilmConvert provides for a wide range of camera types is what sets it apart from other similar programs. This allows users to produce a wide range of styles, ranging from old and classic aesthetics to current and digital images, which ensures flexibility in visual storytelling. The speed with which it renders is another factor that contributes to its allure. When users can save significant time that would otherwise be spent waiting for results, they express their appreciation for the quick rendering process. When it comes to achieving the required visual style for a project, FilmConvert demonstrates that it is a reliable ally by giving full coverage and much more than that.

Positives:

- **An Extensive Selection of Options**: FilmConvert provides customers with a vast selection of options, which enables them to generate subtle and individualized effects for their movies.

- **Rapid Rendering**: Despite its extensive capabilities, FilmConvert functions quickly, producing effective results without forcing users to wait for an extended length of time.
- **User-Friendly Interface**: The tool finds a balance between complexity and simplicity, making it reasonably straightforward for users to explore and use. This is one of the tool's greatest strengths.

Diverse Camera Simulation: Supporting a variety of camera types, FilmConvert enables users to replicate a multitude of looks, spanning different eras and technologies.

Cons:

- **Limited Help Manual:** The available help manual might not provide extensive guidance, but the interface is intuitive enough for most users to navigate without much difficulty.
- **Priced Higher, but Justifiable:** Although considered expensive by some standards, the cost is reasonable considering the capabilities and value it brings to the table.

With regard to the cost, the Adobe Premiere Pro package for FilmConvert can be purchased for a total of $142. It is also possible to purchase comparable packages for DaVinci Resolve and Final Cut Pro at the same price. These bundles include features and functions that are identical across all aforementioned platforms.

4. Neat Video Noise Reduction

When it comes to the video capture process, the digital world is the most popular choice for the majority of artists. This can be accomplished using portable cameras, cellphones, or other devices. Given the current state of the digital world, it is of the utmost importance to own a noise reduction tool that can be relied upon, and Neat Video Noise Reduction is an exceptional option for producers who are looking to improve their films. By removing digital noise or improving visuals that may otherwise look fake or too digital, these plug-in functions as a sort of picture restoration. It can do both of these things. For example, it can alter film that was taken using a smartphone, giving it a more polished and professional image. Quite literally, all that is required to get started with this program is a few clicks, which is one of the most astounding aspects of this software. The automated profile is capable of handling the majority of jobs without any problems; however, individuals who need further control have access to a wide variety of modification choices. The plug-in offers a "Beginner" mode that is designed for novice users, as well as an "**Advanced**" mode that is geared toward more experienced users. Both modes give users access to a wide variety of settings. This disparity in modes can have a discernible effect on a variety of aspects of the video, ranging from the details in the background to the subtleties in the front, such as skin tones.

There is also a collection of presets included with Neat Video Noise Reduction, which makes it easier to control difficulties such as light flicker, dust and scratch removal, artifact corrections, and other similar concerns. It is sufficient for users to choose the appropriate preset, then click a button, and the problem will be remedied. The capacity to thoroughly clean up previously captured video has a huge impact on the quality of the final product. Neat Video Noise Reduction is a dependable tool that can be used by those who require support on their trip toward the quality improvement of video content.

Pros:

- **User-Friendly Interface:** The software boasts an astonishingly simple user interface, making it accessible to all levels of users.
- **Incredible Potency:** Despite its simplicity, the plug-in wields substantial power in enhancing video quality.
- **Wide Array of Presets:** Offering a diverse set of presets, it empowers users to address various video imperfections with ease.
- **Flexibility in Detail Enhancement:** Its flexibility extends to managing a wide spectrum of details, even in low-light conditions or shadowy areas.

Cons:

- **Rendering Time:** While not the fastest in rendering, the preview window facilitates decision-making before committing to changes.

Regarding pricing, Neat Video offers a free demo version. For the Adobe Premiere Pro license, the Home version costs $74.90, limiting resolution to 1920×1080, while the Professional version is priced at $129.90, offering higher resolution capabilities.

5. FlickerFree

Flicker is an annoying part of modern life that can get in the way of people who want to become filmmakers or video editors. There are many places where judder can come from, like bright lights or TV screens, either in drone video or time-lapse photos. Digital Anarchy's FlickerFree has been on the market for a long time and has earned its spot. Most types of flicker can be fixed with it, and the settings help with this. As an example, you could choose slow motion or stage lights as the cause of the flicker and then use the effect to fix it. Yes, there are a lot of settings, so if you want to learn more, it's simple to get your hands dirty and find the settings. Also, if you want to learn more, the FlickerFree website has a lot of guides that can help you. That being said, FlickerFree can't fix all Flicker problems, but it can fix or help with a huge number of them. You won't want to be without FlickerFree once you start using it. It can save footage that you might not be able to use otherwise. You can get a flicker-free video!

Pros

- Simple, effective tool that does what it sets out to do.
- Great range of presets.
- Fine control is easy to achieve.
- Genuinely impressive results.

Cons

- Slow to render.
- Very high-contrast areas for very high-speed objects can be a bit problematic, so it can't fix everything – it's not quite a magic bullet.

Cost

Trial software is completely free. $149.00 for the complete package.

6. Manifesto

If you want to show your video project interestingly, Manifesto can help. It improves the visual storytelling experience by making it easy to make interesting title rolls and slides that smoothly combine openings and end credits. After downloading, Manifesto can be accessed through the Adobe Premiere Pro Effects panel. It makes the process of making titles easier by giving users a variety of choices to customize text and fonts and make sure titles fit the style they want. The easy-to-use interface has simple scroll bars for changing the width and placement of elements horizontally and vertically. You can control these elements precisely by entering specific numbers or percentages based on the size of the screen. Manifesto also has a lot of different animation styles, so users can move text in any way they want. Users can change the fade-in and fade-out effects, which give the names more interesting movements. Aside from not being overly complicated, Manifesto's ease of use makes it possible for users to have creative power over an otherwise difficult part of their project without any problems.

Pros:
- **User-Friendly Interface:** The plug-in is very easy to use and makes it simple to make title slides that look great.
- **A Lot of Text Options:** Manifesto lets users change a lot of things about the text and fonts in titles, so they can make them exactly how they want them.
- **External Text Compatibility:** Manifesto can read RTF files and makes it easy to add external text, which makes managing text in the app easier.
- **Built-In Features:** The plug-in comes with motion blurring and de-flickering tools that make the titles look better overall.
- **Text Masking Capability:** The tool makes it easy to hide text, so users can decide how visible text is.

Cons:
- **Simplicity over Complexity:** Its simplicity is a strength, but some users may find that its features are restricted because it is so simple.

Manifesto is free, and so are all of its title production tools. This makes it an easy-to-use and cheaper option for people who make videos.

7. TimeBolt

When it comes to the arduous task of editing video or audio content, grappling with dead air—those periods of silence—stands as one of the most vexing challenges. TimeBolt strides onto the scene as a solution, aiming to simplify and expedite this otherwise time-consuming and tiresome aspect for video editors. The software works by reading your file on its own and carefully looking for any blank spaces. Once these parts are found, the software highlights them and gives users the option to follow its recommendations, look at them by hand, or make adjustments until they are happy with the results. TimeBolt is great at working with complicated sets and lots of clips at once. It's not just for videos; the program can also remove dead air from audio WAV files without any problems. It also lets users speed up or slow down a scene, add changes, and add their unique information to the background. TimeBolt is a tool that makes one of the most difficult parts of editing a lot easier. Editing can be very time-consuming and careful work.

Pros:
- **Easy-to-Use Interface:** TimeBolt has a design that makes it simple for people to use.
- Thoughtfully Designed Controls: The controls are well-designed, which makes the user experience better and makes edits go more smoothly.
- **A Variety of Tools:** The tools that are offered may seem easy, but they are very useful and have useful features.
- The TimeBolt successfully simplifies the editing process by removing dead air, which relieves editors of a major load.

Cons:
- **Feature Limitations:** While functional, it might lack the breadth of features present in more comprehensive editing tools.

Cost
- You can get your money back in 60 days if you don't like the basic plan, which costs $17 a month. There is a free version that only exports video (no audio) and has a label on it.

8. PluralEyes

There are times when the audio and video don't sync when you're moving a lot of them around. This is especially true when you have a lot of different video clips. This is when PluralEyes comes in handy for video makers. The PluralEyes tool can resync your video and audio clips. PluralEyes is superior to any built-in setting, even though many video editing programs will include an audio resync tool. It's so easy to use PluralEyes because a lot of the work is done for you. The software can easily look at video and audio files, figure out which ones are broken, and tell you how to fix them. It can also handle many cams and audio files at the same time, so you don't have to focus on just one sync problem at a time. You can also mix video clips that are timed and clips that aren't. When audio is out of time, it can be a real pain to fix, but PluralEyes makes the process stress-free and simple. A plug-in does everything you need it to do.

Pros

- Hugely powerful – really unmatchable.
- Better than any built-in option.
- Can handle numerous video and audio files simultaneously.
- Does exactly what it's supposed to, exactly how it's supposed to.

Cons

- System resource heavy.

Price

$299 as a standalone package. Free trials are also available.

9. Separate RGB

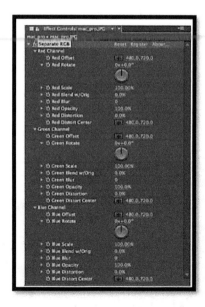

We're going to end our list of Adobe Premiere Pro plugins with a really simple tool that only does one thing. We kept it on the list because it's fun! As you might have guessed from the name, Separate RGB takes out the red, green, and blue colors from your video. Three different colors are used to separate the video, which is then shown next to each other. You don't have to stick to one pattern, though. You can blur, scale, fade, deform, and do anything else you want with the RGB channels. It also has a lens-distorting effect that can be used on one channel or all three. The "chromatic aberration" image is made by this. It will also allow you to use lens shake and other camera moves to give footage that would have been flat otherwise in real life. You can play around with the color channels in Separate RGB as much as you want, whether you want to spice up a fashion shoot or give your footage a cool, retro look. What they found is really cool!

Pros:
- You can change the RGB channels in any way you want;
- You can make really cool visual effects;
- Chromatic Aberration is now easy to get!

Cons:
- It's a bit of a trick, but it's fun!

Cost
- $39.99 one-off-cost.

How to Install Audio Plug-ins for Adobe Premiere Pro

Even though Adobe Premiere Pro video plug-ins is the best choice, it is also very important to make sure that your audio sounds good. Poor video can get by with perfect audio, but great video will always suffer from bad sound. In other words, you need to add more audio plug-ins to Adobe Premiere Pro. On both Windows and Mac, Adobe Premiere Pro works with VST and VST3 plugins. On Mac, it also works with AU plugins. First, get the plug-in and save it to your computer. The plug-in can be downloaded from the developer's site or any other place that has it. Choose Audio from the menu, and then click on the Audio Plug-in Manager. Click the Scan for Plug-ins option, then select the place where your plugins are saved. When you open Adobe Premiere Pro, it will look at the following files. If you want to keep your computer clean, you should copy this information into these folders. You can use any files you want, though.

- /<user>/Library/Audio/Plug-Ins/VST (MacOS)
- /Library/Audio/Plug-ins/VST (MacOS)
- C:\\Program Files\VSTPlugins (Windows)

The time it takes for Adobe Premiere Pro to scan and load the plug-ins may depend on how many you are trying to install. You can access the audio plug-ins after the import is complete by going to Effects, then Audio Effects.

Troubleshooting

Timeline Panel in Adobe Premiere Pro not working?

There are several potential reasons why you might encounter issues with your Timeline Panel in Adobe Premiere Pro. One common factor could be related to outdated software or potential bugs within the application. In such cases, it's advisable to check for any available updates or patches released by Adobe. Ensuring you have the latest version might resolve issues caused by software bugs. Another probable cause could stem from inadequate system specifications on your computer. If your device falls short of meeting the necessary system requirements for running Adobe Premiere Pro smoothly, it could result in software malfunctions, including problems with the Timeline Panel. Issues might also arise due to project-related factors such as corrupted files or incompatible formats. If your project files are damaged or incompatible with the software, it can lead to errors within the Timeline Panel. Similarly, incorrect project settings or preferences might trigger problems. Attempting to reset preferences or creating a new project can help determine if the issue persists due to these settings.

Fix the Premiere Pro Media Pending Error

Let's talk about the media pending. Yes, that annoying yellow box that won't go away. Sometimes having media waiting messages open for a long time can really slow down the editing process. It's possible to fix this annoying issue in some ways, so let's learn how to fix the Premiere Pro media waiting error. What you're seeing is the annoying little cousin of the red media offline warning. Media offline means that a clip is lost completely, usually because Premiere is looking for something in the wrong place or a file has been removed. Media waiting, on the other hand, means that there is a problem reading the data of your video files. It's possible that something was lost in translation, which can make updating take a lot longer. Don't worry—we have three ways to help you get there!

1. Turn off and then on again

First, try this fix. The fastest way to fix the media waiting mistake is to do this.

- Move the playhead to the clip that has the "media pending error" message.

- Highlight the clip by selecting it.
- Right-click on the click and uncheck **Enable** from the menu. This should disable the clip.
- Right-click on the clip and check the box next to Enable again. This should make it work again.
- You could also pick all the clips in the timeline with Ctrl+A or Cmd+A and do the same thing. This will turn off and on each clip in the sequence.

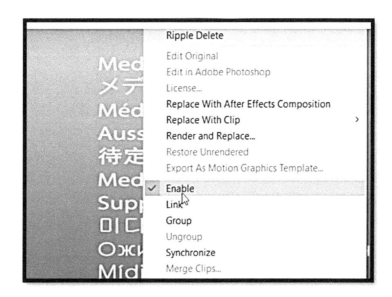

This should fix it, I hope! You can try one of our other options if that doesn't work.

2. Add a Cut

Adobe Premiere Pro will sometimes start up right away after you make a small, unnoticeable change to a clip or the timeline. Try making changes to the video that don't change how it looks, like cutting it.

- Move the playhead to the clip that has the "media pending error" message.
- To cut the clip, press Ctrl+K or Cmd+K.
- You can also use the Razor tool and click on any part of the clip to cut it.
- Do not change any of the times, and watch out that the cut is still there when you keep changing. You're only splitting the clip; nothing is moving.

This small change could be all it takes to get it going again.

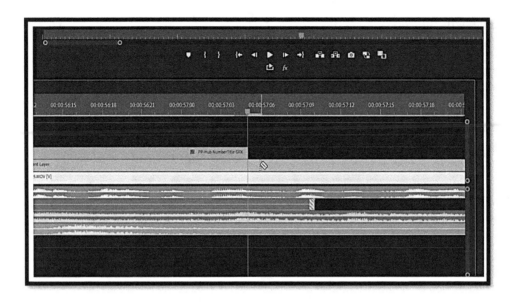

3. Adjust the Duration by One Frame

When you use this method, you only make small changes to your timeline by adding one frame to your clip.

- Choose the file that has the "media pending" message.
- Use **Ctrl++ or Cmd++** to zoom in on the timeline. Then, drag the end of the clip out by one frame.
- Use Ctrl+ or Cmd+ to zoom out again, and try the clip again.

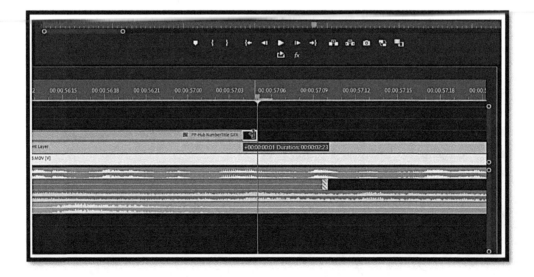

We're hoping that one of these solutions has fixed the problem. If this mistake hurts so much that you don't want to make it again. Don't worry—we have some helpful advice to keep this annoying mistake away.

How to Avoid the Media Pending Error

Some quick fixes can help, but to move forward, you need to figure out why the media pending mistake is happening. Once you know what caused it, you can take steps to make sure it doesn't happen again.

1. Dynamic Links & Nested Sequences
You might have seen problems with automatically linked video and stacked sequences more than any other type. Keep an eye out for those things in your feed first.

- When you're done making changes to footage that is automatically linked, choose Render and Replace to switch the project link for a rendered file.
- If you have sequences inside sequences, try setting the start and end points and saving only that part.
- **Re-import** the exported file.
- Change the sequence that is stacked. There's a dirty way to get around the problem, but sometimes you have to get it done quickly. Do it first, and then look into why it went wrong.

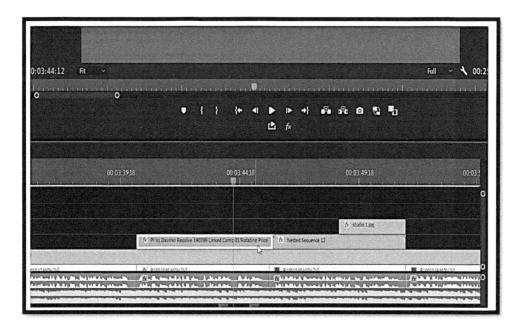

2. Replacing the Sequence

Still having trouble? A permanent media pending problem can be connected to the sequence rather than a clip in particular.

- Make a new sequence that is the same as the one you have now. If you right-click on the sequence, you can choose "New Sequence from Clip."
- Press Ctrl+C or Cmd+C to copy all the videos from the Media Pending timeline.
- To put it into the new sequence, press Ctrl+V or Cmd+V.

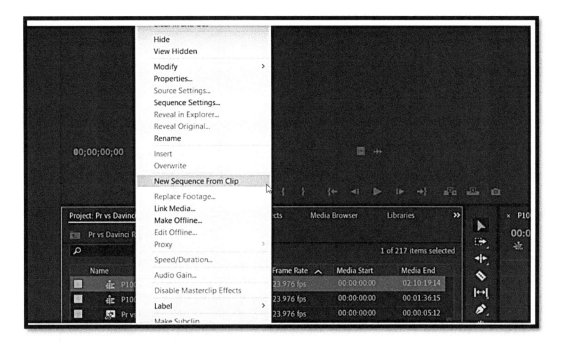

3. Getting rid of cache files

Small files called cache files and sample files are made by Premiere to speed up and smooth out the project. You can sometimes make them wrong, which causes a lasting Media Pending mistake.

To get rid of them, go to the back end of Premiere and delete them.

- To delete the media cache automatically, go to Edit > Preferences > Media Cache > Delete Unused Files.

There can be other things that are giving you trouble if this doesn't work. You can do this by hand by going to your computer's Media Cache Database. In a cache folder, these are generally clearly marked.

- Close Premiere Pro.
- Pick out all the files in the cache area by hand and delete them all. Don't worry about getting rid of the files; just make sure they're marked as cache.
- Open Premiere Pro again.

You might also want to try putting the cache on a different hard drive.

- Go to Edit > Preferences > Media Cache > Browse to find a new location.

4. Deleting/Removing Preview Files

Still no luck? Let's give the preview files a look.

- Close Premiere Pro.
- Find where you saved your project file, a **.prpoj file**.
- Go to the same place as before and look for the folder called Adobe Premiere Pro Video Previews.
- Just get rid of the files in that area.

- Open Premiere Pro again.

Fix Choppy Playback in Premiere Pro

Premiere is a very complicated piece of software, and it can be very annoying to keep running into bugs and other issues. Sometimes choppy playing doesn't stop you from changing, but it can make it hard to test. We're going to look at some possible reasons why your Premiere Pro playback is choppy and how you can fix it.

What to Check When Your Premiere Pro Playback Is Choppy

To fix the issue, it's good to try to figure out what caused it. Since Premiere is such a complex piece of software, it isn't always clear what's wrong.

- **Check your Hardware**: The first thing you should check is the gear on your computer. Does it meet the requirements for running Premiere Pro? You might not have a hardware problem if you've been working on your device for a while and choppy playing is a new problem. It could be a lack of room. Make sure there is enough space where you saved your project for it to open and run.
- **Check for Updates**: Both Premiere Pro and your system software will need to be updated regularly. Editing can go wrong if either is a little out of date. So, the first thing you should do if you're having problems with Premiere Pro is to see if there are any changes available.
- **Check the Sequence and Clip settings**. If the choppy playing is happening on a certain clip or group of clips, there can be a problem with the settings for the sequence and the settings for the clips. For instance, this happens a lot when you add 4K or 50+fps clips to a timeline sequence that has different options.

- To check the settings for a clip, select it in the timeline and go to the Info tab in the Inspector. It's possible that the choppy clip was shot with different settings than the rest of the sequence. You can either make a Proxy clip or separate the clip and export it to match the other footage.
- **There are too many open apps**: One simple problem could be that there are too many apps running on your device. Running Premiere Pro on a slow computer can be slowed down by even a simple web browser. Close as many programs as you can so that you can only use the ones you need for editing.
- **Turn It Off and On Again**: This works for most programs on all devices. Leading Edge can get lost sometimes. Resetting the program and gadget can help it figure out what its doing. Don't forget to save your work before you close the window.

How to Fix Choppy Playback in Premiere Pro

A lot of the time, Premiere Pro's choppy playing is caused by your project being too big or complicated for your device. There are, however, some ways to fix these lag problems right in Premiere.

Consolidate the Project

Having a clear and simple file format for your projects is always a good idea, and Premiere can have trouble if things get complicated behind the scenes. All of your files and videos will be in one place if you use the Premiere Consolidation tool. Putting together a project will let you pick out certain sequences and copy them to a new project in a different saved place. Many things are copied during the process, not just the sequence itself. Project consolidation is a great way to store projects and make them smaller at writing stages.

- Press "File" and then "Project Manager."
- Pick out the sequences you want to copy.
- Make sure you're copying everything you need by going through the other selection option.

- Click on the name of the file to change where it is saved.
- Click the "Calculate" button to find out how big the copy of the project will be.
- Click "OK" when you're done, and then wait for Premiere to finish the combination.
- Look for your new project and open it to keep updating.

GPU Acceleration

You can turn on GPU Acceleration for faster playing if your computer has a graphics card that is only used for video work.

- Open Premiere Pro. To turn on GPU acceleration, you can open any project.
- To open the project settings box, go to File > Project Settings > General.
- In the drop-down menu, change the Renderer to Mercury Playback Engine GPU Acceleration.
- Click "OK" to keep the changes.

Get rid of the media cache.

In the Media Cache folder, Premiere stores files that speed up your editing. These files should make playing smoother. Every time you play something in your project, Premiere Pro will keep adding files. The Media Cache is full of "helper files" that make playing smooth in Premiere. However, the Cache can fill up quickly, taking up a lot of room. When you clear your Media Cache, your Project will have to be rendered all over again. This can greatly improve speed.

Playback Resolution

If you don't choose, Premiere will play back your edit in the sequence settings, which are most likely 1080p or higher. Premiere doesn't have to show as much information for each Frame when the playing quality is lowered. This makes playing easier. In the bottom right area of your Media Viewer, there is a drop-down button that lets you change the size of the viewing.

Toggle Effects

If your project has a lot of effects, grades, or levels, the complexity can make the video jumpy. You can quickly turn off and on the effects for the whole sequence if you need to check how fast an edit is going.

- Look for a "**fx**" button in the menu at the bottom of the Media Viewer.

- Click the plus sign (+) if there isn't an Fx icon.
- In the pop-up box, find the fx icon and drag it to the Media Viewer menu. Once it's there, close the pop-up box.
- Click the "**fx**" button on the menu to turn on and off the effects on the timeline.

How to Fix Stuttering and Glitches Video in Premiere Pro

Many problems in Premiere don't make sense and for which there is no known solution. This quick fix is great for when you don't know what's wrong and have tried everything else.

- Save your work and close the project.
- Press Alt + Command/Control + N on your computer or go to File > New > Project.
- Save the new project in the same place and give it a name that lets you know this is the most recent version.

- Go to File > Import or press Command/Control + I. Then, look for your old Premiere Pro project in the finder window.
- Choose the project file and click "Import." Depending on the size of the project, this process can take time.
- Keep your new project in storage.
- Find the sequence in the Media Browser and open it. We're not sure why this works, but it can fix a lot of problems in Premiere Pro.

Relink Media That Is Missing

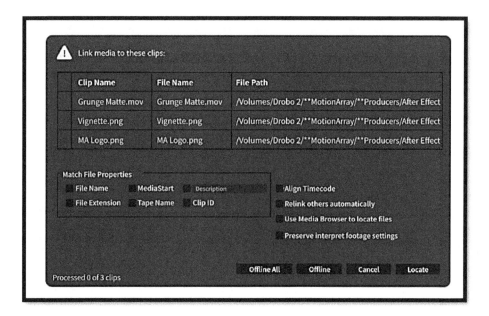

Don't worry if you start a project and see a message that says your media is missing. Let us show you the best way to fix these problems step by step:

When you try to open a project, sometimes it gives you an error because some files are missing.
- In the pop-up window that shows you the lost files, click on "**Locate**."
- On the left-hand side, you'll notice a bunch of folders. Navigate to your **Motion Directory** (this will be specific to what you've named it).
- Click **Search** in the bottom right corner of the chat box. When you search, your video files will be looked through to find the clip you want.
- Select the clip and click on OK once you've found it.
- If you click **OK**, all of the clips will be linked again.

- Adobe Premiere Pro will be able to find other files that might be lost in the same area while it does this. Everything will be fine if it finds all of them.
- If it doesn't, click on Locate again and look through all the folders again. Do this step again and again until you find all of your lost files. You should now be able to continue with your changes without any problems.

Resolve the Offline Error Message

If you already have a project open and see this message, it means that the media is offline. That can be fixed in this way:

- Click on the **Project** Panel.
- Look for the word "**Offline**" in the project panel. This is the best way to find offline media. This will show all the offline sources.
- From the search results, select all of the stored files.
- Click a third time and choose "**Relink**."
- The Find box will show up again.
- Following the steps above, click on **Find and Search** the main folder.
- Click OK when you find the file.
- This will make all the media work again, and you're good to go!

Glossary

Several terms will be used in this book that has to do with audio and video technology, especially with nonlinear post-production. **There are some things you might not know how to change if this is your first time.**

- **Alpha channel:** A nonvisible channel that defines the opacity of a pixel. This fourth channel is stored in a very similar way to the three visible color channels and can be adjusted in a multitude of ways using manual adjustments or visual effects. When you create a greenscreen effect, for example, Premiere Pro adjusts the alpha channel level for your selected pixels to allow a background to be visible.
- **Aspect ratio**: This shows how a picture is shaped by showing the ratio of width to height. 1:1 is a square. A lot of videos are 16:9. The frame will always have the same aspect ratio, no matter what the screen size or picture quality is. Both sequences and images indeed have an aspect ratio. Pixels are usually square, but some video types use pixels that aren't square.
- **Bin**: Bins work and look a lot like folders in the Finder (macOS) or Explorer (Windows). But they are only in the project file you are working on in Premiere Pro.

- **Bit depth**: Your media's bit depth determines how many steps there are between "fully dark" and "fully bright," or "from no blue at all to fully blue." It is the exact number of bits (0s and 1s) that are being used to store the data that is used to describe bit depth.

Scales that are multiples of 2 are made by bit depth, and each extra bit doubles the scale. Most video is 8 bit, which means it can go from very dark to very bright in 256 steps. A 10-bit video has 1024 steps, which is two bits more than an 8-bit video. It's crazy that a 16-bit video can handle 65,536 steps. Since these scales have to start at 0, the real numbers are 0–255, 0–1,023, and 0–65,535. **It's easier to keep high-quality images when using color correction methods to change the levels and avoid posterizing the image, which makes lines of color that can be seen.**

- **Clip**: In the world of media editing, a clip is simply a reference or pointer that points to a particular media file. It is similar to an alias or a shortcut at the same time. Many other kinds of material can be included inside these files, including video segments, graphics, audio tracks, and other forms of multimedia. In the same way that they behave and function as if they were the real media to which they are attached, clips display the features and qualities that are associated with the original file. These properties and details include information about the size of the picture, frame rates (fps), and other relevant characteristics. They play an important role in the development of media projects, serving as vital building elements that enable smooth integration and manipulation inside editing tools.
- **Codec:** The term "*codec*" is an abbreviation for "coder/decoder," and it refers to a technique that is used to store digital information, particularly audio and video. This technique often makes it possible to save data in a more compact form in comparison to its initial size. Codecs, which are analogous to shorthand writing, make it possible to compress data, so lowering the size of files and making storage and transmission more efficient. However, extra processing work is required to decode this compressed data. The majority of the time, video footage is captured by using certain codecs to reduce file sizes without a substantial loss in quality. However, there are instances in which some camera systems capture raw media, which preserves data without requiring considerable processing or compression.
- **Compression:** In the context of the media, compression is a concept that has two distinct dimensions of relevance. To begin, it is a term that describes the process of increasing the efficiency with which information is stored by making use of codecs (coders and decoders) to reduce the size of audio and video files. Through the use of this approach, it is possible to achieve more cost-effective storage and transmission

of media, all while preserving an acceptable degree of quality. The second meaning of compression is that it refers to the decrease in the dynamic range that exists between the loudest and quietest sections of the sound. By reducing the amount of volume variation that exists between levels, this method makes the overall audio level seem to be louder than it is.

- **Cut:** In the context of a sequence, a cut is a mark that indicates the moment at which one clip comes to an end and another begins. The word "cut" refers to a basic kind of transition between distinct parts within a sequence. Its origins can be traced back to the classic celluloid cinema editing process, in which actual film strips were physically cut and spliced together. It is one of the editing methods that is applied the most often because it provides a transition that is both direct and immediate from one clip to another on the screen.

- **Effect**: An effect is a method that is used to modify the visual look of multimedia content or to improve the quality of the audio that is included within it. Video and audio effects are used for a variety of reasons, including but not limited to the alteration of the form or visual features of an image, the adjustment of brightness or darkness levels, the animation of picture locations on a screen, the regulation of audio volume levels, and the implementation of a wide variety of additional improvements and changes. Because they provide creative tools that can be used to change and improve the visual and aural parts of the information, these effects play a crucial role in improving the overall presentation and storytelling within multimedia projects.

- **Export**: After you have assembled your video clips into a sequence inside Premiere Pro, the next stage in the creative process is to export this sequence to build a new media file that can be sent to a more extensive can choose a variety of factors during the export process, including the file format, the codec, and particular parameters that regulate the properties of the media file that is produced as a consequence of the export. During this s can modify the output in accordance with the platform or purpose for which it is intended, assuring compatibility and the necessary quality standards.

- **Footage**: Originally a term rooted in the measurement of film length (in feet), "footage" now broadly denotes the original video content captured during recording. Unlike measuring file size, footage typically quantifies the duration of video content in terms of hours and minutes. It encompasses the raw or unedited video content before any modifications, edits, or post-production enhancements are applied.

- **Format**: The word "format" can be interpreted in two different ways when it comes to the context of media. Even though it is usually used to identify the file type (such as AVI, MOV, MP4, etc.), its more comprehensive definition includes particular features such as frame size (picture dimensions), frame shape, pixel arrangement, and frame rate (measured in frames per second). These criteria, when taken together, determine how the visual content is organized and shown inside a digital environment. As a result, the quality, compatibility, and visual qualities of the media file are impacted.

- **Frame**: In the world of video, a frame is a full still picture that serves as the basic building block of visual content under its existence. Videos are a fast series of these discrete frames, which are shown at a rate that is sufficient to give the appearance of continuous motion. The frame rate, which is measured in frames per second (fps), is determined by the pace at which these frames are played back every second. This rate has a considerable influence on the fluidity and smoothness of motion within the video.

High Dynamic Range (HDR): This refers to the process of quantifying the brightness of a display panel using a variety of metrics, with the nit being the most popular unit of measurement. The term "High Dynamic Range" (HDR) refers to a display technology that, in comparison to conventional displays, provides a greater variety of brightness levels and contrast levels. At one point in time, the maximum brightness of home television displays was around 200 nits, and the maximum brightness of theater screens was approximately 100 nits. Greater dynamic range (HDR) displays, on the other hand, can achieve substantially greater peak brightness levels. This results in pictures that are more vibrant and realistic, with better contrast and a wider spectrum of colors. This ultimately results in a more immersive viewing experience. A measure of the overall range between the lowest level that will still display detail and the brightest level is what this can be taken to be in its most fundamental form. What is known as the Dynamic Range is the range that lies between the two. Standard Dynamic Range, sometimes known as SDR, is defined as a range that is about 200 units in magnitude. The term "High Dynamic Range," or HDR, was coined as a result of the fact that it became feasible to manufacture much brighter panels. The following is a description of a variety of technologies that can be used for cameras, editing systems, distribution standards, and displays that are capable of displaying up to 10,000 nits. It is important to note that the majority of home television sets that are referred to as high dynamic range (HDR) have a dynamic range of about one thousand nits. **This implies that you can make out the color and picture features of fireworks in the sky, as well as notice details in the shadows of a scene that is taking place at night.**

- **Import:** In Premiere Pro, importing a media file is the process of incorporating it into a project without physically transferring the data into the project file itself. Instead,

Premiere Pro generates links known as clips, which serve as references containing essential information about the media. These clips retain details such as file location, attributes, and characteristics of the media content. During editing, these linked clips are manipulated and combined to create the final sequence, allowing editors to work with diverse media assets without duplicating or moving the original data.

- **Keyframe:** A keyframe is a critical marker in the timeline that indicates a single instant in the flow of time when the value of a property, such as spatial location, opacity, or audio volume, is determined. Keyframes are used to show how the value of a property changes over time. Multiple keyframes are set by editors to orchestrate changes in a property over some time. The editors first mark the value of the property at the beginning of the intended alteration, and then another keyframe is set at the endpoint of the desired modification. Premiere Pro makes use of interpolation, which is an automatic process that occurs between keyframes. This causes the values of the property to transition and change seamlessly over time, which enables changes to occur in the media that is both gradual and fluid.

- **Media:** Media comprises both the original and newly generated content utilized within a project. This encompasses an extensive range of elements such as video files, graphics, photographs, animations, music, voice-overs, or specialized audio effects like sword clashes or explosions. It encapsulates all visual and auditory components, both raw and refined, employed in the creation of multimedia projects.

- **Metadata**: This is a term that describes supplementary information that describes the main data or content. Many different types of descriptive data are included in it. These data provide context, information, or qualities about the content that is related here. For instance, the metadata that is associated with a video file may include information about the camera system that was used during the recording process, the name of the camera operator, timestamps, geographical location, resolution, or any other relevant information that provides insights into the creation, composition, or characteristics of the content.

- **Pixel**: A pixel is the smallest individual unit or dot that makes up a digital picture that is shown on a display screen. The color values that are contained inside each pixel are often represented as a mix of red, green, and blue (RGB) hues; however, various color models can be used. The visual appearance of the pixel is determined by these color values, which, when taken together, contribute to the formation of the overall picture that is shown on a screen. Pixels are the fundamental elements with which digital pictures and videos are constructed. They collaborate to produce images that are rich in detail and vivid in color.

- **Project:** In Premiere Pro, a project is a project that acts as a complete container that houses all of the media assets, edits, sequences, and creative aspects that the user has assembled and arranged. All of the creative work that was done is included in this project, which is stored as a separate file. The purpose of this component is to serve as a repository for a variety of components, such as clips, sequences, effects, transitions, audio tracks, and more. Throughout the editing process, the structure, layout, and settings that are applied to the media components are stored and maintained in the project file.

- **RGB Color**: RGB, signifying Red, Green, and Blue, represents the fundamental color model used in digital photography and video display systems. To generate a whole spectrum of colors and to make a complete color picture, these three-color channels are merged in varied intensities to provide the entire spectrum of colors. A broad gamut of colors is produced when various combinations of these hues are combined at variable degrees of intensity. This is important for the production of colorful and realistic visuals in digital media. Each channel represents one of the main colors.

- **Sequence:** The term "sequence" is used to describe an organized arrangement of clips that are built in a specific timeline inside Premiere Pro. Typically, these sequences are made up of numerous layers, which are used to integrate and edit together a variety of different media assets. These elements include video clips, audio tracks, graphics, effects, and transitions. The majority of the editing work, which includes arranging, cutting, applying effects, and making other creative tweaks, is carried out inside sequences. This allows editors to build and develop the visual story or presentation of their project.

- **Timecode**: Timecode is a standardized method that is used to measure time inside recorded media. It offers a precise temporal reference for a variety of frames, scenes, or moments that are included within a video or audio file. To indicate certain timings within the media content, it makes use of units composed of hours, minutes, seconds, and frames. Timecode information is always included in professional video recording systems. This makes it possible to achieve precise editing, correct synchronization, and reference throughout post-production operations. The timecode can have a different number of frames per second depending on the particular media type and frame rate parameters that were used during the recording process.

NTSC broadcast television uses a system that drops frames from the timecode to compensate for the slightly slower playback during broadcast. This is called *drop frame timecode* and is displayed in Premiere Pro with semicolons as dividers. If you are delivering content for broadcast television, you will use an NTSC frame rate, such as 29.97 fps, in preference to a non–drop frame timecode frame rate, such as 30 fps.

- Drop frame timecode looks like this: 00;15;07;19.
- Non–drop frame timecode looks like this: 00:15:07:19.

The difference is subtle but important.

- **Timeline**: The Timeline panel in Premiere Pro functions as a primary workspace that allows editors to see, organizes, and adjusts sequences. Sequences are the chronological organization of clips and media assets. The phrases "timeline" and "sequence" are sometimes used interchangeably, and both meanings relate to the graphical depiction of the advancement of the editing process. Using this panel, editors can organize clips, apply effects, create transitions, and adjust the timing and flow of the project. It also offers a visual depiction of the structure of the sequence.
- **Transition**: A transition is a visual or audible effect that is used to allow a seamless transition from the conclusion of one clip to the beginning of another clip within a sequence. There are many different types of transitions. Even though a normal cut is the most typical transition, Premiere Pro offers a wide variety of transition effects that can be used to provide visual interest, improve storytelling, or indicate changes in time. As an example, a transition that is often referred to as a "dip to black" generally indicates the passage of time or a shift in the narrative. Transitions are an important part of the language of cinema because they enable viewers to comprehend and interpret minor changes or shifts in scenes, time, or mood.
- **Vector-based Graphics:** Images are generally made up of pixels, which are little individual dots that, when applied together, produce the visual information. Vector-based graphics, on the other hand, are distinct from pixel-based visuals (also known as raster or bitmap). The definition of forms and lines in vector graphics is accomplished by the use of mathematical formulae and pathways, as opposed to pixels. The quality of these graphics is not affected by scaling since they are not reliant on the resolution of the display environment. Vector-based graphics, on the other hand, are determined by mathematical equations, which mean that they maintain their sharpness and clarity regardless of the size of the picture. This is in contrast to pixel-based visuals, which may lose clarity when heightened owing to the restricted amount of pixels. Because they possess this property, they are perfect for

designs that need scalability without sacrificing quality, such as logos, icons, drawings, and designs.

When the scale of a rasterized picture is increased by scaling it up, the dots get larger. This can result in the edges of organic forms and curves being more rounded or even jagged. It is not possible to create vector graphics using pixels. In its place, they use a mathematical approach to characterize the pictures. Vector graphics can be shown at any resolution (any size), and they will always be flawlessly crisp since they are produced from scratch each time. This is because vector graphics are generated from scratch. Using this method, for instance, a circle will always be a circle regardless of the resolution (it will not transform into a blocky shape even if you increase its size). Premiere Pro graphics are vector-based, while imported vector-based graphics are processed as pixels. Premiere Pro graphics are developed in the program.

- **Virtual Reality Video**: VR video is a specialized kind of video material that is taken using a camera system that captures 360 degrees of the scene. This creates an immersive spherical image that allows viewers to experience an area as if they were physically inside it. These videos encompass a full 360-degree field of view, which enables viewers to freely glance in any direction, including up, down, or around, creating a more immersive visual experience. Although virtual reality video footage is not strictly considered to be virtual reality, it does provide an immersive watching experience. This is especially true when the information is viewed using virtual reality headsets. Virtual reality often incorporates surroundings that are computer-generated and interactive.
    - **360-degree Video Camera System**: A 360-degree video camera system can record footage in all directions simultaneously, creating a spherical or panoramic image of the local environment. Multiple lenses or a specific configuration are used by these cameras to capture footage from a variety of viewpoints. The different recordings are then combined to produce a video that is integrated and immersive. When watched on appropriate platforms, such as virtual reality headsets or interactive internet players, viewers can explore the whole 360-degree world. This provides a watching experience that is more engaging and participatory than the typical linear video formats.
    - **Virtual Reality Headsets**: Virtual reality headsets are popular among viewers because they allow them to completely experience and immerse themselves in virtual reality video media. Users can enter and explore the 360-degree video world by using these headsets, which are equipped with specialized

displays and motion-tracking sensors. Viewers can replicate a sensation of presence inside the virtual area portrayed in the video by wearing these headsets, which allow them to freely move their heads in any direction.

Many filmmakers and content providers have begun to refer to this format as "VR video," recognizing its relationship with immersive watching and the need for VR gear to successfully interact with the material. This is because the usage of virtual reality headsets to enjoy this sort of immersive video experience has led to the term "VR video" being used. Dedicated visual effects and a viewing mode are both included in Premiere Pro for virtual reality. To further simplify and expedite the process of reviewing information, you can also edit using a virtual reality headset.

Conclusion

As you reach the end of this Adobe Premiere Pro guidebook, take a moment to celebrate your journey from a novice to a proficient video editor. This guidebook was crafted with your learning experience in mind, providing a user-friendly approach that transforms the seemingly complex world of video editing into an accessible and enjoyable adventure. From the basics to advanced features, you've explored the massive landscape of Adobe Premiere Pro, uncovering the tools and techniques that allow you to bring your creative visions to life. The step-by-step instructions, supported by clear examples and visuals, aimed to empower you at every stage of your learning process. Remember, video editing is not just about mastering the technicalities; it's about storytelling and expression. The guidebook delved into the creative aspects of editing, encouraging you to not only manipulate footage but to craft narratives, evoke emotions, and captures your audience's attention. Troubleshooting tips were included because we understand that challenges are part of the learning process. As you encountered roadblocks, the guidebook aimed to be your companion, offering solutions and fostering your independence as an editor. This guidebook aims to keep you in sync with the latest features and updates in Adobe Premiere Pro. Staying current ensures that you continue to grow and innovate, adapting your skills to the ever-expanding possibilities within the software. As you close this chapter, remember that learning is a continual journey. The skills you've acquired here are the foundation upon which you can build, experiment, and push the boundaries of your creativity. Whether you're editing for personal projects, professional endeavors, or simply for the joy of it, may your future edits be filled with confidence and artistic flair. Thank you for choosing this guidebook as your companion on your Adobe Premiere Pro adventure. Here's to the exciting edits that lie ahead!

INDEX

D

F

G

N

Q

R

T

X

Y

Z